Songs to Seven Strings

Songs to Seven Strings

Russian Guitar Poetry and Soviet "Mass Song"

Gerald Stanton Smith

INDIANA UNIVERSITY PRESS
BLOOMINGTON

This book was brought to publication with the aid of a grant
from the Andrew W. Mellon Foundation.

Manufactured in the United States of America

Library of Congress Cataloging in Publication Data

Smith, Gerald Stanton.
Songs to seven strings.

(Soviet history, politics, society, and thought)
Bibliography: p.
Includes index.
1. Protest poetry, Russian—History and criticism.
2. Underground literature—Soviet Union—History and
criticism.   3. Music, Popular (Songs, etc.)—Soviet Union
—History and criticism.   4. Soviet Union—Popular
culture.   I. Title.   II. Title: Songs to 7 strings.
III. Series.

PG3064.P76S6   1984   891.71'044'09   83-49453
ISBN 0-253-35391-2
1   2   3   4   5   88   87   86   85   84

for BH

for BH

The genre of song, created in spite of the reigning silence, fear, and indifference, in spite of official phrases and official music—song, which with the aid of the guitar and tape recorder spread like wildfire and penetrated each and every home, each and every environment—still needs to be comprehended. We stand before a fact that is obvious to every one of us, something that long since became our property and part of our everyday life. . . .

—ANDREI SINYAVSKY (Abram Terts),
"Galich's Theater"

No matter how they fought the guitar,
    the peal of strings kept getting hotter.
No matter how they watered the wine of verse,
    it kept getting stronger.
Who was first to leave,
Who got away with the loot—
That's all mixed up now, all turned into one.

—BULAT OKUDZHAVA,
"A Song about Volodya Vysotsky"

Contents

Preface

I was initiated into guitar poetry and *magnitizdat* on my first visit to the USSR, in 1963. An encounter with a fanatical jazz fan in Leningrad led to a session with his treasured collection of tapes, mostly transcribed from the Voice of America radio station. The tape recorder, made in East Germany, was without a cover; it needed endless cajoling and makeshift repairs. I would later recognize it as the classic vehicle of *magnitizdat*. We sampled the fan's most precious jazz tapes. Sensing that I had heard them all before, he put on a Russian tape, which turned out to be by someone called Bulat Okudzhava, a poet who sang his words to the guitar. The recording was obviously an amateur one, and its technical standard was unspeakably bad. I was fascinated, but regarded it as no more than a curiosity. My comprehension of spoken Russian was poor, and I had no entrée at the time to the literary and intellectual circles in which even by then Okudzhava, and with him the idea of sung poetry transmitted through clandestine tape recordings, had made an indelible impact.

During my student years in the early sixties, I worked vacations as an interpreter for groups of Soviet "young people" (*molodezh'*)—some of them old enough to be my father—who were visiting Britain under the auspices of the old Educational Interchange Council. It was from them that I learned the current repertoire of Soviet "mass songs." On trains and buses and at impromptu concerts, dutifully led by their leaders, they would strike up with "The Buchenwald Tocsin," "Do the Russians Want War?", "Komsomol Volunteers," and other anthems. On less-public occasions they would sing lyrics that at first I took to be traditional folk songs; eventually I was astounded to discover that the haunting "Roads," for example, had been written by Lev Oshanin in 1945 and was just as much an example of a Soviet "mass song" as "Do the Russians Want War?" I also grew very fond of some childrens' songs, such as "The Captain" and "May There Always Be the Sun," and learned that they too were "mass songs," the work of contemporary Soviet songwriters, Vasily Lebedev-Kumach and the same Lev

Oshanin respectively, and written, astonishingly, in 1937 and 1962. The mass song, like guitar poetry, was an aspect of Russian culture that simply did not exist in the curricula of my student courses and my early teaching, and for many years I regarded them both as a diversion, somehow not worthy of the attention of a serious literary scholar.

As my visits to Russia continued through the sixties and seventies, and my sphere of contacts grew wider and my relationships with some people developed into friendships, guitar poetry was never far away from conversation. Eventually it became a framework of reference for shorthand orientation in the subtleties of Soviet life, and a never-failing source of humor. But what was for me an entertainment and an object of study was for some of my friends a mighty resource in their daily struggle with Soviet life.

I managed to bring some tapes home, and got hold of more from the few other foreigners who were listening to guitar poetry. I think it was in 1971 that I first gave a lecture-recital on the subject, and I spoke about it many times in the next ten years, mainly at universities in England, the United States, and Canada. It was always a pleasure to watch a realization of the power in these songs steal over the minds of audiences who may have understood only a part of their literal meaning and nothing of their contextual meaning, apart from what they had been told as an introduction to the particular example I was playing.

As part of the lecture-recital, I prepared translations of the songs and usually copies of the Russian texts, too, because at the time I started there were no printed texts available, except for a few songs by Okudzhava. This endeavor developed into an attempt to translate some of the songs isometrically, so that they could be sung in English to the original tunes. One result has been my collection of Galich translations (Alexander Galich, *Songs and Poems,* Ann Arbor, 1983). The translations in the present book, though, all of which are my own, are not metrical. They aim to be as faithful to the literal meaning of the original as is consistent with the preservation of economy and a tolerable English style. They also set a premium on retaining the same distribution of matter to the line that is found in the originals. But no literary merit is claimed for them. The poetics of guitar poetry is a subject that will doubtless receive proper treatment in the appropriate publications, but one that has had to be largely neglected in this book, in translation as well as in discussion.

In contrast to the situation when I started, at the present time there are abundant texts and recordings available of guitar poetry in Russian.

This fact has laid to rest my anxiety about writing a book on a subject which would not be accessible to interested readers in its original form, an anxiety that has held up the writing of this book for some years.

I have experienced the delight and stimulus of meeting all three of the great guitar poets personally. Aleksandr Galich was very kind and encouraging on several occasions after his emigration in 1974. The last time was after what turned out to be, alas, his final concert, given in Venice as part of the Biennale in December 1977. I met Vysotsky several times in his dressing room at the Taganka Theater, a coup engineered by a group of Moscow friends to whom I will always be grateful. I was with him there one night after he had played Hamlet. I have never seen anyone in so transcendental a state as this quite extraordinary man was on that occasion, the epitome of fulfilled creative energy. I talked to and interpreted for Okudzhava during part of his tour of England in 1977. He was modest to the point of evasiveness, protesting that he could remember only a dozen of his songs. That year, during the course of which I met all three of these great poets, was the last year on earth of guitar poetry in its full panoply: Galich died that December, and was followed by Vysotsky in 1980.

When I talked with the three poets about their work, there was more guarded disagreement between us than anything else. Like all Russian writers I have met, they insisted that there are ultimate areas of their work which are accessible only to their fellow countrymen, and hinted in their various gentle ways that it was impertinent for a foreigner to study and write on something as intimately bound up with an alien language and society as their songs. Perhaps they were right.

The deaths of Galich and Vysotsky, and the withdrawal of Okudzhava from any substantial involvement with writing and performing songs, have brought the first phase in the history of guitar poetry to a close. It may prove to have been not just the first phase but the whole story. But whatever may happen in the future, it is certainly possible and appropriate to take stock now of what has happened so far.

My account is that of an outsider, even though it draws on some firsthand experience of the subject in its native habitat. Since the published evidence is scanty, the detailed history of guitar poetry and the context of song in the USSR can be told only by the people who were actually involved in the process of its creation, promotion, circulation, and reception. It is to be hoped that these people are aware of that, and prepared to do something about it.

This book is about song, an art form that uses words and music together. It is bound to suffer from the limitation inherent in the written discussion of all music: the examples will be abstract and one-dimensional. And the words of the songs discussed here were intended not only to be sung but to be sung by the person who wrote them. Putting them down on the page deprives them of the resonance and authenticity of the poet's own interpretation. It also exposes them to the kind of isolated scrutiny that the written literary lyric receives, and which these texts are not necessarily meant to endure. All of these problems are in addition to the losses that are inevitably suffered when poetry is translated from one language into another. An awareness of these difficulties has haunted the author at every stage of his work on this book.

GSS
Vancouver, B.C.

Acknowledgments

This book has grown out of a lecture-recital I have given in a number of places during the last ten years. I am grateful to have had the opportunity to present my views to so many people and receive their comments.

Martin Dewhirst and Michael Nicholson, master bibliographers, have supplied me with many pages of material. This book could not have been written without their help.

In the years before printed texts became available, Tanya Chambers spent many hours transcribing songs from tape with me. Ilya Serman and Ruf' Zernova guided my steps and forgave my excesses from the earliest days of the project. Victor and Marina Raskin, Mark and Natasha Serman, and Marina Tarlinskaya have helped with delicate points of detail. Vladimir Frumkin kindly used his unique inside knowledge to clean some major errors out of my text. For those that remain, and for all matters of fact and judgment, I take sole responsibility.

I am grateful to Carl and Ellendea Proffer for permission to use photographs of Bulat Okudzhava and Aleksandr Galich from the Ardis Archive and to Igor Vysotski for making available the photograph of Vladimir Vysotsky.

Part of this book was written, and a good deal of the material was organized, during my tenure of a Research Fellowship at the University of Liverpool. I am very grateful to Professor A. B. McMillin and the University Research Committee for their confidence. I was able to finish the book because of the support of Barbara Heldt, to whom I am, literally, more than grateful.

Transliteration

The system of transliteration from Russian Cyrillic used in this book is that of *Oxford Slavonic Papers.* It is economical, relatively elegant, and does not use diacritics. Exceptions have been made in the spellings of the names Tolstoy and Yevgeny Yevtushenko, which are sanctioned in these forms by common usage.

Songs to Seven Strings

Introduction

Guitar poetry[1] was originally a cultural development of the Khrushchev era in the USSR, part of an upsurge in Russian poetry associated with the de-Stalinization of intellectual life in the mid-1950s. It has run its course alongside many other phenomena in Soviet life that were released by this process. The pioneer guitar poet was Bulat Okudzhava (born 1924), who began singing his poems in the late 1950s and made his first public appearance in 1960. Okudzhava accompanied himself on the most accessible of all Russian musical instruments, the seven-stringed acoustic guitar. He soon had imitators, and two of them, Aleksandr Galich (1919–1977) and Vladimir Vysotsky (1938–1980), proved to be indisputably great figures in their own right. The three outstanding guitar poets all came from the intelligentsia of central Moscow, and were members of the capital's literary elite before they began their careers in guitar poetry. They represent three generations of Russian citizens, and to some extent each spoke for and to his own generation. But each used the genre of guitar poetry for his own expressive needs, and as a result the three artists created distinctive individual bodies of song. And they were treated in different ways by the literary and state authorities.

The heyday of guitar poetry occupied the decade beginning around 1962. During this period, all three great poets were at work in Russia, and most of their greatest songs were created. At about the same time, tape recorders were beginning to be sold to the public in the USSR, and recordings of guitar poetry could be copied and circulated beyond the reach of official controls, a process known as *magnitizdat,* "tape recorder publishing."

The result was one of the most important developments in Russian culture of the last twenty-five years. Within the Russian intelligentsia, guitar poetry is generally acknowledged to be such a development. And it has penetrated beyond the intelligentsia more powerfully than any other literary phenomenon. To Russians outside literary circles, guitar poetry is better known than written literature, both official and dissident. For them, Vysotsky is a much more relevant and revered voice than either Yevtushenko or Solzhenitsyn. It goes without saying that this situation is not reflected in Soviet criticism and literary historiography, where guitar poetry is not much more than a target for abuse, if it is mentioned at all. Independent Russian literary historians have devoted some attention to guitar poetry.[2] But among non-Russians there is almost complete ignorance of the subject. Even specialists in Russian literature tend either not to know much about it or to regard it as a subliterary phenomenon. More often than not they do both simultaneously. Guitar poetry has certainly not been accorded the attention it deserves by recent non-Russian literary historians.[3] It is perfectly natural, and indeed highly desirable in the case of modern Russian literature, that the picture of a national literature in the minds of foreigners should differ from the one held by the native readership, its literary elite, and the masters of its media. But the discrepancy in the case of Russian guitar poetry is so remarkable as to be more than enough to justify an attempt to change the situation.[4]

Guitar poetry is a composite art form which interpenetrates the domains of its two constituent elements, poetry and music. Poetry, of course, is one branch of literature. And guitar poetry is not the only art form in which poetry and music come together to make song. The complexities in the perception, description, and interpretation of guitar poetry that spring from these interrelationships are awesome. A consideration of any one of them in isolation would fill a whole book; the same could also be said of a treatment of their aesthetic aspect on its own. And further complexities arise out of the peculiar and novel mode in which guitar poetry is most characteristically preserved and transmitted, that is, through tape recordings made privately and circulated in unknown numbers and combinations. The history of the genre before the advent of publicly accessible tape recorders, and the relationships between the Russian form of guitar poetry and those of other nations, are additional vast potential areas of inquiry.

In narrowing down this range of problems for the present study, the choices have stemmed partly from the author's views regarding the importance of the problems themselves in relation to the subject as a whole, and partly, of course, from the direction of his own personal interests and sense of his own competence.

This book concentrates most consistently on presenting the actual texts of guitar poetry and the song genres most closely related to it. I have taken this approach because of the paramount need to dispel the ignorance of the texts that prevails among non-Russians, and thereby to provide some primary material for further discussion. The extensive citing of texts has inevitably led to a curtailment of the space that can be devoted to analysis, and several hard choices have had to be made. First of all, a certain amount of detail has been offered about the three major talents involved in guitar poetry. That is because of the author's conviction that the work of Okudzhava, Galich, and Vysotsky ranks with the best (and certainly the most interesting) Russian literature of the postwar period. Also, their lives and careers are of great significance from the point of view of the history of Russian literary dissidence in the post-Stalin period. However, this emphasis on the three greats has meant that there is no space left for a systematic account of the lesser guitar poets. They appear here, if at all, only on the periphery, which is especially regrettable in the cases of Yuly Kim and Anri Volokhonsky along with his regular collaborator Aleksei Khvostenko.

Apart from the work and lives of the three major guitar poets, precedence has been accorded here to an account of the literary song as a whole in present-day Russia, with special emphasis on the Soviet "mass song." This material has been presented as a spectrum, whose constituent parts are defined by a political criterion: the relative acceptability of the text in question to the Soviet authorities and its consequent level of access to the media in the USSR. The literary and musical dimensions of these texts have been regarded as secondary. But they are, in Soviet conditions, inextricable from the political. It is quite clear in the author's mind that in the USSR the political process determines the rules (if not all the values) by which the literary process operates, by positive or negative reference. In terms of the criterion of official acceptability, the spectrum of songs begins with texts which positively reflect the Party's call for Soviet culture to expound its ideology. It then runs through a substantial segment formed by texts that are ideologically inoffensive but perhaps not explicitly supportive of official requirements. And the spectrum shades off into songs that are regarded by the authorities as dangerously subversive. The access that song texts have to the media ranges correspondingly from active promotion at the former end to active suppression at the latter.

The necessity for some description of this spectrum of song, and the reason for presenting it as a prelude to a discussion of guitar poetry itself, is that in certain important senses guitar poetry developed, and continues to exist, by reference to it. Guitar poetry was created in the post-Stalin period in large part as a deliberate alternative to existing Soviet culture; and in searching for this alternative, the poets concerned drew on formal and thematic resources offered by traditions of song that the official world had tried to ignore, discourage, or suppress. This process may perhaps be understood in the last analysis as a manifestation of a normal strategy for self-renewal that takes place in the arts, whereby innovation comes about through the introduction into serious art of devices that previously seemed to belong outside it. But the relationships between Russian guitar poetry and the spectrum of song illustrate well the peculiar Soviet symbiosis between the political and literary spheres. This symbiosis is present and active in the minds of Soviet citizens when they experience any cultural artifact, and it may indeed be the primary formant in their response. The relationship between guitar poetry and the spectrum of song is also important in regard to the status of the guitar poets as individuals. The songs of some of them, and with them their creators, have in the course of time emerged from the clandestine world of *magnitizdat* into official acceptance; others have remained underground and even actively persecuted; yet others occupy a middle position between these extremes, shading into both. Guitar poetry may thus be seen from one point of view as constituting a formally marked component of the spectrum of song itself.

This formal marking, whose principal components are the musical characteristics and performance style of guitar poetry, is almost completely its own preserve, and it pulls the genre toward the clandestine end of the spectrum of song. The lone individual with an acoustic seven-stringed guitar in hand is inescapably an antiestablishment figure, a kind of gypsy. Regrettably, a discussion of the musical characteristics of guitar poetry, and their relationships with those of the spectrum of song, has had to be omitted almost entirely from this book. This work is a literary rather than a musicological study. Its emphases, despite the one-dimensionality sometimes entailed, fall consistently on the verbal texts and their literary context. Of the two domains that contribute to guitar poetry, that of poetry is far and away more important than that of music; indeed, the unevenness of this relationship may constitute the distinctive characteristic of guitar poetry as a species of song.[5]

It follows that of greater importance than the relationships of guitar poetry with other species of song are its connections with Russian literary poetry intended for declamation or reading. Guitar poetry is not detached from the main body of modern Russian poetry, but is rather an extension of it that uses additional means. This continuity and interpenetration begins at the level of the individual poet. All three great guitar poets have created poetry for reading as well as songs. With Vysotsky and Galich, the proportion is relatively small; but Okudzhava has written at least as much poetry for reading as for singing. Novella Matveeva, though, is only marginally a guitar poet; and the minor guitar poets include none who are recognized as significant regular poets. They have tended to be active in other aspects of literature for performance.

The most interesting area of contiguity between guitar and literary poetry is formed by the substantial body of songs that has been composed over the years by recognized Russian poets, for whom the song is a venerable and viable lyric genre. Nearly all the important Russian poets have written songs at some time in their career.[6] These songs fall outside guitar poetry, because they have not as a rule been performed by the author to his own accompaniment on the guitar. But they are stylistically and functionally similar to guitar poetry. And they contribute to the same body of sung folklore if, as is the case with some texts that originated as guitar poems, they become detached from their authors and take on an independent existence within the folk memory. We shall cite examples by such eminent modern Russian poets as Yaroslav Smelyakov and Gleb Gorbovsky, as well as examples by authors for whom one or two phenomenally successful songs form their sole poetic achievement, such as Akhill Levinton and Yuz Aleshkovsky. Songs by these authors have been taken up by guitar poets, even the great ones at the early stages of their careers, but they usually form part of the repertoire of minor and amateur singers to guitar accompaniment.

The aspect of guitar poetry's relationships with orthodox Russian literary poetry that has been singled out for discussion here reflects the main difficulty that foreign literary scholars experience in dealing with Russian poetry in general. This aspect is its "seriousness," its credibility as a literary monument capable of evoking a profound human response and meriting careful study. Guitar poetry sounds and looks "light" to the foreigner. Heard in performance, seen on the page, and particularly in translation, it has that same lack of textual complexity, that naiveté wrapped up in archaic-looking highly regulated forms, that many foreign readers of modern Russian poetry find second-rate, even embarrassingly so. An attempt has been made in the final chapter of this book to analyze the causes of this problem and face their consequences. It is worth emphasizing now, though, that for the Russian audience the problem of the genre's "seriousness" hardly arises, any more than does the question of the political resonance of the texts. It is only in a book aimed toward an anglophone readership that these questions need to take precedence over others that are usually more central to studies of poetry.

The essence of guitar poetry is the poet's singing of his own words to his own guitar accompaniment, a kind of creative expression that goes back in Russia, as elsewhere, to long before the twentieth century.[7] In Soviet Russia it acquired a new dimension and was transformed as a genre when tape recorders began to be available for private use in the 1960s. Tape recordings were instantly seen to offer a new method of preserving and circulating texts, one that would bypass the system of controls attendant upon access to the media, over which the state, guided by the Party, exercises an ideologically determined monopoly. With the advent of the tape recorder, the poet also had at his disposal for the first time a convenient means of preserving the impact and authenticity of his own voice. The tradition of oral literature, more central in Russia than in other European countries, acquired a permanent medium for the first time. Alongside *samizdat,* the time-honored Russian method of circulating clandestine literary material, appeared *magnitizdat.* This novel and specific mode of transmission and circulation for a body of literary texts helped to define guitar poetry as a genre and also created new problems of interpretation and categorization. Like folklore in the preelectronic age, guitar poetry is aurally perceived and orally transmitted, but unlike that folklore it is created and performed by known individuals who are both the original creators and the performers of the material. This factor further complicates the network of problems referred to earlier that derive from guitar poetry's situation between poetry and music. Its ramifications have been considered too vast and probably too specialized to be allotted anything but the most perfunctory discussion in the present study.

There is a considerable need for thorough analysis of the various problems that have just been mentioned, in isolation and in their interconnections. The serious investigation of Russian guitar poetry has hardly begun. The present study, it is hoped, will provide some primary evidence and a rough chart on whose basis the more detailed work of the future may take its orientation.

The Spectrum
of Song

Part One

In the Sov. period there has been an intense
development of various genres of s. in both
folkloric and lit. forms. The her. history of the
Sov. people, the thoughts and feelings of Sov.
man have been graphically reflected in the s.

S. G. LAZUTIN, "Song,"
in *The Concise Literary Encyclopedia*

1   Song in State Service

A LEAD ARTICLE ON THE front page of *Pravda* for Friday, 12 September 1975, unsigned and therefore unimpeachably representing the current line of the Communist Party of the Soviet Union, provides an authoritative introduction to the idea of song as a component of official Soviet culture:

> "A song helps us build and live" has become a well-known saying. It contains an acknowledgment of the great social role of this most mass-oriented genre of art. The revolutionary song resounded at the early illegal May Day meetings, on the barricades of class battles, the fronts of the Civil War. Its heir, the new Soviet song, accompanied the people who built cities and factories, upturned virgin soil for the collective farms, and waged war against the Fascist aggressors. Today, the best creations of our songwriters are helping the Soviet people build, and are making life more interesting and spiritually richer.
>
> Songs have a large civic resonance, and they reflect in vivid and graphic form the main things by which the toilers of the Land of the Soviets live today; they are taken up by millions. They are becoming a means for the ideological-political and moral-aesthetic education of the broad masses.

The article enunciates a categorical principle:

> All work connected with the creation and propaganda of song must issue from the demands formulated by the XXIV Congress of the CPSU: "The Soviet people have an interest in the creation of works that truthfully reflect reality and with great artistic power confirm the ideas of Communism."

And it closes with what is normal in *Pravda* editorials, a peremptory specification of what the people want:

9

Soviet people expect from poets and composers new, inspired songs that
give genuine joy to millions, songs which are helpmeets in our Communist work of construction.[1]

The line quoted at the beginning of the article, "A song helps us build
and live," actually is familiar to literally every Soviet citizen. The text
it comes from may fairly be used to introduce what is known in the
USSR as a "mass song" *(massovaya pesnya)*. This term covers just
about everything considered suitable for publication, apart from folk
songs and *Lieder.* The song was written in 1934 for the Komsomol by
Vasily Lebedev-Kumach (1898–1949), one of the most revered of
Soviet songwriters, and is entitled "Merry Children's March" ("Marsh
veselykh rebyat"). Two of its more striking verses are the following:

> Our hearts are light from our merry song,
> It never lets us get bored;
> Villages and hamlets love the song,
> And big cities love it, too.
>
> Stride forward, Komsomol tribe,
> Joke and sing, let your smiles blossom!
> We are conquering space and time,
> We are the young masters of the earth!

The last verse runs:

> And if an enemy in stubborn battle
> Should want to steal our vital joy,
> We'll sing a martial song,
> We'll stand and fight for the Motherland!

And the song's refrain, from which the line quoted by *Pravda* actually
comes, carries the main message:

> A song helps us build and live,
> Like a friend, it summons us and leads us forward;
> And whoever strides through life with a song
> Will never be lost anywhere![2]

The *Pravda* article and the "Merry Children's March" illustrate the
primary function and the nature of the "mass song" in Soviet society as
seen by those who run that society. For them the song is a component
of Soviet culture, and as such is subject to the same requirements and
restrictions as any other aspect of that culture. Uppermost among the
requirements is that the work should use the "basic method" of all

Soviet art, Socialist Realism. This "method" was first promulgated with reference to literature, in the original Statute of the Union of Soviet Writers when it was established in 1934, and defined in the following way:

> Socialist Realism, the basic method of Soviet belles-lettres and literary criticism, demands of the artist truthful, historically concrete representation of reality in its revolutionary development. . . .
>
> At the same time, truthfulness and historical concreteness in the artistic representation of reality must be combined with the task of ideologically remoulding and training the labouring people in the spirit of socialism.[3]

What Socialist Realism actually does mean is a problem that has given rise over the years to some of the most tortured theoretical writing ever produced in the USSR.[4] The explicitly aesthetic element in the phrase, "Realism," itself indefinable in an unambiguous or constructive way in any context, has in practice managed to encompass a wide variety of styles. In the last twenty years in particular it has been subjected by writers to considerable expansion.[5] However, no matter how sincere the originators of the method were about its aesthetic aspect, and no matter how Soviet critics may agonize about its true meaning and manipulate it as the literature itself evolves, the fact remains that the fundamental reason for the existence of the doctrine is political. It asserts the principle that the artist's ultimate loyalty shall be to the Party's requirements in the interests of building Communism, rather than to his art or himself. The interpretation of the formula can then be manipulated as required to encourage or discourage according to the Party's current political concerns.

This attention to the Party's concerns and requirements, and subservience to them, are what is essentially meant by the concept of "Party-mindedness" *(partiinost')*, which is another requirement that has been exacted of the arts since the early 1930s. And there are several other features which are usually considered to be "inextricably bound up with" Socialist Realism. The one that produces the most salient results is that in their effort to help the Party in its task of bringing about Communism, the arts should provide a human model for emulation, in the form of the "positive hero," who should be endowed with those characteristics that fit him to participate in the Party's work. He should be strong and balanced both physically and psychologically, socially aware, enthusiastic, and optimistic. Surprisingly, this general formula has managed to encompass over time quite a broad range of literary characters. Stemming inevitably from the requirement that the arts reflect and aid the Party's purpose is that they should embody its view of human history, which is, of course, a progressive one. The detectability of this view within the work of art enables it to be regarded as satisfactory in terms of "ideological awareness" *(ideinost')*. Triviality or inconsequentiality is impermissible within Socialist Realism.

Party-mindedness, ideological awareness, the positive hero, and the progressive view of human history are prominent features of Socialist Realist works of art. But there are several other characteristics of Soviet art which are less strongly emphasized in theory, but which to the non-Soviet observer are just as noticeable. Chief among them is patriotism. The Motherland must be revered, and it is not permissible to lose faith in her, nor to doubt that her best interests are enshrined in the Party and its plans. There is also the requirement that the work of art must be comprehensible and morally beneficial (in the definition of the Party) to the average person. Soviet art works hand in hand with the state system of education in the inculcation of Party objectives. The didactic quality of Soviet art, overt or covert, is understandable in the context of mass literacy recently and laboriously achieved. But in its institutionalized form it has the effect of stultifying experiment and producing a uniform middlebrow art. The idea that the function of art (much less its *sine qua non*) might be to challenge and subvert is anathema to Socialist Realist thinking.

The establishment of a monolithic artistic method was one aspect of the totalitarianization of Soviet cultural life that was undertaken by the Party under Stalin in the early 1930s. It introduced a new element into the age-old Russian institution of censorship. The imposition of a system of censorship, which had been abolished after the February Revolution, was one of the first acts of the new Soviet government when it seized power in October 1917. During the 1920s the system was proscriptive, and fairly permissive on the whole, functioning as under tsarism to suppress matters which officialdom did not wish to have publicly discussed. With Stalinism and totalitarianism, censorship also took on a prescriptive element. It now acts as the final instance in a network of inducements, incentives, and prerogatives designed to get out the cultural products the Party requires and whose specifications it stipulates.

There can be no doubt that after fifty years in continuous operation, the system of prescriptive and proscriptive censorship works well, especially in combination with the self-censorship it now engenders as second nature in creative artists in the USSR.[6] Lebedev-Kumach's "March" is an example of the results, and it bears the hallmarks of Soviet Socialist Realism in practice, in one particular aspect of the arts. It uses simple, accessible language and a form that is not in any way disturbing or experimental. It has a clear message, is optimistic, and has a note of patriotism. Perhaps the most striking thing about it to the foreign eye, especially in view of the term *Realism* in the official formula, is the total lack of specificity, in place or time, or in reference to persons and events. This song is one of the staples of the Soviet repertoire. It is included in just about every one of the dozens of songbooks that roll off the Soviet presses year by year in mass editions. An examination of one of these songbooks will make it possible to amplify the impression of the official song that the Komsomol march presents.

The collection *Russian Soviet Songs, 1917–1977*,[7] published during the sixtieth-anniversary year of the Revolution, is claimed by its compilers to present "a poetic chronicle of the Russian Soviet song over the sixty years of its development." A recent American commentator has found this claim to be largely justified.[8] The anthology begins, as do all Soviet mass songbooks, with what might be called the Old Testament of revolutionary song, the anthems of the labor movement before the October Revolution. The main ones are the Party's anthem, "The International," followed by Leonid Radin's "Bravely, Comrades, in Step" ("Smelo, tovarishchi, v nogu," 1896), Gleb Krżyzanowski's "Warsaw Song" ("Varshavyanka," 1897), Petr Lavrov's "Workers' Marseillaise" ("Rabochaya Marsel'eza," 1905), and Grigory Machtet's "Tormented by Oppressive Bondage" ("Zamuchen tyazheloi nevolei," 1876). These songs are familiar to every Soviet person. They are performed and recorded endlessly by every kind of ensemble and are heavily featured on TV and radio, and in concert performances, by amateurs and professionals alike.

After them come the classics of the Civil War; then the anthems of the construction period of the 1930s, like Lebedev-Kumach's "March"; then the songs of the Second World War; and then a lesser number of songs from the period up to the mid-1950s, their paucity reflecting the current unacceptability of the copious references to Stalin that songs of the time obligatorily contained; and finally, there are some songs of the post-Stalin period that are already considered classics. These songs as a whole reflect the same stages of evolution that have been undergone by other aspects of Soviet culture since the

Revolution: the bravado of the 1920s, increasingly ponderous solemnity in the 1930s, a rapprochement with genuine popular aspirations during the war, strangulation in the last years of Stalinism, uncertain and always precarious reinvigoration under Khrushchev, and finally a slide into grayness as Brezhnev's sclerotic stagnation took hold. An objective history of the Soviet mass song has yet to be written; such a work will one day provide a valuable sidelight on the history of Soviet literature and culture.[9]

The uppermost layer of mass songs consists of anthems or hymns (the word *gimn* is actually used in Russian.) These are songs that have been adopted for particular institutional or ceremonial purposes by Party or state. The most famous of them is also by Lebedev-Kumach. It was written in 1935 and is called "Song of the Motherland" ("Pesnya o rodine"). Even before the war it was being published in editions of twenty million copies.[10] The opening notes of its portentously swelling tune have for years been used as the station identification of Radio Moscow. It begins with a refrain:

> Broad is my native land,
> With many forests, fields, and rivers.
> I know of no other land
> Where a man can breathe so freely!

The first verse runs:

> From Moscow to the very furthest borders,
> From southern mountains to northern seas,
> Man strides like the master
> Of his boundless Motherland.
> Everywhere life flows free and bountiful,
> Like the Volga in spate.
> The young can always make their way,
> The old can always find respect.

The second verse continues in the same vein of chauvinistic bombast. But we should not forget that behind the words stands the sinister reality of Stalin's call for loyalty to the Party to take precedence over loyalty to relatives, a policy that poisoned human relationships for many years:

> The eye can't encompass our wheatfields,
> We have too many towns for the mind to grasp,
> Our proud word "Comrade"

Is more precious than any fine words.
With this word we're at home everywhere,
We have no whites and blacks,
Everyone's familiar with this word,
And with it we can find relatives everywhere.

In the text published in 1977, absolutely no trace has been allowed to remain of the verse that came third in the song for twenty years after its creation:

No-one is left out at our table,
Everyone is rewarded according to his services.
In golden letters we are writing
Stalin's nationwide law.
No years can erase
The grandeur and fame of these words:
"A person always has the right
To study, rest, and labor!"[11]

This "un-verse," of course, remains loud in the memories of every Soviet citizen who has any recollection of things as they were before the mid-1950s.

The fourth and final verse of Lebedev-Kumach's anthem contains a belligerent threat similar to the one in his "March." We shall see that this threat is a mandatory element in the full-blown Soviet hymn:

Nobody in the world knows better than we
How to laugh and love.
But we'll sternly knit our brows
If an enemy should wish to smash us—
We love our Motherland as if she were a bride,
And cherish her as if she were an affectionate mother.
[*RSP,* 167–68]

The function of this song and those like it is to promulgate and propagandize a set of myths and dogmas from the orthodox ideology, just as religious hymnology does. The first and last verses together with the refrain of Petr Gradov's "We Are Party Members" ("My—kommunisty," 1958) will demonstrate the occasional startling similarity of tone between Soviet hymns and those of militant Protestantism. Here is the Soviet equivalent of "Onward, Christian Soldiers":

There are millions in our ranks,
We are the sons of Lenin.

Above us flutter victoriously
The banners of glorious October.

We are Party members,
Strong in our truth.
The aim of our life
Is the happiness of simple folk.
The aim of all our struggle and our life
Is the happiness of simple folk.
. . .

O Party of the brave and steadfast,
We are all proud of you.
We were first at the new construction sites,
And the first to go into war.

We are Party members,
Strong in our truth . . .

Here we have, expressed in song, the Party's view of itself as "the vanguard of the working people in their struggle to build a Communist society." Divorced from its tune and its context, the song reeks of the same odious self-congratulation that is given off by the slogans the Party puts up to itself all over Russia.

Perhaps the most perfect all-round example of a Soviet mass song of the "hymn" type, and of special interest from the point of view of its presentation of the "positive hero," is Konstantin Vanshenkin's "I Love You, Life" ("Ya lyublyu tebya, zhizn'," 1956). The song is known by heart by every Soviet citizen, and is sung to a stirring, inspirational march tune. It begins:

I love you, Life,
Nothing new in itself,
I love you, Life,
I love you over and over again.

The hero is first identified as a conscientious member of the toiling masses:

Windows are already lit
As, tired, I stride home from work;
I love you, Life,
And I want you to get better.

He is not discontented with things as they are, though:

Much have I been granted—
The earth's breadth and the sea's expanse;

And I've long been familiar
With masculine selfless friendship.

In the clamor of each day,
How happy I am not to be at peace!
I have a love.
Life, you know what that means.

What it does mean is excruciatingly priggish:

When the nightingales sing,
The half-dark. A kiss at daybreak.
And the pinnacle of love,
That great miracle—children!

With a mature sigh, he sketches in the continuity of the generations:

With them once more we will go
Through childhood, youth, stations, and harbors;
Then there will be grandchildren,
And everything will begin again.

The tonality deepens as a constant awareness of the victims of war, one
of the mandatory attributes of the positive hero, makes its appearance
before the song ends:

Ah, how the years fly by.
We get sad as we notice our gray hairs.
Life, do you remember the soldiers
Who perished defending you?

But matters cannot end on this note; having asserted his credentials as
worker, family man, mature citizen, and patriot, he can sign off with
even a touch of selfishness to round off the rabble-rousing:

So exult and rise
In the trumpet-tones of a vernal hymn!
I love you, Life,
And I hope that's mutual.

[*RSP,* 548–49]

Here again we have the hallmarks of Soviet Socialist Realism. The
language is transparent; the form is straightforward; the imagery is
vague to the point of almost total abstraction, safely avoiding anything
historically specific. We note the cozy lighted windows in the first verse
(mercifully, though, Vanshenkin's nightingales are not sitting in a birch
tree.) The tone is one of uplift and commitment. The positive hero has

an optimism which it would be an exaggeration to call facile, but which is unclouded by worries about ultimate social, political, moral, or ethical problems. He identifies himself with his country and people, seeing himself as one of a group, a collective, rather than exploring his individual identity.

Patriotism is implied rather than stated in Vanshenkin's song, which is dealing with love for an abstraction even greater than the idea of the Motherland. At the other extreme is the homely treatment of patriotism in a very famous song by Mikhail Matusovsky (1915–), "Where Does the Motherland Begin?" ("S chego nachinaetsya Rodina?" 1967):

> Where does the Motherland begin?
> From a little picture in your spelling book,
> From the good and faithful comrades
> Who live in the next courtyard.
> But perhaps she begins
> From a song our mother sang us,
> And from the thing no possible trials
> Can ever take away from us.
>
> Where does the Motherland begin?
> From that dear old bench by the gates,
> From that same birch tree that grows
> Out in the field, bowing in the wind.
> But perhaps she begins
> From the springtime song of the starling,
> And from that country road
> Whose end cannot be seen.
>
> Where does the Motherland begin?
> From windows that glow in the distance,
> From our father's old Civil War cap
> We once found in a cupboard.
> But perhaps she begins
> From the pounding of carriage wheels,
> And from the vow that in your youth
> You swore to her in your heart . . .
>
> Where does the Motherland begin?

[*RSP,* 485]

This text has the reflective, elegaic note that is Matusovsky's trademark. It exhibits the sentimental rather than the stridently chauvinistic aspect of Soviet patriotism. But it has the same vagueness of focus as the hymns, even though its surface texture seems to be full of objects. There is nothing in it that can be identified with the actual appearance of modern Russia, and we can already recognize some clichés—the birch tree, of course, and the lighted window seen from afar. The veteran father and the devoted mother are also favorite accessories in the official song.

The most prominent single theme in Soviet "mass songs" remains, thirty-five years after the end of hostilities, that of World War II, or "The Great Patriotic War," as it is officially known in the USSR. In this respect the mass song parallels all other branches of the arts. Nobody would seek to deny or belittle the tragic reality of the Russian experience between 1941 and 1945, one of truly historic heroism and sacrifice. But it would be equally unreasonable not to recognize the wholesale exploitation of this theme in Soviet official literature. It is perhaps the only major subject on which official and popular opinions coincide; both sides claim that the Soviet cause was just, and that the war was won by the colossal efforts of a people united. It was an occasion when for the first and only time since 1917 there was national solidarity, with internal bloodletting set aside. In the enormous attention that is given to the war theme in all branches of the Soviet arts, the Party's line is relentlessly hammered home. During the war, it claims, its leading role in national life (the only claim it has to legitimacy) was put to the supreme test and justified. Of course, tremendous modifications have had to be made to war mythology as a result of de-Stalinization, but the essential points of emphasis remain unchanged.

The exploits of the Red Army are endlessly extolled. Plenty of attention is given to the ordinary private soldier who leaves his native hut in the country or courtyard in the town, saying goodbye to sorrowing mother and/or wife. He fights all the way through to Berlin, and then returns, medaled, gray-haired in his twenties, to that same hut or courtyard (or the place it used to be) to pick up his life. His military experience has case-hardened his labor discipline. He is an example to his fellows and the object of admiration by the patient mother or fiancée who has waited faithfully for his return and will now build a family with him. Or—the preferred scenario—he sacrifices his life at the front, and is still awaited by a mother or widow faithful to his memory and by her grieving but proud children. Besides its justification of the Revolution and the subsequent history of the country, including collectivization and industrialization, the moral of the war is that it justifies Soviet patriotism. The Motherland is sacrosanct and must never be yielded to an invader. A song by Sergei Vasil'ev, a poet born in 1911 who has an immaculately orthodox literary pedigree, finds a maximally simple image to articulate this message. It is that same hardworking birch tree. The song is called "The White Birch" ("Belaya bereza," 1950):

> I remember a birch tree being wounded
> By a bomb splinter one dawn.
> Its ice-cold sap ran like tears
> Down its mutilated bark.
>
> Beyond the wood the guns thundered,
> Powder smoke billowed up.
> But we stood firm for the capital
> And saved that birch tree that grew near Moscow.
>
> And then one very early spring
> The white birch once more
> Was dressed in new leaves
> And made the earth beautiful.
>
> And since that time to all threats
> There's only one thing we say:
> We'll never allow anyone to hurt
> Our dear Russian birch again.
>
> [*RSP,* 401]

If one phrase could express the essence of the interpretation of the war theme in the Soviet arts, it would be "justified sacrifice." The theme manifestly accommodates that part of the people's religious impulse that is not absorbed by the Party's cult of Lenin. The motifs that appear with the greatest regularity are the concept of laying down one's life for one's neighbor, and the moral obligations imposed on later generations by those who made the supreme sacrifice. Here is a song by Lev Kuklin, written in 1965, and unusual in that the singer is female. The song is an illustration of the permissible limits of tragedy:

Song of My Father

> I don't know where you are buried,
> Far away from your beloved home.
> Over you the branch of the birch doesn't bend,
> Bitter grasses have grown up there.
> In that victorious year of '45
> We all waited for you on the porch.
> If you served with him, soldiers,
> Tell me about my father!
>
> Was he gray-eyed, like me?
> I know nothing about him.

I never saw my father even once.
I know no pictures of him . . .
Like wounds, the sunsets burned,
He went forward in fire and lead.
If you fought beside him, soldiers,
Tell me about my father!

A soldier's fame is anonymous.
But I believe in my father.
And it seems to me that the trees and grass
Whisper his noble name . . .
Perhaps he didn't live long in this world,
But I know he was honest to the end.
I want to be like my father,
I want to be worthy of my father!

[*RSP,* 662]

Here again we have imagery that is commonplace to the point of
cliché: the birch tree yet again, the porch, the sunset; and again, nothing is specific. Everything swims in a thick soup of sentimentality.

Of course, by no means all Soviet "mass songs" are overtly political.
There is a large corpus of approved songs about love. The archetypal
Soviet love song is one of respectable, requited love, leading to stable
home and family life, as in Vanshenkin's "I Love You, Life." It could
be claimed that the mass love song is an even more powerful advocate
and repository of "middle-class values" than Soviet fiction.[12] An unhappy end to a love affair is sanctioned only, it seems, if the man is
killed in action defending the Motherland. Infidelity, triangles, crimes
of passion, philandering, sex for its own sake, are almost totally absent. As an example we may take "Evenings near Moscow" ("Podmos-
kovnye vechera," 1955) by Mikhail Matusovsky, whose "Where Does
the Motherland Begin?" was discussed earlier:

Not even a rustle can be heard in the garden,
Everything has fallen still until morning.
If you only knew how dear to me
Are those evenings near Moscow.

The river moves and then stops moving,
All made of the moon's silver.
A song can be heard and then it can't
In those quiet evenings.

My dear, why do you give me a sidelong glance,
Bowing your head down low?
It's hard to say, but not to say,
Everything that's in my heart.

And dawn keeps getting lighter,
So please be kind, and like me,
Don't you forget these summer
Evenings near Moscow.

[*RSP,* 472]

It is not surprising that when this song became something of an international hit in the late 1950s, it left its words behind in Russia. Again they
have the elegaic quality in which Matusovsky specializes, but they are
quite typical of the approved Soviet love song: saccharine, sentimental, extremely vague, and naive. They bring in an affinity between
human beings (who behave with impeccable decorum) and a natural
scene which is very vague (garden, river, moon) but which is safely
identified with a patriotic locale in the refrain line.

At its best, the mass love song is timeless and utterly simple. Here is
a very popular song, again by Matusovsky, one that uses the ritual
threefold repetitions of folklore. It is called "The Old Maple Tree"
("Staryi klen," 1961):

The old maple tree, old maple tree, old maple tree knocks on the
    windowpane,
Asking me to go out for a walk with you.
Why, why, why do I feel so fine?
Because you simply walked down the street.

The snow, the snow, the snow has been gone for long,
It looks as if spring has come to visit us again;
Why, why, why are things so good?
Because you simply smiled at me.

Look, look, look at the sky,
See it shine, cloudless and clean.
Why, why, why is that accordion singing?
It's because someone loves the accordionist.

[*RSP,* 477]

Of course, things are not always as straightforward as in this song.
There are mass songs about the eternal sad subjects of song: parting,
separation, unhappy first love, nostalgia for lost places and times. But
joy, acceptance, or at least the positive consequence of an unhappy
experience, such as wisdom after the event or stoicism in the face of
adversity, are always dominant, even in the rare mass songs about
unrequited love. There are only a couple of them in *Russian Soviet
Songs, 1917–1977.* One of them, Nikolai Dorizo's "So Many Golden
Lights" ("Ognei tak mnogo zolotykh"), written in 1953, contains an

incipient triangle and even potential adultery. But the female principal of the song is going to be strong in her resolve not to disturb the marital status quo:

> There're so many golden lights
> On the streets of Saratov.
> There's so many bachelor boys,
> But I love a boy who's married.
>
> Ah, he started a family early! . . .
> It's a sad story!
> I hide my love from myself,
> And even more from him.
>
> I want to run away from him
> As soon as he appears;
> But what if everything I keep silent about
> Should speak out for itself?
>
> I ought not to see him,
> For I'm afraid he'll like me.
> I'll come to terms with love on my own,
> For we can't do that together!

[*RSP,* 450]

The awesome gap between the attitude expressed here and normal Soviet sexual relations will be apparent to anyone with even a superficial knowledge of Soviet life as it really is. But in the mass song, the nuclear family is sacrosanct. Only death in war condones the absence of a spouse and a resulting one-parent family.

Even more sacrosanct, and having unmistakable parallels with avowed religion, is the image of the mother, in song as in other aspects of Soviet official art. It is quite unthinkable to find a negatively portrayed mother in official songs. It is even more unthinkable to find a song dealing with the grinding harshness of motherhood in present-day Soviet conditions. In song, the preferred mother is elderly, and if possible a war widow. The dominant convention is to deal with the subject from the point of view of the erring son, whose mother never forgets, always forgives, is patient, not very well dressed, and above all *tired.* A good example is Nikolai Starshinov's "To My Mother" ("Materi," 1959):

> The slushy snow is dark on the street,
> Water's starting to drip from the roofs.
> You've been busy all day and you're tired,
> And now you're sitting by your window.

She is alone; she had a big family, but they have all left her and gone their own way, and she stoically hid her tears as she saw them off. They all "forgot to write," and she waited for months on end for news of them. Finally:

> Now I'm embracing you again.
> I'm so happy we're together today!
> I didn't write. I forgot. I understand . . .
> Forgive me, please. It's my fault . . .

[*RSP,* 605]

Perhaps the ultimate "mommy song" is Igor' Shaferan's "Our Mommies" ("Nashi mamy," 1974):

> That springtime looked as if it would be eternal—
> And from the frames on the walls looked down
> Our mommies in their wedding dresses,
> Our mommies, still quite young.
> Their eyebrows like spread wings,
> Not a single wrinkle by their eyes;
> Who would believe there was a time
> When our mommies were younger than we are now?
>
> We're still soaring up in our dawn dreams,
> Our mommies are out of bed before it's really light.
> We're rushing away again somewhere—
> Our mommies stand and wave behind us.
> And the sons' sadnesses lie
> Like white snow on their temples;
> If we could choose our mothers
> We would still choose our own.
>
> You can travel all over Russia,
> Spend many days on the road,
> You'll never meet anyone more beautiful,
> You'll never meet anyone more dear.
> So send them a telegram more often,
> Try and warm them with a letter.
> Our mommies can do anything in the world,
> Except not grow old.

[*RSP,* 652]

The large proportion of songs in which concern is expressed for an older woman who is alone reflects, of course, a central demographic fact about Soviet society. But the matter goes deeper than that; the "guilt of the erring son" theme has profound roots in classical Russian literature.

Besides official songs of the "hymn" type, patriotic songs, love songs, and "mommy songs," there are several other prominent thematic divisions within the Soviet mass song. For instance, there is a whole corpus of what might be called "theme songs" for the various professions and the branches of the armed forces. As an example we may take "The Geologists," written jointly by Sergei Grebennikov and Nikolai Dobronravov in 1959. The protagonist is female.

> I've gone away into the sultry steppes,
> And you've gone to explore the taiga.
> Above me is only the burning sun,
> Above you there's only the cedars in the snow . . .

Its refrain goes:

> But the road is long and far,
> And there's no turning back.
> Hold on, geologist, be strong, geologist—
> You're the brother of wind and sun!

Another verse of this song must contain the most agonizingly wrought metaphor ever produced by a songwriter desperate for something to make his words catch the attention of his intended public:

> I'll never find a better friend.
> The two of us are geologists;
> In life we know how to tell
> Precious ore from empty ore!
>
> [*RSP*, 607]

There is also a very large body of mass songs whose purpose is to laud the virtues of particular places; "Evenings near Moscow" has an element of that, and there are many others about the capital city. Leningrad too has been the subject of many songs, whose accessories can be guessed without straining the imagination too much—the white nights are the most frequent prop. There are also some songs in praise of more out-of-the-way corners of the "wide native land"; they usually manage to bring in one or more of the favored themes. Nikolai Dorizo's "It's a Long Time Since I'd Been in the Donbass" ("Davno ne byval ya v Donbasse," 1956) is a real grab bag:

> It's a long time since I'd been in the Donbass,
> And I felt drawn back to my native places,

Where to this day has been left on the shelf
That coal-mining youth of mine.

It's stayed the same,
Even though I've been far away.
And there has to be a girl called Galya
Living in her factory town there.
. . .
At last I got to the Donbass,
And there was her little white house. . .
A gray-haired housewife on the clean terrace
Was calmly doing the washing.
. . .
Forgive me my cruel memory
Of the plaits you used to wear,
And that as the years pass, men
Stay younger than their girl classmates.

Forgive me for those moonlit nights,
And that it was not in this place
I searched for and found someone
Just like you in your faraway youth.

[*RSP,* 458–59]

Whether a song can become genuinely popular as a result of sheer promotion by the media and other systems in the USSR is as difficult a question to answer as whether in capitalist society a song can be made into a hit through "hype," or through promotional effort. There would probably be agreement between the people professionally involved in both systems that nothing at their disposal could make a song into a hit if the public, the people itself, did not make the decision to accept the song. But there is the same difference between the situation in Russia and the West in this regard as in all others. In the USSR, the Party-state axis has an economic monopoly, and there is no real competition inside the public system. A Soviet song that has official approval can receive promotion on a scale undreamed of by public relations executives in the West. Its impact can saturate society from top to bottom, and even include the education system, which is subject to the Party's mandate as much as if not more than any other area of national life.

To write a song that achieves official approval and promotion in the USSR is a path to immense fame, privilege, and riches, greater potentially than for any novelist or poet. There is, not surprisingly, a corps of specialized lyricists (*tekstoviki*) and composers whose careers are based on the mass song, and who are very protective in their attitudes toward it—as we shall see in greater detail when we examine their attitudes toward the rise of their amateur rivals in the 1960s.[13] Their prototype was Lebedev-Kumach, who has already been mentioned. The doyen in the 1960s was Mikhail Isakovsky (1900–1973), one of the true classics of Socialist Realist literature, the author of "Katyusha" (1938), the only Soviet "mass song" to have become genuinely popular on an international scale. There is Evgeny Dolmatovsky (born 1915), Shostakovich's librettist on several occasions, and author of such classic Soviet songs as "Komsomol Volunteers" ("Komsomol'tsy-dobrovol'tsy," 1957), a stirring march whose chorus runs:

> Komsomols and volunteers,
> We're strong in our true friendship.
> We'll go through fire, if need be
> To open up our youthful paths.
> Komsomols and volunteers,
> We have to believe and love wholeheartedly;
> Sometimes to see the sun before dawn—
> That's the only way to find happiness!

[*RSP,* 229]

Then there is Lev Oshanin (born 1912), currently a very high official in literary politics. His "Lenin Is Always with Thee" ("Lenin vsegda s toboi," 1955) illustrates one of the most cherished and most heavily promoted Soviet themes:

> The years run past, day after day—
> The dawns of new generations.
> But nobody anywhere
> Will forget Lenin's name.
>
>> Lenin is always alive,
>> Lenin is always with thee—
>> In grief, hope, and joy.
>> Lenin is in springtime,
>> In every happy day,
>> Lenin is in you and in me.
>
> A long time ago, amid stern gloom,
> At the dawn of Soviet power,
> He said that on earth
> We would build happiness for people.
>
> We walk behind the Party,
> Praising the Motherland with our deeds,
> And throughout our great journey,
> In every deed Lenin is with us.
>
>> Lenin is always alive . . .

[*RSP,* 320]

The parallels with Christian hymnology are too obvious to require comment.

A much less well-known Soviet lyricist, but one who has made a considerable contribution to the repertoire, specializing in lyric songs about love and nature, is Aleksei Fat'yanov (1919–1959). Similar in stature to Fat'yanov but specializing in the opposite kind of song, the heavily official, is Vladimir Kharitonov, author of such songs as "Russia Is My Motherland" ("Rossiya—Rodina moya," 1950), "A Son of Russia" ("Syn Rossii," 1954), "March of the Communist Brigades" ("Marsh kommunisticheskikh brigad," 1958), and "My Address Is the Soviet Union" ("Moi adres—Sovetskii Soyuz," 1972).

Several poets of the generation born in the decade immediately preceding the war have contributed songs that have already become classics of the official repertoire. Of them, the best-established is Robert Rozhdestvensky, born in 1932 and in print since before 1950 with what is now a very weighty oeuvre of highly acclaimed verse. He tends to be the poet with whose work Party-minded Soviet youth identify most closely as an expression of their ideals. His songs in the official repertoire include "Ballad about Colors" ("Ballada o kraskakh," 1970). This song is about a mother who has two sons, one red-haired and the other black-haired. They go to war in 1941, and she is the only mother for three villages around whose sons come back. But both now have the same color hair—gray. Rozhdestvensky's "The Enormous Sky" ("Ogromnoe nebo," 1971) is a copybook example of an "optimistic tragedy," a song about two friends, both Air Force pilots. They sacrifice their lives by refusing to bail out when their plane gets into difficulties over a city—they remain on board and make sure it crashes into a wood (inevitably, a birch wood). The idealism that permeates Rozhdestvensky's songs at times becomes indistinguishable from religious mysticism, which is the case with many official songs about the ultimate destiny of the individual. A particularly interesting example is "On the Far Side of the Clouds" ("Tam, za oblakami," 1973):

> The young rain is rippling in the sky,
> The winds fly over the sleepless plains. . .
> If only I could know what awaits me beyond the distant boundary,
> On the far side of the horizon.
>
> Not for nothing did I seek the high heaven,
> And sleep under the cover of the big snows;
> But I did find out what the dawn is like
> On the other side of the clouds.

I believe that in putting up with all my failures,
Giving up my life to my friends and my journeys,
I will recognize love, I will encounter you
On the far side of a turning.

If something terrible happens to me,
Don't pace out the melancholy earth,
Just know that you can always find my heart
On the far side of the clouds.

[*RSP,* 585]

Rozhdestvensky is an accomplished poet with a sincere and questing intellect. Even his most orthodox songs contain what could be seen as the seed of their own destruction in his persistent leaning toward sadness and mysticism. After Rozhdestvensky, the most eminent contributor of the prewar generation of poets to the repertoire of official mass song is Yevtushenko, a rather more vulgar and facile poet than Rozhdestvensky who has a record of face-saving conflicts with the literary authorities. His "Do the Russians Want War?" ("Khotyat li russkie voiny?" 1961) is a very good example of the mass song on a military subject. It promotes the official line that the Russians because of their past sufferings are by nature peace-loving and not aggressive, but that when the Motherland is threatened by an external enemy, they will fight to the last man:

Do the Russians want war?
You just ask the silence
Over the broad expanse of plowland and field,
The birches and poplars.
You just ask the soldiers
Who lie there under the birches,
And their sons will tell you—
Do the Russians want,
Do the Russians want,
Do the Russians want war?

It was not just for their country
That soldiers perished in that war,
But so the people of all the earth
Could sleep peacefully at night.
As the ones who did the fighting,
And who embraced you on the Elbe
(We remain faithful to that memory)—
Do the Russians want,
Do the Russians want,
Do the Russians want war?

> Yes, we know how to make war,
> But we do not want our soldiers
> To fall in battle once more
> Onto their bitter soil.
> You just ask the mothers,
> You ask my wife.
> And then you really will have to understand—
> Do the Russians want,
> Do the Russians want,
> Do the Russians want war?
>
> [*RSP,* 616–17]

This song is ideologically immaculate. In addition, it has two excellent examples of what Western pop professionals would call "hooks." The first is the reference to the Red Army's meeting up with the Allied armies on the Elbe in 1945, and the implication that whereas the Soviets have remained faithful to the idea of cooperation against evil, the Western allies have let them down. The second, on a more sneaky level, is the reference to "my wife," which turns the whole song around by implying that it is sung by a ghost.

The references to nature in Yevtushenko's song are also worth noticing. As in so many official songs, we find the birch tree, which is joined here by the poplar, and a reference to Russia's broad expanse of plowed land and fields. The landscape evoked in the song is for most Russians a bucolic dream that has nothing to do with the conditions under which they actually live. In part, the imagery of the official mass song derives from a carefully selected, burnished, and bowdlerized version of Russian folk song.

The study of folklore is a massive academic industry in the USSR, taking in the collection, publication, and study of texts.[14] Folklore is studied under the same conditions as the rest of Soviet scholarship: it has a Party mandate to work to. It supplies an image that fits hand in glove with the Party's conception of the history of Russia as one of centuries of the peoples' suffering, relieved at last by the October Revolution. Traditional folklore is selected and edited in order to produce an image of Russia and the Russians that conforms with the norms of the Party's expectation from literature of the Soviet period, and it is manipulated to express the same attributes that we have seen in the official mass songs. Folklore is not only collected, published, studied, and taught. It is also performed, and with a vengeance, throughout the entertainment industry of the USSR. Never a day goes by without Moscow Radio's churning out yet another women's choir from the Sverdlovsk region, a group of balalaika players from Ust-Ilimsk, or the Old Bolsheviks' Choir of the Kirov Region, singing the same old staples from the folk repertoire. The use of stylistic and thematic elements from folklore in the mass song is highly approved of, and is always mentioned as a positive element when songs are discussed.

The approved repertoire of official mass song is promoted through a system of controls. Singers in the USSR have a "repertoire sheet" that lists the songs they are permitted to perform. The songs on the list form the subject of the same sort of fierce bargaining that writers have with their editors and editors with *Glavlit*, the state's organ of censorship for the printed word. This bargaining takes place between the singer (or his agent) and the representative of the appropriate local branch of *Glavrepertkom*, the "Main Committee for Repertoire," which is responsible for controlling the repertoire of all aspects of the performing arts in the USSR. If a singer is caught performing songs not authorized on his list, he may be punished in a number of ways, chief among them being denial of the opportunity to give concerts, or restriction to less lucrative or prestigious work.[15] Again as in the case of writers, the material self-interest of the performer in the USSR is a major stimulus working for self-censorship and the promotion of officially approved material.

The official mass song has an approved repertoire, and it also may be said to have an approved style of performance. Despite the breakthrough that was made in the late 1950s with the arrival of Mark Bernes, the first Soviet crooner, Soviet singers still have a pompous, stiff aspect compared with their Western colleagues. The archetypal performers of the mass song are the huge choirs maintained by various institutions of the Soviet state, the most famous being that of the Red Army. The adipose, self-important dignity of the state and its massive apparatus can be strongly sensed in their style.

Such, then, is the official Soviet "mass song," playing its appointed part along with the other branches of the arts in embodying the Party's ideology in images acceptable to it, actively shepherding the country's people along the road the Party decrees, reinforcing the Party's version of its history, creating an icon of the new Soviet man at work and in his private life.

It will be obvious that the official song as represented in this anthology leaves vast areas of human experience and emotion untouched. It has no satirical element, nor could it have without bringing about the destruction of the whole edifice of conventions. Its capacity for humor of any kind is severely limited. It is highly stylized in language and imagery, using elements divorced from common speech. It draws compulsively on a few favored images that come from a version of archaic rural folklore rather than the urban life familiar to the majority of the present-day population of the country. More important still, its emotional range is restricted. Joy, happiness, determination, pride, fidelity, and defiance are amply provided for, even required. But despair, anger, lust, hopeless longing, revenge, and many other fundamental drives and emotions can find no place in it, not to mention the entire middle range of emotions centering on contented passivity. The official song deals with life as seen through ideologically tinted spectacles; it offers examples for emulation rather than recognizable aspects of lived experience. The real life of real people in the country from day to day has very little connection with what the Party wants these people to sing about. In the song, as elsewhere in the Soviet arts, there are extensive aspects of the country's historical experience that cannot be publicly discussed at all, and many others (such as the war) that can be discussed only in a certain way.

But to sing about the whole range of experience and emotion seems to be a universal human need. And the Russians gratify this need—but not through the official mass song.

2   The Middle Ground and the Amateurs

THE SOVIET "MASS SONG" produced by the corps of professional songwriters and composers, and the officially approved folklore and literary heritage that go along with it, receiving active promotion from all the enormous resources that the Party-state axis commands, form a large segment at one end of the spectrum of song in modern Russia. There are no clearly definable boundaries separating this body of song from the next area on the infinitely gradated and constantly shifting spectrum that leads ultimately to the underground song at the opposite end. But there is an area of this spectrum that needs some examination as a point of reference, even if it cannot be defined with any great precision. This "middle ground" lies between what is actively promoted and what is actively persecuted by the authorities.

Part of the difficulty of definition arises from the fact that the very concept of ideological neutrality is officially unacceptable in the USSR. The principle that "he who is not for us is against us" may sometimes be held in abeyance for quite long periods, but it is never forgotten. Also, it is axiomatic that anything actually published in the USSR, whatever the medium, is in a real sense "official," since the state has an economic monopoly of the media and controls access to them through its system of censorship. Nevertheless, in song as in all the other branches of the arts, the controllers tolerate a good deal of material which, while not explicitly promoting official attitudes, does not actually say anything that could be interpreted as hostile to them or incompatible with them.

The limits of toleration in the USSR, as everywhere else, are the focus of a continuous contest between the producers of cultural artifacts and the interests involved in the media. In the West, what is transmitted by the media is the result of a very long series of compromises involving artists, managers, producers, editors, trade unions, accountants, sponsors, lawyers, and agents, all of whom have their own motives and interests. In the USSR, the agencies that intervene between the artist and the public are probably not as complex or as insidious, but they are certainly more effective as interference, certainly more rigid and doctrinaire, and certainly more firmly rooted in a monolithic ideology. One can never be certain of the extent to which a text that is published in the USSR represents the author's intention—assuming, that is, that there is a final product at all, and that it has not come to grief somewhere within the control system, or been dismissed as unrealizable by the author at the moment of conception. But within the system there is a certain amount of give-and-take, and the threshold of toleration shifts sometimes even from month to month as the result of the interplay between the creative process and the factors that are interposed between its products and the public.

There are also in the USSR, as elsewhere, various levels or degrees of publication, which are especially important in the case of songs. The most common location of a song belonging to the "middle ground" is not words on paper but more ephemeral modes of publication. The vast output of Soviet radio and TV includes songs which may have come in for bitter criticism by established songwriters because of the low standard of their words and music. Just as is the case everywhere, an overwhelming proportion of the material spewed out every day by the broadcasting media is trash, ephemeral both in the intentions of its creators and in the consciousness of its consumers. It is enough to listen to the Youth channel of Moscow Radio for a couple of hours to realize that if the material were deemed worthy of really serious checking by the ideological controllers, it could not possibly be passed. It is not actively subversive, but it is almost completely lacking in the positive qualities expected of Soviet art. However, rather than in radio and TV, it is in the theater and films that ideologically suspect or even hostile material persists and gets a public hearing.

One perhaps trivial example is the scene in Bulgakov's play *The Days of the Turbins (Dni Turbinykh),* which has been in the repertoire of the Moscow Arts Theater for years, when the tsarist national anthem is played and the White officers on stage stand rigidly to attention. Everybody in the audience knows what the music is, and in this way an ideologically hostile cultural artifact has been preserved in the consciousness of Soviet audiences. Similarly, films which take prerevolutionary Russia as their subject abound in all sorts of songs, especially religious ones, whose words could not possibly be published within the domain of the Soviet system of censorship.

Perhaps the most striking example of this kind of "publication" was the use, in the production of Pasternak's translation of *Hamlet* by the Taganka Theater in Moscow, of the Russian poet's lyric also called "Hamlet." It is the first in the set of poems appended to the novel *Dr. Zhivago* as the work of the eponymous hero. Some of these poems, unlike the text of the novel, have been published in the USSR more than once, but "Hamlet" was not published until 1980.[1] Its text movingly explores the plight of the persecuted intellectual, making an analogy with the agony of Jesus in the Garden of Gethsemane. The Taganka performance began with an absolutely bare stage, stripped right back to the bricks of the outside wall behind it. As the stage lights gradually came up in synchronization with the dimming of the house lights, after the audience had taken its seats, the figure of Vladimir Vysotsky became visible. Dressed in his all-black Hamlet costume, he was sitting with his back against the bricks, and quietly strumming the guitar he cradled in his lap. As the lights grew stronger, he got up and walked to front center stage, and then sang Pasternak's lyric to a soft guitar accompaniment. The effect was breathtaking—the underground poet-singer performing in his own inimitable way the most profound underground words of the great persecuted poet. This production of *Hamlet* was in the repertoire of the Taganka Theater for eight years and has been seen by thousands and thousands of Soviet citizens—who know the poem by heart anyway from *samizdat* copies. And yet, technically, strictly speaking, this poem was banned and unpublished in the USSR. Paradoxically, through its use by the Taganka Theater, it is well known and has been brought to the consciousness of an uncountably greater number of people than spare a glance for, say, the latest bunch of Yevtushenko lyrics in a large-circulation newspaper like the *Literary Gazette (Literaturnaya gazeta)*.

In the middle ground there is also a considerable body of non-Soviet songs, Russian and translated, that for various reasons have been published and recorded in the USSR. Perhaps the most interesting example is the work of the great cabaret singer Alexander Vertinsky (1889–1957). Vertinsky emigrated after the Revolution, but he returned to Russia in 1943 and was active as a performer until the end of his life. His performances were not genuinely public but were restricted to "closed" occasions with the audience either carefully selected or with entrance available only to members of the specific institution sponsoring the performance. The exotic strangeness of Vertinsky's decadent songs and style—something like those of Noel Coward—in the USSR in wartime has been described by Alexander Shtein.[2] The popularity of Vertinsky's songs in the 1960s was documented by Mikhailo Mikhailov.[3] That was long before Soviet recordings of Vertinsky were released, which happened on a small scale in the 1970s.

Songs like those of Vertinsky have a clandestine, or at most semipublic, existence. But the decadence and escapism of his songs are not entirely absent from "official" song. Outside the USSR, attention has always naturally focused on the exceptional, untypical, problematical, or "scandalous" products of Soviet culture. The run-of-the-mill, the average, tends to be ignored. However, the nature of this material is not what most people would think it is—stiff, heavily official work on approved themes like Lenin and the Party, tractor drivers and milkmaids—although there certainly is plenty of this dreary hackwork, exuding the uplifting philosophy that was attested in the official hymns. It comes as something of a surprise to learn, for example, that even in the years when Stalinism was at its most oppressive after the postwar clampdown, in Soviet poetry the dominant theme was one of escape, as Vera Dunham's pioneering work has demonstrated.[4] There was indeed some factographic work about the war, but there was even more of what Professor Dunham called "rhymed mushrooms"—verse about an artificial, "style-russe" countryside with echoes of a mythical Slavonic past. And the most frequently expressed aspiration by poets was for silence and peace, rather than for commitment to the communal political tasks of the present day. Findings such as these suggest that it may in fact be the "middle ground" of tolerated failure to write the Party's bidding that actually makes up the bulk of Soviet art.

In terms of the song, it is the treatment of love that seems to offer the maximum leeway for publishing authors to depart from optimism, commitment, and positive thinking. One of the most popular recent Soviet love songs is "Weeping Willow" ("Ivushka," 1958), by the otherwise obscure wordsmith Vasily Alferov:

> A golden evening sunset
> Shines over the river.
> Dear weeping willow,
> Calm my heart.
>
> Green weeping willow,
> Bending over the river,

Tell me, tell me without keeping secrets
Where is my love?

There were meetings with my darling
Under your boughs.
And every evening the nightingale
Sang us songs.

But my sweetheart has gone away
And he won't come back.
With the song of the nightingale
Love too has ended.

Green weeping willow,
Bending over the river,
Tell me, tell me without keeping secrets
Where is my love?

[*RSP*, 592]

This unremittingly sad song is publishable probably because of its immaculate folkloristic accessories. The timelessness and conventionality of the style make the otherwise unacceptably gloomy message and tone acceptable. But it is possible to go even further in print. An established poet can, it seems, publish work that would appear to be quite incompatible with official canons. For example, Robert Rozhdestvensky, whose work was mentioned earlier in the context of official song, has the following lyric from 1974. It is called "Sweet Berry" ("Sladka yagoda," 1974):

The sweet berry lures you into the wood,
Amazes you with its ripe freshness.
The sweet berry makes your head spin,
The bitter berry sobers you up.

I don't know what's happening to me,
Why they grow the way they do—
The sweet berry only in spring,
The bitter berry all year round.

Oh, cruel fate, like a mountain,
Has tired me out and used me up.
Of the sweet berry only a handful,
Of the bitter, two bucketfuls.

Go on, laugh at my trouble,
From the window watch me go.
We picked the sweet berry together,
The bitter berry I pick alone.

[*RSP*, 386]

The protagonist in this song, as the grammatical form of the Russian makes clear, is a woman. Rozhdestvensky here uses traditional Russian folk imagery to articulate a lament for the loss of sexual innocence and to assert a resigned view of woman's life as timeless and tragic. The text of this song appears along with the same poet's calls to do one's duty by the Komsomol, march in step with right-thinking youth, and so on, in the anthology from which all the examples of official songs have been taken so far. Rozhdestvensky's song shows that the "middle ground" can stretch a long way away from the official, even within the work of a single author.

One song that became extremely popular among young people in the early 1960s is "If I Should Fall Ill. . . ." Its words were written in 1949 by Yaroslav Smelyakov (1913–1972), a very talented poet whose life was one of continual persecution and privation, including two periods of arrest and one term as a prisoner of war. He eventually emerged, toward the end of his life, into high official standing.

> If I should fall ill,
> I won't turn to any doctors.
> I appeal to my friends
> (Don't start thinking I'm delirious):
> Make up the steppe for me like a bed,
> Hang mist at my windows,
> And at the bedhead set
> The night star.
>
> I always walked straight ahead,
> I wasn't known as a namby-pamby.
> If I am wounded
> In fair fight,
> Bandage my head
> With a mountain road,
> And wrap me up in a blanket
> Patterned with autumn flowers.
>
> Powders and drops—
> I need neither.
> In my tumbler
> Let sunrays shine.
> The hot wind of the deserts,
> The silver of the waterfall,
> Those are the best medicine.
>
> From the seas and mountains
> Comes a strong scent of passing centuries;

You only have to look at them to sense
That we live forever.
My path is not strewn with white capsules [*oblatkami*]
But with clouds [*oblakami*].
I will leave you not down a hospital corridor
But down the Milky Way.

[*RSP,* 463–64]

The religious impulse that has been so rigorously channeled into secu-
lar themes since the Revolution is here simply bursting for expression.
The poem expresses a yearning for an untrammeled, direct, un-
mediated life, in contact with natural forces, a yearning that is central
to many Soviet lyrics. In this respect, the song does contain, implicitly
at least, a note of dissatisfaction with the bureaucratization, in-
stitutionalization, and urbanization that are characteristic of Soviet
life. But the text cannot be interpreted unambiguously in this way. It
has the same vagueness, the same lack of focus and specificity, as the
official songs. Refreshingly, though, it lacks any of the accessories that
crop up so often when nature comes into official song. There is no birch
tree, for example. And there is a generally optimistic, life-enhancing
ring to the poem. But it would be difficult indeed to see it as a positive
exemplification of Socialist Realist art.

A Soviet critic writing in the mid-1960s asserted that "the most popular song at present . . . justly called the anthem of tourists, climbers,
geologists, and students" is "The Globe."[5] The song goes as follows:

I don't know where you and I
Will happen to meet again,
The globe goes round and round
Like a sky-blue balloon . . .
Cities and countries flash past,
Parallels and meridians,
But the dotted lines haven't been made yet
Along which we will wander the world.

I know there is an undiscovered
Latitude of latitudes,
Where a wonderful friendship
Is bound to bring us together . . .
And then we'll discover that boldly
We were both taking on a great cause,
And the places where you and I went
Have been marked on the maps of the world.[6]

The general optimism of this text, in which the protagonists are aware of themselves as individuals but also socially conscious, makes it acceptable for public performance in the Soviet media. But its central idea says nothing that explicitly supports Socialist Realism or any other particular ideology. The song finds a satisfyingly concrete expression for a universal longing for justified trust in a friend and confidence in one's professional activities in the face of the unknown. Whether the "undiscovered latitude of latitudes" is a coy reference to life after death is a tantalizing question.

Almost as popular as "The Globe," again according to Dobrovol'sky, is another song that for many years was not sponsored by the media but existed as folklore, mainly among campers and hikers. It is "The Brigantine" ("Brigantina") by Pavel Kogan, a poet who was killed in combat in 1942 at the age of 24:

> We're tired of talking and arguing,
> Of loving tired eyes . . .
> In a far-off filibustering sea
> There's a brigantine making sail . . .
>
> The captain, windswept like the cliffs,
> Has gone to sea without waiting for us . . .
> Raise in farewell your goblets
> Of tart golden wine.
>
> We drink to the malcontents, the unlike ones,
> The ones who've despised a cheap refuge.
> The Jolly Roger flaps in the wind,
> Flint's people are singing a song.
>
> That is how we say goodbye
> To our silvery, most sacred dream,
> Filibusters and adventurers
> By blood which is taut and thick.
>
> If trouble, joy, or sadness comes along,
> Just narrow your eyes a bit, that's all.
> In a distant filibustering sea
> A brigantine is making sail.
>
> The Jolly Roger flaps in the wind,
> Flint's people are singing a song.
> And, our glasses ringing, we too
> Begin our little song.
>
> We're tired of talking and arguing,
> Of loving tired eyes . . .
> In a far-off filibustering sea
> There's a brigantine making sail . . .[7]

Apart from the direct reference, in the person of Captain Flint, to Robert Louis Stevenson's *Treasure Island,* enormously popular since its first translation into Russian in 1886, this text is heavily marked by the spirit of the most eminent Russian poet of adventure in exotic lands, Nikolai Gumilev, who since his execution for being a counterrevolutionary in 1921 has remained unpublished and almost completely unpersoned in the USSR, but who nevertheless exerted a strong influence on prewar Soviet poetry. What is also striking about Kogan's song is that it was written in the dread year 1937, at the height of Stalin's Great Terror. To understand its appeal in terms mainly of escapism, comparable with the novels of Alexander Grin (1880–1932), is obvious but unavoidable. The song is apolitical, implies values that have nothing to do with official ones, and has the appeal of a simple, morally direct code that makes life carefree and straightforward, far away from familiar surroundings.

"The Brigantine," in the way that successful songs often do, spawned a number of successors. One of them neatly ties up the ethos of the song with the milieu in which it characteristically flourished. It is by the successful official songwriter Mikhail Tanich, and was written in 1966. It is called "City of Tents" ("Palatochnyi gorod"):

> We live in mosquito country
> And want no easy life.
> We love our tent,
> Full sister to the brigantine.
>
> > In the taiga the insects swarm,
> > And the post takes its time.
> > Forward once more
> > Like a fleet under sail
> > The city of tents sails on!
>
> In our rucksacks are cities
> And the crests of concrete dams.
> River water splashes
> Against the canvas hull of the brigantine.
>
> > Our long route in the taiga
> > Will be marked on the map in time to come.
> > Forward once more . . .
>
> You can come if you want—risk it!—
> To our canvas discomfort,
> Where there aren't many lights,
> And guitars sing at night.

> At night paraffin burns
> On the decks of all the brigantines.
> And forward once more . . .

> Far-off places will be settled,
> The tents be sent to a museum,
> And the streets here be named
> After our friends.

> But all this will be later on,
> After we've gone from here.
> And forward once more . . .

> [*RSP,* 638–39]

"City of Tents" is one of a very large number of modern Russian songs about what might loosely be called the romance of pioneering. The theme became a subject of intense official promotion during the "Virgin Lands Campaign" of Khrushchev. This policy gave birth to dozens of songs in which young people fly away from the cities into the *taiga* wastes, full of joyful anticipation, eager to work and build. But these songs also express a theme of universal appeal that this time coincided with the official drive to recruit young people for voluntary service in Siberia—the romantic urge to escape into wild nature. And the milieu created in the virgin lands was an important one for the creation and transmission of unofficial songs. Lev Kopelev made the connection between the great guitar poets and the culture of the virgin lands:

> . . . the eminent singers were preceded by and coexisted with the amateur activity *(samodeyatelnost')* of geologists, tourists, and the student brigades of "virgin-landers" *(tselinniki).* As they put distance between themselves and the ruling, "industrially" standardizing civilization, the gloomy clichés of propaganda, and all kinds of cultural work done according to plan, these groups of traveling young companions often became hotbeds of freedom and liberty. On the road in their leisure time they sang songs, as people always sing in these circumstances in Russia and The Ukraine, yes, and probably in all the other regions of our country. And most often there's a guitar to accompany these singers.[8]

The popularity of the last three songs that have been quoted, and their rise into the middle ground, were part and parcel of a tendency in the arts during the post-Stalin phase away from solemnity and rigidity, away from the mandatory concern with man as a social animal, confident and aggressive. These songs were not written for the official media and supplied with music by recognized composers according to normal process with the mass song. In the case of Smelyakov's text, the words were not even specifically intended to be sung. The words of these songs were taken up "by the people" and became detached from their authors. They did not exist through the public media as entertainment or propaganda but were sung mainly on informal occasions, away from the metropolitan centers or on the fringe of the official network of cultural activity.

This fringe, in which the "middle ground" of song comes into its own, is difficult to define with any precision. The public part of it is located in those facilities that exist in the USSR for leisure activities of a cultural nature. They include cafés, the clubs that are attached to practically every industrial enterprise of any size, and the Houses of Culture, the institutions that serve (and organize) cultural activities on a local level. What goes on in these establishments is referred to in Soviet jargon as *samodeyatelnost'*, "doing it yourself," with connotations something like those of the word "amateur" in English.[9] The term covers anything not performed by professionals, even though professionals might be and probably are involved in a supervisory capacity. Insofar as *samodeyatelnost'* exists within institutions like the clubs, efforts are made to bring it within the control system. For the most part, *samodeyatelnost'* involves collective or group activities such as choirs, theatricals, dance, and musical ensembles (particularly ones using folk instruments like the balalaika); creative writing groups exist, too. For all these things, professional advice and practical help are channeled by the appropriate unions as part of their professional activities. Thus, for example, poets are expected to provide a roster of visits to creative writing groups in their area. This professional intervention forms the lowest level of the pyramid of state-sponsored artistic activity in the USSR.

Less formal than the clubs and Houses of Culture, and less susceptible to organization, are the opportunities that such leisure activities as camping and hiking offer for the singing of songs. In fact, "The Globe" and "The Brigantine" are especially popular in this milieu, and apparently existed within it during the years intervening between their composition and their emergence into a more public role in the 1950s.

The individual's singing of songs to his own guitar accompaniment is a mode of performance that has existed in these environments since time immemorial. (The military is also sometimes said to be another environment in which guitar-accompanied solo song has persisted.)

The reasons are obvious. A working technique on the guitar for accompanying the vast majority of songs is fairly easily acquired; the instrument is a fully adequate accompaniment in itself and is portable and, obviously, it leaves the vocal organs free for singing. At the end of the 1950s, guitar-accompanied solo song was taken up by several poets and developed into a new "serious" art form. What had been for years a subcultural activity, not much more than mere entertainment, began to seem appropriate to more serious, more demanding artistic purposes.

The most important stimulus was the general atmosphere of the early Khrushchev period.[10] The "Secret Speech" of 1956 seemed to imply that the way would be opened for more informal, individual work, which would not have to fulfil all the requirements that had strapped the arts under Stalin. The emergence of poets who sang alongside those who declaimed their work was part of a general opening up and loosening in the arts, with opportunities for more direct contact between artist and public. The most celebrated manifestation of this tendency was the institution of Poetry Day, the first of which was held in September 1955. It is defined in the *Short Literary Encyclopedia (Kratkaya literaturnaya entsiklopediya)* as follows:

> Poetry Day: The day of the mass meeting between Soviet poets and their readers, a form of active propaganda of poetry . . . it is held every autumn in Moscow, Leningrad, Kiev, and other cities; organized by workers in the book trade and poets. On Poetry Day poets stand behind the counters of bookshops and sell books, read their work, answer readers' questions, sign autographs. Poets also give readings, make appearances in squares, clubs, and so on, sometimes getting an audience of more than 75,000 listeners. . . .[11]

The reaction of the public to the early "Days" was ecstatic. In his *Precocious Autobiography,* Yevgeny Yevtushenko, one of the leading lights in this movement, has given an account of how in the later 1950s poetry was in the vanguard of the revitalization of cultural life. The absolute high point at the time he was writing was the attendance of 14,000 people at a poetry reading at the Palace of Sport in Moscow. Among the writers he considers to have been on the side of change and movement at the time, Yevtushenko identifies Pasternak, Dudintsev, Yury Kazakov, Aksenov, Akhmadulina, Voznesensky, Rozhdestvensky, and "the poet Bulat Okudzhava," who

> in the evening sat with two or three friends, a glass of vodka and a guitar, singing his lyrics, without suspecting that in a few years they would be heard on thousands of tape-recorders.[12]

Another Poetry Day activity was observed in 1967 by Olga Carlisle:

> Last fall in the vicinity of the Pushkin monument I heard several beat-niklike young men, so much like their Western counterparts with their beards and guitars, sing Esenin's menacing lyrics:
>
> > I too will cut a throat
> > to the whistling of autumn.
>
> Certain singers continue this tradition; they write their own songs in the popular vein, drawing mostly on contemporary urban folklore.[13]

By the mid-1960s, the poet accompanying himself on the guitar had become a familiar phenomenon in Soviet cultural life. Its rising popularity had to be officially dealt with and accounted for. But commentators were rather at a loss as to how to deal with it, or even what to call it. The earliest substantial discussion of the subject was by the well-known critic Yury Andreev. It appeared in January 1965 in the right-of-center literary periodical *October (Oktyabr')*.[14] Andreev felt compelled to defend his interest in the subject against colleagues who thought it unworthy of the attention of a serious literary critic. The remarks he attributes to his detractors are interesting, because they reflect attitudes that have persisted to this day:

> What are you on about, those semiunderworld [*polublatnye*] little songs they were singing at that concert at our institute?
>
> Listen, drop that bright idea of yours! Life's too short, there's so much to do, it's simply criminal to waste time studying all kinds of vulgar froth. . . ."
>
> "Surely not the modern 'minstrels?' We can't find space for that!"—snapped the deputy editor of a "thick journal" categorically.[15]

The term Andreev uses for the object of his study is *samodeyatel'naya pesnya,* perhaps best translated as "amateur song." He also uses the term *ashug* to refer to the poet-singers; it is the Kazak word for a singing folk poet, an appealing term which has not caught on. Andreev lists a total of 26 "ashugs," making no distinction between them in terms of ability or talent. The list includes both Okudzhava and Galich (but not Vysotsky); also Gorbovsky, Kukin, Ancharov, Matveeva, Vizbor, Kim, Aleshkovsky, and Klyachkin, as well as a rump of authors who have never been heard of before or since.

Andreev's analysis of the actual content of the amateur songs is constructed in terms of their thematic range's being so wide as to take in all the colors of the rainbow. There is the red of "our life": the "civic, courageous lyric," about the casualties of war, perhaps, but always optimistic and enhancing. Then there is the green of nature, where the singer rejoices in the beauty and wonder of the natural world that surrounds him. There is the yellow, or rather pure gold, of "fantasy and dream, romantic invention" (the field leader here is Pavel Kogan's "Brigantina".) Then there is the orange color of love, associated in this way by Andreev because orange is the most prominent color, just as love is the most prominent theme. In an insert into his main scheme, Andreev mentions what to an outsider is probably the most distinctive thing about the amateur songs he is discussing, namely, their "antibombastic" nature, their "nonacceptance of sugariness and false exaltation." Andreev does not, of course, spell out exactly where in Soviet life the main source of the target of this negative quality might be located! He identifies this quality with the rich humor that the songs possess. When he goes back to his spectrum of colors, it is to deal summarily with the range from violet to black. He primly refuses to "name names" with regard to the authors of any "violet" songs. Andreev concludes his article by asking about the nature of the amateur song as a Soviet cultural phenomenon. He realizes that the reason for its rise and flowering is that "professional songwriters at this particular stage have not been able sufficiently to express the moods and feelings of young people."[16] However, Andreev's discussion runs into the ground as he asks whether or not these songs can count as folklore (thereby implying positive cultural value). His inevitable conclusion is that in terms of the older criteria for validating folklore (collective composition, anonymity, oral transmission, variability of texts), they do not fit the bill. Finally, he wonders if in modern conditions, after the Soviet cultural revolution, now that there is universal literacy, the time has perhaps come to revise the criteria for folklore in order to take in the amateur song.

Andreev's article has the general merit of being fairly open-minded about a phenomenon that for an establishment critic like him is fraught with all sorts of difficult implications concerned with defining the limits of tolerability in a particular art form. But he is not traducing the material when he finds that the bulk of it is quite compatible with Soviet criteria of acceptability. In fact, it is even highly orthodox thematically, informed by the same positive, optimistic, progressive views as the official song, and quite acceptable stylistically.

More objective and comprehensive than Andreev was B. M. Dobrovol'sky, whose essay appeared in 1968 as a contribution to a very serious volume dealing with all aspects of the use of folklore in "amateur artistic activities" *(khudozhestvennaya samodeyatel'nost')*.[17] Dobrovol'sky uses the rather clumsy phrase "urban youth's contemporary songs of everyday life" *(sovremennye bytovye pesni gorodskoi molodezhi)* to label his subject. The main point of his essay was to assert, with numerous examples, that there is no evidence of an interest in traditional Russian folklore among contemporary urban youth. These people have their own songs, whose origins and history have not been studied and whose texts are unpublished, but which have just as good a claim on the interest of scholars, on an aesthetic and every other ground, as traditional Russian folklore. Dobrovol'sky gives a valuable, concise historical survey of the evolution of the repertoire, citing songs from before the Revolution and from each successive period of Soviet history. And he examines the reasons why certain songs have stayed in the repertoire and others have not.

Dobrovol'sky says that in the late 1950s and early 1960s a new kind of song appeared, the "author's song" *(avtorskaya pesnya)*. The conditions fostering its growth were as follows:

> The opening of "youth cafés" (with volunteer labor, another form of amateur activity) and song clubs; the organization of concerts by enthusiasts among the authors, collectors, and active listeners, and of amateur arts festivals and competitions; and the circulation of songs in taped copies and duplicated manuscript collections led to a remarkable expansion of the audience, and made "author's songs" known to the public at large.[18]

The singers Dobrovol'sky regards as the founders of the author's song are Yakusheva, Vizbor, Matveeva, Klyachkin, Gorodnitsky, Vikhorev, Poloskin, Dulov, Kim, "and many others."

Dobrovol'sky has high praise for the artistic merits of songs by Matveeva, Gorodnitsky, and especially Kim. But he treads warily when he comes to the far end of the repertoire of song. He asserts that a special category among the songs known by contemporary urban youth is "songs for listening." These are "songs which are accepted by the audience only in the author's performance," those of Klyachkin and Poloskin being Dobrovol'sky's cautious examples. The reason why they can still properly be considered "mass" songs is that they are so "thanks to circulating in amateur tape recordings." Finally, Dobrovol'sky attempts to define the specific characteristics of "author's songs." In one important respect he is absolutely right, if rather clumsy:

The distinguishing feature of the creative activity of urban youth with regard to contemporary song is that now the author of the song is most often the creator of the entire musical-poetic complex.

And he describes the way the song enters the folk memory:

. . . . it begins as part of everyday life—on tourist and climbers' hikes, on geologists' expeditions, at student evenings and so on. . . . The next stage is the encounter between the song and the masses in youth cafés, clubs, and Houses of Culture. These meeting-concerts are "amateur" *(samodeyatel'ny)*. They take place as a result of the initiative of youth groups—lovers of song, who make up the evening's program, set up the premises, design and distribute the tickets, and so on.[19]

Dobrovol'sky's article will remain a valuable contemporary testimony to the actual conditions under which the guitar-accompanied solo song began to emerge and took a firm hold in Soviet culture.

The terminological difficulties encountered by Andreev and Dobrovol'sky have never really been resolved. The guitar poets are still referred to by a large number of terms: *poet-singer (poet-pesennik), chansonnier (shanson'e), balladeer (balladnik), minstrel (menestrel'), bard (bard),* even *troubadour (trubadur)* and *minnesinger (minnizinger).* The history of this group of words has been discussed by a leading Soviet lexicologist, A. A. Bragina, in a passage that incidentally says quite a lot about the history of middle-ground song.[20] The word *shanson'e* is attested in Russian as early as 1864; a century later, says Bragina, it has the meaning "a singer who pays attention to the word, to the content of his song." Bragina notes the increasing use of *menestrel'* and *bard* as synonyms for the age-old native Russian word *pevets; bard* is first attested in the eighteenth century, *menestrel'* in the mid-nineteenth. She quotes an advertisement for a concert in the Palace of Sport in Luzhniki, Moscow in May 1966, at which there is to be a section devoted to "bards and minstrels." Her most revealing sample of the word is as follows:

There has been much writing and argument about the contemporary *bards* . . . their songs have been condemned more often than they have been praised . . . just try to buy a guitar these days—you'll have no luck. . . . Undoubtedly, this phenomenon is connected with the widespread impact of the songs of the *bards,* which are sung exclusively to the guitar. . . . But let's remember that the songs of the *bards* started getting popular in the late forties and early fifties (now the amateur singers can be divided into generations—there is an older one and a middle one, and a young one has already appeared.)[21]

In the mid-1960s, then, Soviet literary critics were trying to describe and explain a new force in Russian poetry and song, the essence of which they saw in its amateur nature. This movement was not without parallel outside the USSR.

Popular music in the West has been transformed in the last twenty years with the rise of rock music in all its forms. The essence of the rock revolution in the beginning was, however much subsequent developments may have traduced this factor, to thrust a lack of professionalism, an unschooled, rough, jagged kind of content and form, into the smooth, overslick, and therefore insincere-sounding popular music of the fifties. The USSR was not insulated from this impulse. But the roots of the turn against officially approved, establishment professionalism grew in native soil whose fertility was even greater potentially than that in the West. It was, as we have said, the soil turned over by the de-Stalinization of Russian life and culture in the wake of Khrushchev's "Secret Speech" to the XX Congress of the Party in 1956.

However much the political factor may have been the real but unspoken issue underlying concern with the rise of guitar poetry, it was on the grounds of professionalism that resistance to it was mounted. Of course, in song as in literature and all the other aspects of the arts, there is in the USSR a powerful vested interest in the maintenance of the status quo. The established professional has his credibility and status at stake. It would be a mistake to think that the relative lack of pressure from the marketplace means that the official songwriter in the USSR is insulated from extraartistic pressure. He is without doubt most consistently pressurized by the ideological watchdogs. But he has his own professional concerns, too.

The route by which an issue is brought to public debate in the USSR is never entirely clear. It is most likely that concern expressed inside the Union of Writers or the Union of Composers about the rise of amateur songmaking, perhaps stimulated by Andreev's article, led to an editorial in the *Literary Gazette* on 15 April 1965 entitled "Youth, Song, Guitar" ("Molodost', pesnya, gitara"). This editorial gave an overview of the current situation, recognizing that young people were turning away from the offerings of the official providers of "mass songs" and starting to create their own material. The titles alone of the "responses" to the editorial speak volumes. First came L. Pereverzev with "The Modern 'Bards' and 'Minstrels' " (15 April), an indication of the official line accompanying the original stimulus for the debate by a recognized musicologist. Then came I. Dzerzhinsky, a composer, with "Ought We Really Begin with Advertisements?" which appeared on 24 April and proclaimed that there was a real issue, which was not being tackled in the right way. M. Tabachnikov, also a composer, published "The Guitar Is Not to Blame," also on 24 April, drawing attention to what he saw as the fundamental issues: content rather than form. Next, on 29 April, came a salvo from on high, in the form of an article by Lev Oshanin, "The Birth of a Song," full of ponderous official platitudes. Then came a restatement of the need for the official songwriters to shake up their ideas, with the singer V. Goncharenko's "What Ought They to Sing?" on 13 May. Another singer, M. Mikhailov, stated that the official line would prevail: "The Song Will Remain with Us" on 20 May; then came the composer Mokrousov with a smug view from the winning side whose victory was a foregone conclusion, "The Victor Is Not Judged" ("Pobeditelya ne sudyat") on 27 May. Finally, there was a ponderous broadside from the most senior living writer of official "mass songs," Solov'ev-Sedoi, on 3 June. He reused the title of the original editorial, for which he had almost certainly been a consultant, if he was not indeed the actual author. His concern was to condemn recent trends in the field of song. He reported among other shocking things that he had recently heard a group of students singing near one of the Neva harbors; he said that their songs were "musical do-it-yourselves, with primitively put-together melody and incoherent text. Something hopeless, pathetic, taken from dance-hall tunes."[22]

The function of this spate of articles was to call attention to the presence of a problem consisting essentially of the threat of an emergent cultural element opposed to the professional establishment. There were some further manifestations of official concern in the later 1960s. In February 1967 the venerable composer Dmitry Kabalevsky complained about "jazzification" as a disease that was rapidly infecting the body of Soviet music.[23] Writing soon after, in March 1967, Mikhail Isakovsky expressed his anxiety that the official mass song had lost its way. He was echoing a complaint that had been made by his colleague Konstantin Vanshenkin in a *Pravda* article of 4 March about the decline in the standards of Soviet songwriting. Composers, Isakovsky complained, had started imitating Western popular songs, and singers had started imitating their Western counterparts, so that listening to an up-to-date Soviet song "makes you feel as if you've swallowed a frog." Radio and television were to blame, said Isakovsky; they had lowered standards while increasing demand. One estimate was that the Youth

(Yunost') radio station in Moscow alone was using about three hundred new songs a year; and a corps of hackworkers had arisen to meet the demand. As a result, things "on the song front" needed to be set to rights. The 2,185 poets who were members of the Union of Writers at the time (20 February 1967) should surely be able to produce a few good songwriters, argued Isakovsky. His peroration is a good example of Soviet rant:

> And so, what we need to do is *bring back music into the song and bring back the genuine poetic word*—these are the two main conditions on which the future fate of the Soviet song depends. The song our people needs and loves so much.
>
> It is impermissible and simply unthinkable to reconcile ourselves to the music-and-song garbage that to our shame has accumulated in our country in such a great amount. This garbage needs to be decisively and permanently swept away.[24]

When the Union of Soviet Writers held its IV Congress in Moscow from 22 to 27 May 1967, the delegates were addressed on the fifth day by Lev Oshanin, whose "Lenin Is Always with Thee" was cited earlier. He gave a concise résumé of the history of the Soviet mass song since the Revolution. It had gone through three peak periods, said Oshanin: the mid-1930s, during the war, and then the late 1950s and early 1960s. Among the songs of this third period had been "many bright, profoundly human patriotic works." Lyrics had appeared that successfully countered the turbid wave of "hits" coming from the West. Genuine feelings had returned to the song, and life in all its multiplicity had been reflected in it. From ritual tribute Oshanin turned to ritual denunciation. He quoted one example of a vulgar song, by A. Gorokhov with music by V. Kuprevich, about a cosmonaut's nightmare, a piece that had somehow been broadcast. However, the point of Oshanin's speech, as is usual with these things, was to call the attention of officials to the unsatisfactory state of affairs revealed by the measures recently undertaken by the relevant organizations. In this case there had been, Oshanin reported, a joint meeting of Secretariats of the Union of Writers and the Union of Composers of the RSFSR. Various proposals had been made to tighten up editorial standards and raise the quality of the songs that were being let through, especially on the radio.[25]

A further indication of the seriousness with which the problem of song was being taken in official circles came in the late 1960s. No less a personage than a Deputy Minister of Culture of the USSR,

V. Kukharsky, published an article on the subject in the composers' journal *Soviet Music (Sovetskaya muzyka)* late in 1968. This article is directed against amateur singers and their works. It is shot through with one of the cardinal fears of the Soviet bureaucrat, the fear of "drift" *(samotek),* implying that the Party has failed to fulfil its function as leader and controller of everything that happens.

> What is sung most often at these meetings of "bards" "who have made a name for themselves," what songs are recorded by lovers of the cheap musical fronde on their tapes and records, which are then sold by speculators who are growing fat on these goods at three rubles a go? It's murky rubbish.

Kukharsky cites some lines from songs by Galich and Vysotsky, and accuses the latter of advocating a specific political program: "propaganda, which consists in sowing doubt, spiritual disarmament, and laying youth to waste."[26]

One noticeable blow in the opposite direction to the official onslaught came from the Leningrad musicologist Vladimir Frumkin, who in the late 1960s was actively involved in promoting guitar poetry. In 1969 Frumkin succeeded in publishing an article on the subject in the composers' journal. Making use of a listeners' poll he had conducted and his own professional musicological analysis, Frumkin subtly ridiculed some settings that the prestigious composer Matvei Blanter had written for a batch of Okudzhava songs. Okudzhava's own "amateur" music was found to be much more appropriate and effective than Blanter's.[27] At about the same time, publication permission was withdrawn for Frumkin's musical edition of some Okudzhava songs. The fundamental reason, Frumkin had no doubt, was the consternation of professional composers at the success of the guitar poets, and of Okudzhava in particular.[28]

The newspaper *Literary Russia (Literaturnaya Rossiya)* reported in November 1970 that the Secretariat of the Directorate, RSFSR Union of Writers, had conducted a meeting the previous December between poets and composers. One result of their discussions had been to call for the establishment of a special commission to deal with problems of "song production." The commission was established, and Lev Oshanin was appointed chairman. A second meeting of poets and composers was called late in January 1971 to deal with the problem of songs in films. Its next meeting, held in May 1971, dealt with the problem of military and patriotic songs; the work of certain poets was recommended for use as texts. But, as far as the published reports enable a judgment to be made, these meetings failed to come to grips with the shortcomings of official song and to propose measures to counter the growing influence of guitar poetry.[29]

Manifestations of concern such as these on the part of official bodies continued throughout the 1970s. As in all the other branches of the arts, there has been an unending and occasionally very bitter struggle between the authorities (including the artists who side with them) and the various sources of dissidence. The "cultural front" in the USSR is like a battlefield, on which the occupying official troops, with vastly superior equipment and an unmatched intelligence service, are engaged against a numerically superior peasant jacquerie. The former tend to be hampered by their rigid tactics and clumsy command structure, and even more by their outmoded ideology. The latter are helped by the continuous emergence of gifted individual leaders, their flexibility, and their open-mindedness toward innovations in tactics.

If we look at what official opinion was actually objecting to in the attacks on "amateurism" in the song that we have just examined, we may find some surprises.

As we can see from the information given by Andreev and Dobrovol'sky, and from the scraps of evidence contained in the publications of the musical establishment, the songs that evoked such consternation and complaints about falling standards in fact belonged to the "middle ground." They did not explicitly contradict official attitudes, but neither did they support them. What has subsequently happened to the majority of the people involved in early guitar-accompanied poetry is that although they may have begun by arousing official condemnation and being found to lack the professionalism expected of Soviet songwriters, they have survived. Their work of the time either has been consigned to oblivion or has expanded the body of song that exists in the middle ground. The most signal example is Okudzhava. At the beginning, some of his songs came in for severe criticism, especially because of the pacifism they allegedly advocated. But by the end of the 1970s a large proportion of his repertoire was or had been in print in the USSR, and recordings of his work were available.

The same is true of another poet who emerged singing songs to a guitar in the early 1960s. She is Novella Matveeva (born 1934), who has been steadily publishing lyric poetry since the late 1950s and has several albums issued of guitar-accompanied performances to her lyrics.

She has been criticized from time to time for the sin of escapism but has not encountered any really serious persecution.[30] Her most famous song is "The Land of Delphinia" ("Strana Del'finiya," 1964), which she sings in an appealing, rather winsome, little voice:

> The dark blue waves come rolling in.
> Green ones? No, dark blue.
> Like millions of chameleons
> Changing their color in the wind.
> The glycine blossoms tenderly,
> It's more tender than hoarfrost. . .
> And somewhere is the land of Delphinia
> And the town of Kangaroo.
>
> It's a long way away, but what of it?
> I too will go away there.
> Oh, my God, my God,
> What will happen when I'm not there?
> The palms will dry up when I'm not there,
> The roses will fade away when I'm not there,
> The birds will fall silent when I'm not there. . .
> That's what will happen when I'm not there.
>
> Yes, but how many times now has the good ship *Porcupine*
> Sailed off without me?
> How can I erase a disaster like that
> From my memory?
> But yesterday there came, there came, there came
> To me a letter, a letter, a letter
> Postmarked from my Delphinia,
> Franked "Kangaroo."
>
> White envelopes from the post
> Burst open like the buds of a magnolia,
> They have the scent of jasmine, but
> Here's what my relations write:
> The palms there aren't drying up while I'm away,
> The roses there aren't fading while I'm away,
> The birds aren't falling silent while I'm away. . .
> How can this be while I'm away?

[*RSP,* 658–59]

This song has been published and recorded many times in the USSR, and toleration of its apolitical nature, escapism, even pessimism may be explained by reference to its absolute vagueness. There is no possible way of interpreting it as a reproach against actual conditions. It expresses only an undirected sadness and longing; the imagery, however, is exotic but conventional, sketching out some locations perhaps to a Russian identifiable with the Crimean coast.

Matveeva continues on her way, the most "overground" of the important figures involved in the guitar-poetry movement. She is not the only one, though. Plenty of songs by other members of the first wave of balladeers were published in the USSR in the 1960s. The most interesting collection of their work was a small anthology, just over one hundred pages long, called *How Reliable the Earth Is (Kak nadezhna zemlya)*, which was published in Moscow in 1969. It was immediately spotted and reprinted under a new cover in the West, with the substitute title *The School of Okudzhava (Shkola Okudzhavy)*.[31] This title is more informative than the characteristically vague affirmation of the original, and it also takes advantage of the popularity, even notoriety, of Okudzhava's name in the late 1960s. The anthology is not a collection of "pure" guitar poetry. Besides the work of the true "bards," responsible for words, music, and performance, it includes a fair number of pieces by teams of composers and lyricists. However, the book gives the most representative picture available of the situation of guitar poetry in the USSR at the end of its first decade of existence. It has the words and music of four songs by Okudzhava, and smaller selections by Ancharov, Yakusheva, Vizbor, Kukin, Klyachkin, and Dulov. Among them are some of the most popular of all the early songs. The claim to the greatest popularity, perhaps excepting the work of Okudzhava and Matveeva, goes to a song by Aleksandr Gorodnitsky about the Atlantes that support the facade of the Hermitage in Leningrad:[32]

> When your heart is weighed down
> And your breast feels cold inside,
> To the steps of the Hermitage
> Make your way at dusk;
> There, without drink or bread,
> Forgotten down the ages
> The Atlantes hold up the sky
> In their stone hands.
> . . .

These stone effigies, the song goes on, stand and selflessly carry out their demanding task, while human history goes on around them. The moral of the song is contained in the last verse:

> They're standing there forever,
> Their foreheads propped on disaster,
> Not gods, but men

Accustomed to heavy labor.
And hope should go on living
For as long as
The Atlantes hold up the sky
In their stone hands.

[*ShOk*, 8–9]

This song has optimism and humanism. One of its middle verses contains a splendidly patriotic reference to the blockade of Leningrad. But the song is an occupant of the middle ground rather than a full-fledged official "mass song" by virtue of the absence of any specific Socialist Realist features. It also contains an insidious analogy between the Atlantes, with their thankless and permanent strain to do no more than keep things as they are, and the Russian people. This analogy, of course, is quite unacceptable in terms of the official progressive ideology, with its vision of "the bright future for all mankind."

The anthology accurately reflects the connection between guitar-accompanied song and the open-air movement, because of the substantial number of camping and hiking songs it contains. They include Gorodnitsky's "My Cities of Tents" ("Moi palatochnye goroda") and the significantly named "The Last Brigantines" ("Poslednie brigantiny") by Yu. Andrianova. There are some love songs, and even some "mommy songs" that are entirely worthy of the official prototypes, especially notable being G. Zaidel's "To My Mother" ("Materi"), which is about a gray-haired griever whose pilot son has perished in a flying accident.

Apart from Okudzhava and Matveeva, most of the authors represented in the anthology had had their day by the late 1960s and early 1970s and then faded away into other spheres of work or into oblivion, leaving perhaps one or two songs in the repertoire of the "middle ground." Only one of them, again leaving aside Okudzhava and Matveeva, is represented in *Russkie sovetskie pesni, 1917–1977*. He is Mikhail Nozhkin, with his highly patriotic mass song of the hymn type "Russia" ("Rossiya," 1967; *RSP*, 685). Mostly, the authors concerned have become lyricists and occasional writers, supplying texts for songs used on radio and TV and in the theaters. Their work has never been brought together and studied in the USSR and is not regarded as part of the country's literary history. As we shall see, the involvement of writers who became dissidents has cast a shadow over the entire movement.

The "middle ground," then, is a significant sector in the spectrum of song. It finds its audience through the more ephemeral media of radio, TV, plays, and films. In doing so, it may meet a very large public indeed, perhaps larger than the public that would take notice of something officially published, recorded, and promoted. The middle ground includes songs written by professionals and performed by other professionals, like the official mass song. But it also has a strong proportion of poets writing their own words and music, and performing them to their own accompaniment, as is the case with Okudzhava and Matveeva. The latter were in the forefront of a move toward amateurism that began in the late 1950s, a move that eventually succeeded in bringing a new element into the middle ground.[33]

The songs of the middle ground have several thematic characteristics. They can deal effectively with love, especially the sadder aspects of it. They also have a strong escapist element. The distinguishing tonality is one of relative understatement—an absence, as Andreev pointed out, of the high-flown rhetoric of the official song. Again, though, certain modes are out of reach of the middle ground. Satire and anything but the most benevolent humor are absent. Plenty of thematic and emotional areas also remain that neither the official song nor the middle ground can deal with under Soviet conditions.

3   Underground Song

THE RANGE OF SONGS lying at the opposite end of the spectrum from the official mass song, and separated from it by the nebulously fringed middle ground that has just been discussed, forms part of underground Russian culture. It is made up of songs that in principle are not carried by the media and are not permitted a public hearing—in the unlikely event that anyone in his right mind would actually present them for publication or broadcast and try to get them through the control system. We shall see that there actually are some ways of doing that, and circumstances under which it is allowed to happen. But the essential condition is that the song should not be presented in its own right, as it were, but as coloring or as an appendage, or as a negative example, in some other undertaking. Underground song is part of that elusive and constantly evolving entity, modern urban folklore, and in the USSR it exists mainly within and for the use of the metropolitan literary and cultural intelligentsia. It has several separable constituents, some of them surprising at first sight.

To begin with, we should consider an aspect of Soviet official culture that by its very nature is not open to precise definition or even examination, because it exists inside the private consciousness of people who are as a rule extremely sensitive to the political implications of their observed conduct. We are all familiar with the notion of "doublethink." It does not really baffle us any longer that a Soviet citizen—perhaps even one who is doing a term in a labor camp—can stand and sing Lebedev-Kumach's "Song of the Motherland," including the couplet

> I know of no other land
> Where a man can breathe so freely

without irony. He almost certainly does not know any other land anyway. But it would not occur to him that he is bending his conscience to sing these words, any more than only the most fanatical of British republican atheists would refuse to sing "God Save the Queen" if the occasion demanded. The words are functionally sanctioned as the appropriate social behavior in a particular context. Life is too short, and most human beings are sufficiently able compromisers by nature not to need to ask ultimate questions about sincerity before committing every single one of their social acts. But it is difficult for anyone who is not a Soviet citizen to grasp the comprehensiveness and sheer all-pervading presence of the official ideology in the USSR. It is commonly observed that Russians now have as second nature the ability simply not to notice such things as the slogans on red bunting that are draped across their streets, reared on scaffoldings on all their highest buildings, repeated over and over again by all the media, and drummed into them by the education system: "Glory to the CPSU!" "Party and People Are One!!!" "Peace to the World!" and so on. The saturation is such that a person would need to confine himself entirely to the private environment of his own apartment (if he is lucky enough to be so self-contained and self-sufficient) and keep all the media firmly switched off and excluded, if he wanted to insulate his mind from these things. But for thinking people, slogans, and the whole vast ocean of "agitation and propaganda" of which they are the surface expression, actually contain the seeds of their own destruction. Only the slightest whiff of irony, only the most elementary confrontation between the slogan and reality, is needed for the entire system to begin to negate itself. First among their strategies for self-preservation, passive resistance, and even reprisal, the Russian people have recourse to political humor. The first line of the universally known official march of the Soviet air force (by P. German and Yu. Khaik, 1928) goes: "My rozhdeny, chtob skazku sdelat' byl'yu" ("We were born to turn fairytale into reality"). By making a couple of tiny adjustments to the *skazku*, "fairytale," the Russian intelligentsia both subverts the official myth of Communism's "radiant future" and asserts its familiarity with ideologically alien culture: "My rozhdeny, chtob Kafku sdelat' byl'yu" ("We were born to turn Kafka into reality").

Official culture, of course, is not static. There is constant movement into and out of the category of officially acceptable song, as with all other categories of official art. And what moves out is not forgotten. Nothing in Soviet life is potentially so subversive as the official culture of the past, especially the "un-past" that has been decreed unmentionable. A vast hymnology, iconography, and hagiography of Stalin was accumulated during the years now dubbed with characteristic mendacious evasiveness "the years of the cult of personality" (the phrase itself, with its pointed exclusion of Stalin's actual name, provides a very good illustration of the technique of unpersoning.) This huge stockpile of artifacts has been consigned to oblivion. A few items from it, as we saw in the case of Lebedev-Kumach's "Song of the Motherland," have been purged of the offending name and recycled. The Soviet national anthem was popularly referred to for many years as "The Song without Words," for although the tune of the original Stalinist anthem was retained, the words could not be publicly performed because of their laudatory references to the leader. A whole generation of Russian schoolchildren grew up singing "Russian and Chinaman Are Brothers Forever." Every Soviet citizen over the age of forty has in his mind a huge detritus of what is now quite scandalously subversive information acquired on his way through the education system in Stalin's time. He copes with his memory by means of doublethink, neglect, humor, or dismissive derogation. But the old official songs form a significant element in the undergrowth of song. And, as we will see, they can be evoked and exploited by skillful authors.

Although the state has continually sought to bring song under its control and keep it there as a means of propagandizing its own values, it has never been successful in taking over the whole of the spectrum—notwithstanding its economic monopoly of the media, its system of prescription and proscription, its hold on the education system, and its intrusion into leisure activities. Just as in other spheres of human activity, but perhaps even more successfully and intensively, the private, unofficial element has managed to persist and to renew itself. It will not be possible to give anything like a complete account of this process until recent émigrés consider the subject worthwhile, or until it becomes feasible for Soviet citizens to be more forthcoming. But it is possible to point with a fair amount of confidence to certain important elements in the undergrowth of song.

The Gypsy Song

One important type of unofficial song that has continued to exist despite occasional condemnation is the gypsy song or gypsy romance. The concept is used very vaguely in Russian to refer to songs that may have no overt reference to actual gypsies in their subject matter. They are performed most characteristically by a solo singer to his own guitar accompaniment, with many liberties permitted with regard to both variation on the melody and departures from consistent tempo. The gypsy song or romance usually deals with illicit, unbridled passion and has an element of debauchery in its setting.

The gypsy choir and gypsy singers are continuously attested in Russia from the last third of the eighteenth century. They helped to popularize the seven-stringed guitar, which has become standard in Russia.[1] The gypsy choir as an element of high-society entertainment reached its peak in Russia in the 1830s, the most famous one directed by Ilya Sokolov, who died in 1848. Gypsies captured the imaginations of Russian poets at least as far back as Derzhavin (1743–1816), and they were used as an image around which the poet could weave a picture of a life untrammeled by the restraints of urban society. Several major nineteenth-century Russian poets, such as Apollon Grigor'ev (1822–1864) and Aleksei Apukhtin (1840–1893), wrote lyrics drawing on gypsy life and its supposed passions. The cult of the gypsy reached its height with the popularity of Bizet's *Carmen* (1875), which took Russia by storm soon after the turn of the century. However, by this time

> . . . the repertoire of the gypsy choirs and their style of performance had turned into what is referred to as "that gypsy stuff" *(tsyganshchina)*—songs of decadent content and low artistic quality. The "gypsy romance," which had first been close to Russian sung romances, by this time had lost all its artistic value. It became widespread in petty bourgeois circles, where it was usually performed as a solo song with guitar accompaniment.[2]

The gypsy song thus became a kind of emblem of bourgeois decadence, and it was the target of particularly hostile criticism when Soviet popular music was brought under Party control in the 1930s.[3] The gypsies themselves were brought within the Party-state system of entertainment with the organization in 1931 of Romany *(Romen),* the State Gypsy Theater, which exists in Moscow to this day. Along with the circus, the gypsy theater is commonly regarded by the intelligentsia as one of the very few institutions that the Soviet state has not managed to deaden.

The most famous example of a Russian gypsy song—recorded countless times, commonly regarded by non-Russians as the epitome of Russian song in general, and a staple of the cabaret and amateur repertoire since well before 1900—is "Two Guitars" ("Dve gitary"). The words are as banal in the original as the translation suggests:

> Two guitars in another room
> Begin their plaintive moaning,
> A refrain I've known since childhood,
> My darling, can it be you?

The song's refrain is the Russian equivalent of "tra-la-la," literally:
"Ah, once, and once again! Many, many more times!" *(Ekh, raz, eshche
raz,/Eshche mnogo, mnogo raz!):*

> It *is* you, I recognize
> Your modulation into D minor,
> And that melody of yours,
> Its frequent repetition.
> > *Ekh, raz . . .*
> How could I not recognize you?
> Upon you lies the mark
> Of passionate merrymaking
> And stormy hangovers.
> > *Ekh, raz . . .*
> It *is* you, you devilish rake,
> By the punchbowl,
> And your melody
> To that Hungarian strain.
> > *Ekh, raz . . .*
> Ah, it aches, oh, how it aches—
> My head from too much drinking . . .
> We've been drinking, and we'll go on drinking
> The whole week through!
> > *Ekh, raz . . .*

This translation has been made from a text of the song as first published
in Moscow before the Revolution; the exact year is unknown.[4] The
song and all its numerous variants actually go back to a lyric poem by
Apollon Grigor'ev, first published in 1857. The first stanza of the original poem, which is still often sung, goes:

> Oh! Won't you have a talk with me,
> My seven-stringed friend!
> My soul is full of such longing,
> And the night is so moonlit![5]

The content, the actual words, of this song are of very little significance
in themselves. They vaguely sketch a lifestyle of bohemian debauchery. The permanent appeal of the song derives from its combina-

tion of sentimental words and plaintive melody, the most common catchall minor tune that has been used again and again. It is also an excuse for the open display of emotion; but self-parody is never far away when the song is performed.

The gypsy element in guitar poetry as it emerged in the 1960s rarely becomes explicit; it exists rather as a submerged component in the musical style. One characteristic manifestation of it is Galich's title "Bol'nichnaya tsyganochka," which does not mean "The Gypsy of the Hospital," as would seem to be the case. The word *tsyganochka* is an affectionate diminutive meaning "gypsy (song)," and the title means something like "A Song in Gypsy Style about a Hospital." Of the major guitar poets, it is Vysotsky who most overtly used the gypsy style. He sometimes performed the classic gypsy songs; his version of "Dark Eyes" ("Ochi chernye") is the epitome of the modern Russian intellectual's idea of unbridled, passionate gypsy emotion.

It is in the gypsy song and the gypsy style of performance that guitar-accompanied solo song has its strongest root in Russia. By the early twentieth century the seven-stringed guitar had become a Russian folk instrument.[6] Even Lenin is said to have played the guitar during his exile in Shushenskoe (1897–1900), in addition to playing chess and shooting game. Two graphic testimonies to the prevalence of amateur guitar-accompanied song may be found among the most beloved Russian dramas of the twentieth century. Chekhov's *Uncle Vanya* is punctuated by snatches of song and strumming on the guitar from the decayed gentleman Telegin, nicknamed "Waffles." And at one stage in the proceedings, when they are far gone in drink, both Dr. Astrov and Vanya himself show that they can take up the guitar and sing at least a fragment of a sentimental romance. Mikhail Bulgakov's *The Days of the Turbins* (1926) was mentioned earlier because of the use in it of the tsarist national anthem. As the play opens, Nikolai Turbin, the eighteen-year-old youngest son of the family, is singing improvised words to his own guitar accompaniment. He sings snatches of song throughout the play; the final example occurs just before the end and provides a touching musical frame to the play's action. Both *Uncle Vanya* and *The Days of the Turbins* have been staples of the Moscow Arts Theater's repertoire for many years.

The popularity of the seven-stringed guitar and the gypsy style of playing to accompany song is in large part due to the ease with which the technique is acquired. The seven-stringed Russian guitar is tuned

D-G-B-d-g-b-d; its open strings produce a G major chord, and the related D and C chords can be produced with very little dexterity, which is why the seven-stringed guitar is the most widespread accompanying instrument in Russia. It also helps to create the "amateur" aura that guitar-accompanied song has; even when the strumming is being done with consummate skill, the result still sounds easy to attain and unprofessional.

The Cruel Romance

The second important kind of song that is found in the undergrowth of modern Russian culture is the "cruel romance," to translate the Russian term literally *(zhestokii romans)*. The cruel romance is a ballad-type song, usually with a strong narrative element telling a melodramatic story of unrequited love or infidelity. Quite often revenge leads to a violent outcome. The style is one of open sentimentality, and the text frequently concludes with a direct appeal for sympathy from the audience. However, self-parody and irony are never far away. The manner of the cruel romance is very familiar to English speakers from such songs as "She Was Poor but She Was Honest," with its bleeding-heart last verse sung by the song's heroine-victim herself:

> "It's the same the whole world over,
>   It's the poor as gets the blame,
>   It's the rich as gets the pleasure—
>   Ain't it all a bleeding shame!"[7]

There exists no adequate account of the origins and history of the cruel romance in Russia.[8] It seems to have evolved as a parody of the high art *Lied,* or "romance" *(romans)* as it is called in Russian, somewhere toward the end of the nineteenth century. The cruel romance was cultivated by cabaret singers and was especially popular in the cabarets of St. Petersburg in the years before the Revolution. It has been used as an object of parody and also as a serious stylistic source by several Russian poets.

Valery Bryusov, for example, in the section entitled "Songs" ("Pesni") in his epoch-making *Urbi et orbi,* the volume which in 1903 established the theme of the modern city in Russian poetry, used the cruel romance as source and model.[9] Aleksandr Blok also made use of the genre. There is an interesting reference to the cruel romance in Marina Tsvetaeva's memoir of her friend, the actress Sonya Holliday (1896–1935), who was particularly fond of this kind of song. One poem of the cycle Tsvetaeva dedicated to Holliday is a brilliant parody of the genre:

> The rain is knocking at my window,
> A workman leans over his squeaking lathe;
> I was a street singer
> And you were the son of a prince.[10]

The cruel romance also seems to have flourished in the period immediately after the Civil War, the NEP period, when the resumption of private enterprise in small-scale undertakings led to a boom in night life. The late poetry of Sergei Esenin (1895–1925), especially the cycle "Tavern Moscow" ("Moskva kabatskaya," 1924), provides the most striking literary embodiment of this style. The most famous example from the NEP period, remembered and sung to this day with great gusto and generally considered to be a folk song, is a cruel romance cast in the form of a street-vendor's cry, called "Bubliki." The word refers to the speaker's wares, the ring-shaped hard bread roll something like a pretzel:

> Buy my bubliki,
> Hot bubliki!
> Chase your rubles
> Toward me quick!
> And in this filthy night
> Take pity on
> Unhappy me
> And my trade.
> My father's a drunk.
> And proud of it,
> One foot in the grave
> And he still drinks!
> My mother's on the streets,
> My sister's a fallen woman.
> And I'm a smoker
> Watch me do it![11]

This song was in fact composed by one Yakov Yadov for the Odessa cabaret singer G. Karsavin.[12]

It is very difficult indeed to find any evidence about the fate of the cruel romance during the 1930s. As Stalinism took hold and consolidated, public reference to a phenomenon as a-Soviet as the cruel romance was something to be avoided. There are some scraps of evidence that refer to wartime, however.

A good example of a song in the style of the cruel romance is the following, by an unknown author. The song was mentioned by Mikhailo Mikhailov, and a full but imperfect text was first published in England in 1964.[13] It obviously dates from World War II.

> I was a battalion scout,
> And he was our HQ clerk;
> I was answerable to Russia,
> But he was sleeping with my wife.
>
> Wife of mine, poor Shura,
> Surely you've not stopped caring?
> What made you, you poor fool,
> Swap your eagle for that shit?
>
> An eagle and handsome figure of a man,
> I wouldn't even stand by his side,
> From Moscow to Berlin I strode
> Over corpses for three years.
>
> I strode, and then in the hospital
> I lay in death's embrace,
> And the nurses wept in the ward,
> And the surgeon's scalpel trembled.
>
> My brave neighbor was also in tears,
> A colonel, three times Hero of the Soviet Union,
> He wiped away his tears
> With his hardened soldier's hand.
>
> An accursed shell fragment
> Had pierced my bladder.
> Once I leaned down for my false leg
> And there under the bed was the HQ clerk.
>
> I battered his white breast
> And tore off his medals,
> Take a look, people of Russia,
> Observe, my native land.
>
> My poor wife Shura
> I adored madly;
> My false limb wouldn't stand for her
> And my crutch tore her to bits.[14]

This song exhibits several hallmarks of the cruel romance. The singer makes an emotional appeal to his audience (in this case, the entire Russian nation) because he feels he has been treated unjustly and wants redress. Clichés like "death's embrace" and "soldier's hardened hand" are used deliberately, as are some elements from classic

Russian folklore (the hero as "eagle," the "white breast" of the victim). The protagonist has an ironic attitude toward his own plight. What makes the song especially appealing is that it takes an irreverent, worldly attitude toward the war theme—which, as we have seen, is sacrosanct in official song.

A second, more modern, song that exhibits strong elements of the cruel romance is a unique text which was taken down by Vladimir Markov from the lips of a deported Russian woman in a labor camp in Nazi Germany:

> Everything's finished, everything in the world is lies;
> My happiness is shattered, I'll never get it back.
> In a house with shining windows and a well-lit room,
> The waltz sounds out and the ball begins.
> Couple after couple, but my man's with someone else,
> My heart is jealous, I'm sorry he's not with me.
> . . .
> My dear women friends, what a mistake I made,
> He loves another and doesn't love me any more.
> Loves her, kisses her strongly, presses her to his heart,
> But he doesn't know there's a baby growing up.
> The child will grow up and ask where its father is,
> And here is what I'll answer him:
> Your daddy's dead, my sweet child,
> And a tear will drip from my eye.
> Stop crying, mommy, stop pouring tears,
> If daddy's dead there's no bringing him back.
> Your daddy hasn't died, my poor child,
> He loves another and doesn't love me anymore.
> Whose grave is this, overgrown with grass,
> A poor girl died from poison at seventeen years old.
> Men, you men, you have such scheming hearts,
> Your love is all words, but never is it deeds.[15]

Markov's concise description of this song's origins is interesting. He calls it

> . . . a love song, among the true descendants of the cruel romance, which are still sung at the lower depths of musical culture by laundry-women, seamstresses, prostitutes, and others. No one collects or records these songs now, for obvious reasons, and they never leave the dark social corners of the cultural periphery. The melody is always borrowed from a well-known song, and the text is never the same. The lyrics, a helpless imitation of "high" poetry, full of grammatical errors and ridiculous stylistic blunders, are nevertheless sometimes charmingly naive and touching.[16]

It needs to be added that however much these songs may be taken seriously on the cultural periphery, they are well remembered, preserved, and performed by intellectuals in Russia. Their attraction is due to the naive charm that Markov points out, and also to a genuine straightforward admiration for them as an alternative to official, politicized culture. They constitute a kind of high camp, regarded with an inextricable mixture of condescension and affection. And, of course, they are functionally differentiated from serious, "high" literature; they are not placed at a lower level of the same hierarchy but occupy one of their own, the function of which has to do with entertainment, relaxation in informal circumstances.

An interesting cruel romance, apparently of recent vintage, the authorship of which has not been established, is "Anna Karenina." The song, a vulgarization of the great novel's plot which brings in the characteristic "begging" motif of the cruel romance, was very popular among Soviet university students in the 1960s:

> In Moscow there lived the heroine of a novel,
> She came of ancient gentry stock.
> Her name it was Anna Karenina,
> Her patronymic was Arkad'evna.
>
> She had no desire to work hard;
> With a criminal passion in her blood,
> This lady lived without the slightest care,
> Suffering from Russian love.
>
> Then along came Vronsky, a terrible cad,
> And an officer to boot.
> He'd been nurtured by a different epoch,
> And he hadn't lived in the USSR.
>
> Old man Karenin was severe and unkind,
> But Anna was beautiful and sweet.
> She couldn't take that kind of family life,
> And she started an affair with Vronsky.
>
> But Vronsky, the rat, was very conceited,
> And he forgot his promise.
> He turned out to be ideologically backward,
> And not on her wavelength at all.
>
> Inside Anna a deep wound opened up;
> It's no secret for us, after all,
> That she left her tyrant husband
> And her twelve-year-old son.

So proud Anna went off to the station,
And proudly lay down on the tracks.
In those far-off days of capitalism
Nobody thought of saving her.

And that's how those empty coquettes met their end,
Who'd seen the regime of the tsars;
But we who've lived through the seven-year plan
Won't put up with a fact like that.

Give, citizens, gents and ladies,
Even a crust of bread,
For that Anna Karenina
Left behind an orphan son.

He wanders about like a fledgling,
Abandoned by one and all.
Give, brothers, and give, sisters,
It's Sergei Karenin who's asking.[17]

The juxtaposition of Tolstoy's plot with the incongruous snippets of Soviet jargon and the revelation of the singer's identity in the final verse make this song very appealing. At about the same time that "Anna Karenina" was popular, there was another song that was often sung back-to-back with it. This song is about Tolstoy himself:

Our great Russian writer
Lev Nikolaich Tolstoy
Wouldn't eat fish or meat,
And walked barefoot down the alley.

His wife, Sofiya Tolstaya,
On the other hand, liked eating;
She didn't walk barefoot,
But kept up her gentry honor.

And this here Sofiya
Who bore the surname Tolstoy
Liked neither the philosophy
Nor the simple nature of her husband.

In his life he had upsets,
He endured the blows of fate,
And you can't read his novel *Resurrection*
Without shedding a tear.

He had his brushes with the government,
Even though he was the idol of the people,
Because of his novel *Anna Karenina*
And his other one, *War and Peace.*

Give, give, give, citizens,
I am his illegitimate son . . .[18]

The "begging" motif here is obviously just tagged on out of deference to genre convention. This inoffensive little song, incidentally, is a good example of what official critics have in mind when they condemn a text for lack of "ideological awareness" *(ideinost')*. It is not acceptable to talk about the great figures of Russian culture, however inimical they may be to Communist ideology, in this flippant, subliterary way. All these songs in the tradition of the cruel romance have a note of irony, a gently fun-poking attitude toward the various dilemmas and unlucky lives that they describe. This note keeps them in the underground of song and also makes them a valuable repository of an alternative tonality to official song.

The Criminal Song *(Blatnaya pesnya)*

The third principal genre that exists in the undergrowth of Soviet culture is the criminal song, to give an admittedly inadequate translation of the Russian term *blatnaya pesnya;* "underworld song" is perhaps equally good. The word *blat,* from which the adjective in the phrase derives, means "crime" itself but also has in modern Russian the meaning of "pull" in the sense of "illegal influence." The word also means "thieves' cant." The term *blatnaya pesnya* is often used to refer to the entire range of unofficial song, but here it will be used in a narrower sense, to refer to songs about life on the wrong side of the law. Typically, the criminal song deals with stories of betrayal and revenge and illustrates the inflexible code or "law" *(zakon)* of the criminal world, a code which demands utter hostility toward the law of the state and complete solidarity within the criminal fraternity.[19]

No adequate description or history of the criminal song in Russia has been written, and relatively few texts have been published. Though the picture may be distorted by the operation of chance in publication, it would seem to be the case that the Soviet period inherited a good number of criminal songs from prerevolutionary times. The criminal song then had a period of flowering (like the cruel romance) during the NEP period, when there was scope for more underworld activity than at any other time in Soviet history. It was still possible at that time to publish reasonably objective studies of this kind of song and the culture in which it had its roots. Perhaps the most remarkable publication was an article of 1926 by N. Khandzinsky.[20] This article has a copious supplement of texts and even a lexicon; it also cites such things as the graffitti on the walls of prison cells. Khandzinsky collected his material in Irkutsk and the surrounding area in 1925 and 1926. His discussion notes the essentially urban character of the songs and poems, and the links—perhaps amounting to direct dependence—between the "folklore" of criminals and respectable literary verse. The collection of songs appended to Khandzinsky's article includes the texts of several songs whose popularity is attested in written sources thirty and more years later. There is, for example, the notorious song entitled "Gop so smykom," a phrase that Khandzinsky registers in his lexicon as "not established." It has elsewhere been explained as the nickname of the song's hero.[21] This song is the defiant credo of a dedicated thief, a paean to his independent, dissolute, and immoral life, his determination never to sink into the ranks of law-abiding citizens. The second half of this extremely long text—one hundred and six lines altogether—concerns the hero's intentions regarding the afterlife. He declares that even in hell he will continue with his calling, to the extent of robbing Judas of his pieces of silver. The song is clearly of literary origin. It has a tone of delicate irony and conscious undermining of its own outrageous braggadocio. "Gop so smykom" has become a kind of epitome of the criminal song, cited by Soviet critics whenever they wish to castigate vulgarity and degeneracy, the absence of Soviet idealism. In this respect, its only rival as a whipping boy is a song usually referred to by the name of its heroine, "Murka":

> The thieves big and small, the evil captains,
> Were electing a new committee.
> And a girl took the floor
> Called Murka,
> She was stern and bold.
>
> They needed to get on with the job, they wanted a drink,
> So they went to an elegant restaurant.
> A guitar was sounding and a couple dancing,
> It was Murka and some young fop.
>
> I rushed up to her and grabbed her arm—
> "I've got to have a talk with you."
> But she just laughed and pressed closer to her dude—
> "I can't live with you any longer."
>
> In a dark alley Kostya met Murka,
> "Hello, my dear, and goodbye!
> You've shopped our entire gang,
> And for that you answer with your life.

Before, you used to love 'No. 3' cigarettes
But now, you won't even need any tobacco.
Before, you used to like a drink of vodka with us,
But now you won't even need cognac.

Hello, my Murka, dear Murka,
You shopped our entire gang
And now you get your lot."[22]

The motifs of betrayal and immediate personal retribution central to the tale of Murka are the hallmark of the criminal song.

With the growth of the Soviet labor camp system to an extent unprecedented in world history, a situation developed that was favorable to the preservation and transmission of underworld song. In an atmosphere where lip service to the ruling official ideology was still exacted, criminal elements were deliberately mixed in with political prisoners, who tended to be intellectuals. There was therefore an ideologically aware meeting between literary and subliterary cultures. It may be that the high proportion of Russian intellectuals with direct experience of criminal life is the distinctive feature of their social group, when compared with the intelligentsias of other countries. However, censorship has choked the reflection of this situation in literature.[23] The published evidence concerning the cultural life of the GULag is small, and the place allotted to song is a fraction of that. There can be little doubt, however, that song loomed large in the prisoners' lives. As early in the life of the GULag system as 1929, Maksim Gorky paid a visit to the convict settlement at Solovki on the White Sea. He heard the convicts singing traditional Russian folk songs—but with new words, the subversive nature of which filled him with alarm.[24] In Soviet literary works dealing with the GULag, criminal songs have tended to be used in negative characterizations of people before they are "reforged" thanks to the conscientious toil of the security organs. However, not much, if anything, of the songs' texts is ever actually published on paper. In Nikolai Pogodin's famous play *The Aristocrats* (*Aristokraty,* 1934), for example, which is about the convicts who built the White Sea Canal, the third act ends and the fourth begins with scenes of revelry. In performance, the actors concerned sing songs whose words could not be published under any circumstances.[25] And in *The Road to Life* (*Putevka v zhizn'*, 1928), Ekk's classic film about the rehabilitation of young people, several startling examples of criminal song are used to portray the corrupt state of the heroes before Soviet morality comes to their deliverance.

The real life of the camps, as opposed to their use as an example of Soviet social progress, has been an "un-subject" in Soviet-published literature throughout its history. It was allowed to sneak into this literature only for a few years up to 1962, the date of Aleksandr Solzhenitsyn's "One Day in the Life of Ivan Denisovich." And quite apart from the necessarily oblique representation of camp culture in literary sources, the time may never come when folklorists in the USSR are allowed to publish and analyze the objective evidence relating to the history of their subject in the camps. It may already be getting too late even to collect this material, unless a good start has been made unofficially. It is therefore to émigré and unofficial sources that we need to look in order to form an impression of the part played by song in this massive segment of the history of modern Russian culture.

Perhaps the most striking testimony of this kind is contained in the memoirs of Aleksandr Vardi, *A World under Guard* (*Podkonvoinyi mir*), which concerns the Soviet camp system in the immediate postwar period. Among many remarkable sequences illustrating song as part of the convicts' cultural life is the following:

> When they had eaten their fill, the older criminals climbed on to the middle bunk, sat around in a circle Turkish style, and started playing cards. Their bodies, naked to the waist, were covered with all sorts of pornographic tattoos and scars.
>
> Below, Senya Garkavy, a boy grown old before his time, piped up in a trembling alto:
>
>> We saw, we chop, we stack,
>> We curse all the grasses.
>> Oh, why did our mothers have us!
>
> Slyly winking at Pivovarov with his pale faded eye, he went on:
>
>> Listen and take heed, lads,
>> Why we'll pay them back in full:
>> They stood us up against tree stumps,
>> Stripped us and beat us up.
>> Oh, why did our mothers have us!
>
> The dashing song rang out louder and louder, the despairing underworld [*blatnoi*] little tune warmed up and got more devil-may-care, and the singer's sad eyes grew more comprehending and expressive.
>
>> You yourselves, my friends, know the reason
>> Why we've always made the vow:
>> "I'll be a reptile and I'll never forget
>> That rotten commander
>> And his belly waiting for the knife!
>> The knife!"

"Senya, be a good lad and sing about Vorkuta for us," rasped Trofimov, clearly deeply moved.

"Right, about the Arctic Circle and about the queen," said the others in support, "Go on, Senya, let it all go!"

Barely audible, full of suffering, the song floated up from the gloom of hopeless longing:

> Beyond the Arctic Circle, in that godforsaken land,
> The nights above the earth are as black as coal.
> The wolfish howl of the snowstorm won't let me get to sleep.
> Oh, for just one ray of light in this darkness and horror!
>
> I often remember that old, old threshold,
> Those long eyelashes and that brown face,
> I know you're not spending your nights alone,
> You're thinking sadly of faraway me.
>
> Beyond the Arctic Circle life doesn't last long.
> The savage winter blizzard will cover up my tracks.
> Don't look for me, don't trouble and torment yourself.
> If you get a chance, just remember me.

And on without pausing, but with a change of melody:

> I'm silent in the countless crowd,
> But there's a cry in my heart,
> Eternal interplanetary cold
> Has entered my soul.
>
> In the polar darkness over the crowd
> Your image is before me.
> There's only you in the whole world,
> Zosenka!

The carriage fell silent. The criminals put aside their cards and fell into a sorrowing silence, and the voice—weak, flickering like the flame of a candle tossed about—complained and grieved:

> Even though I fall down in the formation
> I'll get up.
> Wait for me and I'll come back,
> I'll come back.
> I'll get up and I'll come back.
> I'll hug my darling to my heart. . .
> Zosenka, Zosenka,
> There's only you in the world,
> Zosenka!

And then, suddenly, jumping up from his place, gesticulating not just with his hands but with every muscle in his body, Garkavy began to cry out in a fit of sobbing:

My mother starved to death,
My dad got his in the war,
As for me, the guards drive me
Across this tortured land.
> Smash! Slash! Tear! Burn!
> Get revenge for your mother!
> Don't forgive anything for your sisters!
> Smash! Slash! Tear! Burn!
Smash! Slash! Tear! Burn!
Truncheon the bastard till he's deaf!
The murderer, collaborator, the boss,
Stick your knife through his liver!

And Garkavy went on with his dance to the roars, singing, shouts, and clapping of those around him. He clapped his hands against the floor and the soles of his shoes, mercilessly pounded his skinny, wiry sides, even found a way of sticking his filthy fingers into his mouth so as to make pops and whistles. His entire body writhed and shook. Any gypsy would have envied the abandon and expression of his dancing:

We fought the war and came through
But we're done for now.
We saw the Fascists into their coffins
And we'll see the Chekists too.

On our bunks we'll fiddle-de-dee
Under them we'll fiddle-de-dee,
But as for working for the bosses
We'll never do it, never.

Smash! Slash! Tear! Burn!
We'll have the bosses' guts!
Cut the bloodthirsty leader up,
And make borshch for everybody!
Smash! Slash! Tear! Burn![26]

The book contains many other scenes such as these; there is no reason to doubt their authenticity. The songs have a deliberately antiliterary style. Their language is coarse, but obscene only by implication from time to time. What makes them striking is the savagery of the emotions they express: a lust for revenge, a burning sense of outrage and offense. At the same time there is a sentimental, nostalgic attitude toward the idea of home and family.

The songs performed by Garkavy are without doubt of literary origin, composed by an individual poet on a specific occasion, but having then "become folklore," detached from their author and known as part

of a common stock of songs. The environment they reflect is that of
men in confinement. But the confinement they depict has no specific
features that would identify it as the Soviet GULag.

There is no lack of songs that do reflect this specific environment,
however. By far the most famous of them all is "Comrade Stalin,
You're a Real Big Scholar":

> Comrade Stalin, you're a real big scholar,
> You saw what was what in linguistics,
> But I'm a simple Soviet convict,
> And my comrade is the gray Bryansk wolf.
>
> What I'm in for, I swear I don't know,
> But the procurators are right, it would seem,
> And so here I sit in the Turukhansk region
> Where you sat in exile under the Tsar.
>
> Here I am in the Turukhansk region,
> Where the guards are severe and rude,
> Naturally, I understand all this
> As an intensification of the class struggle.

The singer goes on to assure Stalin that he sympathizes with his heavy
responsibilities, and calls himself a fool for not being able to escape
even once, when Stalin managed to do it six times from his exiles. . . .

> Yesterday we buried two marxists,
> We didn't cover them in red bunting;
> One of them was a right deviationist,
> The other, it turned out, had nothing to do with anything.
>
> And before he passed away forever,
> He willed you his tobacco pouch and all his words,
> He asked you to get to the bottom of all this here,
> And screamed out quietly, "Stalin's so clever!"
>
> Live a hundred years, comrade Stalin,
> And though it may be my fate to kick the bucket here,
> I only hope the production of steel can rise
> Per head of population in the country.[27]

The thoroughgoing irony of this song masks a reality that is hard to
acknowledge even for the most inured dissidents—that Party members
did in fact remain loyal to the Party and Stalin even in the camps, and
remained convinced that when the great, all-wise leader found out
about the crimes that were being perpetrated in his name by the se-

curity organs, he would sort things out and return the country to normal.

"Comrade Stalin" became a genuine folk song and was registered as such many times.[28] Eventually, it became generally known that the author of the song was Yuz Aleshkovsky (born 1929), whose checkered life history had included many different trades and professions, including taxi driver. He had been published in the USSR as a children's writer, but none of his songs or his prose was ever published there. Aleshkovsky eventually became an émigré in 1979. Besides "Comrade Stalin," he is the author of two other songs that have certainly become folklore: "A Song from Places Not So Far Away" and "Soviet Easter Song." Both of them became anthems of the camps.

An anonymous song that became the theme song of the Far East GULag, centered on Kolyma and the city of Magadan, is this one:

> I remember the port of Vanino,
> The gloomy look of the ships,
> When they loaded us aboard
> Those stinking, black holds.
>
> Mist was coming down over the sea,
> The maritime element roared,
> Our destination was Magadan
> The capital of the Kolyma region.
>
> Not songs but a plaintive groan
> Was torn from every breast.
> "Farewell, Mainland Russia, forever"
> Bawled the ship, beside itself.
>
> The prisoners suffered from the swell;
> Embracing like brothers,
> Unbidden from their tongues
> Hollow curses were torn.
>
> Curse you, Kolyma,
> You who are called the planet of paradise,
> It's impossible not to go mad,
> And there's no way back from here.
>
> Death has made friends with the scurvy,
> The wards are packed like sardines,
> And maybe this spring
> I'll be in this world no longer.
>
> Don't cry, mother and wife,
> Nor you, my sweet children,

It seems that my lot in this world
Is to drink a bitter cup to the dregs.

I'll die and they'll bury me,
I won't get put in a coffin,
The blizzard will cover me with snow,
Cover me like a white shroud.

Winter's raging in the snowstorms,
And my strength's melting like a candle,
Curse you, Kolyma,
Grave of freedom and happiness![29]

This song has no element of irony whatsoever. It is a plain, straightforward cry from the heart about the intolerable conditions that were encountered by the people who were sent out to the Far East segment of the GULag. The classic testimony to the experience is the two books of autobiography by Evgeniya Ginzburg, both called in Russian *A Precipitous Route (Krutoi marshrut)*. The song does contain, however, an element of sentimentality, which again centers mainly on the nostalgia for home and family. It is tempting to see this song as in some ways a deliberate antithesis of the official "mass song," a kind of anti-hymn. It has the same high-pitched emotional tone, and an insistent hopeless pessimism that is the mirror image of the official song's blatant optimism. The song has in common with official song, though, the use of the first person as spokesman for the collective, in this case the collective of the oppressed.

One of the most piquant episodes in the published history of the camp song in Russia concerns the following text:

We're freezing to death in this godforsaken camp,
Eating and boozing, going out of our minds;
Our hell and our heaven
Are the polar darkness of Kokosalma.
We're murderers, a bloody herd,
The forest and tundra have become our prison,
We will never come back from hell,
We will never return home.
Like stinking, rotten slime
That rots on the cliffs of a bay,
On our cheeks there is dirt and bristles,
We're not human beings, we're scum of the swamps.
Hairless and black-mouthed
We carouse like madmen with the witch scurvy,
The lice gobble us and whisper at night

"You'll never go back home!"
We have lost our battles,
On our positions are lying
Mountains of corpses. Probably no one will remember
The names of these dead soldiers.
The ones who're still alive will go insane,
Their souls will be twisted forever.
We will never go back from here.
We will never return home.

This song was published in the Soviet journal *Banner (Znamya)* in 1958. It was said to be from a copy found in the pocket of a dead German soldier from the Northern Division of the SS, killed by Soviet troops in the forests of Karelia during the Russo-Finnish war. However, as the émigré critic B. Zhabinsky showed,[30] the song was in fact a Soviet camp song dating from the construction of the White Sea Canal in the early 1930s. It is not known who was responsible for the minor changes in the text (such as the second line, where the original, obviously impossible as it stands, says "We're puffed up from hunger and going out of our minds"). Whether the Soviet critic who published this song was deliberately trying to pull a confidence trick will probably never be known.

No collection of camp folklore can yet be published in the USSR, any more than can objective historical accounts of the GULag. Meanwhile, the songs published in the context of memoirs by survivors outside the USSR may or may not include the most important and best-known songs. They probably represent only a fraction of what must be the most vital component of Russian folklore in the postrevolutionary period.[31]

The persistence of convict songs in Soviet life during the Stalin period is attested only fragmentarily. Perhaps the most striking example is the following, where Nadezhda Mandel'shtam is writing about an apartment building inhabited by writers and secret policemen in Moscow in 1937, at the height of the Great Terror:

One day, into the courtyard of the building came some wandering singers. They sensed the need of the moment and sang the best, classical convict songs—from Siberia and Baikal, and thieves' songs. . . . People (not the writers, of course) immediately thronged the balconies. They joined in with the singers, threw them money. . . . That lasted about half an hour, until one ideologically staunch inhabitant ran down and drove them away. . . .[32]

There is much more published evidence about the late 1950s and early 1960s, when visits by foreigners, and especially graduate students with a knowledge of the language, began again after a gap that had lasted since the time of the Communist-inclined pilgrims of the 1930s. One of the most perceptive was Mikhailo Mikhailov, born the son of Russian émigrés in Yugoslavia. He spent the summer of 1964 in Moscow as an exchange student and published the first really well-informed description of private life among the Soviet intelligentsia in its post-Stalinist phase. In a special section of his book, Mikhailov describes a party in a student dormitory at Moscow State University.[33] Songs had been sung, and much liquor had been drunk, and then a young Siberian came into the room, carrying a guitar. He began to sing.

> What staggered me most of all was the actual songs. I had never imagined that anything like that existed in the USSR. He sang all sorts of convict songs—happy ones, despairing ones, and cynical ones . . . through them spoke the Russia we know from the works of Tolstoy and Dostoevsky; there were genuine "earthy" [*pochvennye*], profoundly national works, not stylizations—not the sort that gets broadcast on Soviet radio—but raw, sometimes naive but always profound, very melodic and profound.

Mikhailov cites about a dozen songs. Among them was the first publication in English of "Comrade Stalin, You're a Real Big Scholar"; and also "A Song from Places Not So Far Away," "Soviet Easter Song," and several others. Mikhailov concludes that these songs represent "the most significant folk creativity of our times, and it is understandable why they have been created in Russia rather than anywhere else."

One major formant in the domestic culture Mikhailov describes was the absorption into the cultural life of Moscow and Leningrad of numerous members of the intelligentsia who had been in the camps—a powerful contributory factor to the dissatisfaction with official Soviet culture that was so evident in this period. These people had seen a reality that made it impossible for them to accept slogans anymore. In his story "This Is Moscow Speaking" ("Govorit Moskva," written about 1960 and published abroad under the pseudonym Nikolai Arzhak), Yuly Daniel describes the return from the GULag and associates it with a rise in interest in camp songs as part of a counterculture. The story is set in the late 1950s.

> It was the time when songs from the camps were becoming popular. They were gradually seeping through from Siberia and the Far North,

and you kept hearing snatches of them in refreshment rooms at railway junctions. It sounded as if the amnesty decree were being sung through clenched teeth. They wound their way round the suburbs like the vanguard of an advancing army. Suburban trains pounded out their rhythm. At last they marched into town on the backs of the "rehabilitated" offenders. There they were picked up by the intelligentsia. . . . There was something rather piquant about a cosy chat on the Comédie Française being interrupted by the melancholy dirge of some poor devil on his last legs, and about the way the bright boys of the Faculty of Literature discussed the alliterations and assonances of this outlandish style. Ladies, flushed with vodka, mouthed delicately:

> Hey, boss, hey, boss,
> Let me go home.

And if one of them suddenly winced and choked on a word that had hitherto lain fallow in her vocabulary there was always some connoisseur on hand to say: "But darling, this is literature!"

Then everything was as clear as daylight. The mad howling of the wolves, the louse-ridden vests, the sores, the tattered foot-rags, the so-called rations, which fell into your aching guts like a lump of clay—it was all literature.

But sometimes one of these well-washed, well-fed types would feel a sudden pang, a superstitious fear. "My God, what am I doing? Why am I singing these songs? Why am I asking for trouble? It's all coming at me from a dark corner of the room. Only one thing is missing—the traditional knock at the door. . . . Who am I to smile at the naïveté of these words? After all, it's really immensely serious. This is what it was like. Goodbye Moscow! Goodbye everybody! They'll pick up a rifle, press the trigger and shoot me dead. Nasty!"

But the song went on and people smiled and those ominous shades from the past skulked out of the room, through the lobby and on to the landing. And there they stayed.[34]

Of course, Daniel's assertion is a simplification. Members of the intelligentsia formed a significant part of the population of the camps, and they knew these songs first-hand rather than "picking them up" after other people had brought them back to the towns.[35]

The popularity of the *blatnaya pesnya* into more recent times is attested in a sanctimonious poem by Yevtushenko:

> The "intelligentsia" is singing *blatnye pensi*.
> It doesn't sing the songs of Krasnaya Presnya.
> On it goes to the accompaniment of vodka and dry wines,
> About that same old Murka and about Enta and the rabbi.
> They sing to

　　　　　　　shishkebab and to sausages,
Doctors sing, actors and actresses, too,
Writers at their dacha in Pakhra sing,
Geologists and
　　　　　　　　　even atom scientists sing,
They sing,
　　　　　as if there were a general conspiracy among them,
or as if they were all from a criminal background.
Ever since
　　　　　I was very little,
I never ever loved
　　　　　　　the folklore of thieves,
and a revolutionary melody
is my
　　　　guiding
　　　　　　melody.
And without calculation,
I would prefer that there always showed, crimson and high,
something from the revolutionary song
in my poems,
　　　　　simple and tough as a flagpole. . . [36]

Criminal songs also became a fairly common accessory of Soviet fiction in the late 1960s. The guitar-strumming youth became a stock character at this time, and he was usually provided with at least a fragment of a song to perform. Tendryakov's "Three, Seven, Ace" ("Troika, semerka, tuz," 1966) has such a character in Bushuev, who is, significantly, an ex-convict. Aksenov's story "A Pity You Weren't with Us" ("Zhal', chto vas ne bylo s nami," 1969) contains some good examples. Perhaps the most remarkable appearance of a song in this respect occurs in the first of a pair of stories by Vasily Roslyakov; the story features a party scene. The participants sing Pasternak's poem "The Snowstorm Swept o'er All the Earth" ("Melo-melo po vsei zemle"), one of the Zhivago poems that has been published in the USSR, and also Radin's revolutionary march "Bravely, Comrades, in Step" ("Smelo, tovarishchi, v nogu"). One solitary line of another song also appears—"And I'm only a simple Soviet convict"—which, as we know, comes from the most famous camp song of all, Yuz Aleshkovsky's "Comrade Stalin, You're a Real Big Scholar."[37]

The history of the actual creation of underground songs by poets who did not themselves sing in the years preceding the emergence of guitar poetry will probably never be known in detail. Even the history of unofficial written poetry during these years, a subject rather more tangible than that of the song, is not known with any certainty.[38] However, as part of a uniquely vivid story, Ruf' Zernova mentions the creation of one song in Leningrad in the darkest days of the late Stalin period:

In 1948, when the country ran out of anecdotes, he wrote a song. Using the tune of "Cut-Glass Goblets":

> I was standing in my place,
> Looking for pockets to pick,
> When suddenly up to me came
> A citizen I didn't know.
> Quietly he said to me
> "Where should I go
> So as to spend this evening
> Having a real good time?
> I need girls and more girls,
> I need wine and yet more wine;
> And I don't give a damn
> How much it all costs!"
> I answered him:
> "Just yesterday they closed
> Our last remaining dive,
> On the Ligovka it was!"
> But he said, "In Marseilles
> They have such bars
> They have such liqueurs,
> They have such cognacs!
> The girls dance there naked,
> The ladies wear ermine,
> The footmen bring you wines
> And the thieves wear tailcoats!"
> He offered me French francs,
> And a glassful of pearls,
> If I would hand over
> The plans of a Soviet factory.
> We grabbed this subject,
> Took away his suitcase,
> His money in francs,
> And the glassful of pearls.
> And then we handed him over
> To the powers of the NKVD.
> And ever since then around the jails
> I've never seen him again.
> The powers congratulated me,
> The procurator shook my hand,
> And immediately placed me
> Under strict surveillance.

And since that time, lads,
I've just one aim in life:
If only I could set eyes on
That Marseilles in the West!
What girlies they have there,
And what bars,
What liqueurs,
And what cognacs!
The girls dance there naked,
The ladies wear ermine,
The footmen bring you wines,
And the thieves all wear tailcoats![39]

The author of this song was Akhill Grigor'evich Levinton, who at the time was a research student in the Faculty of Philology at Leningrad University. He simply appeared one evening at his friends' house and sang the song, which he had just composed. Zernova comments:

> . . . the song was impeccable. It gradually entered folklore, *samizdat,* and the thesaurus of the language (I mean "The plan of a Soviet factory" as a cliché). . . . Suddenly, in that most godforsaken, accursed, astounded year of 1948 there spilled over the great open spaces of the motherland this miraculous colossal Odessan "Glassful of Pearls." It had everything: the thirties and the roaring forties; spies, thieves, our glorious Chekists, and the dream of foreign parts, too, which is a myth about life beyond the grave. And it turned out that it was actually possible to make fun of all that. But the main irony was that this Glassful of Pearls poured out over Leningrad, which had been beaten and beaten again, eternally seditious, eternally insulted, gloomy and cheerless, which had long forgotten Lenka Panteleev, its very own Robin Hood. And then suddenly it was there: "the dive on the Ligovka" . . . and every other two lines in the song there was something unexpected, a gift, an explosion of guffaws, truth.[40]

The song is indeed a work of near-genius, and is indeed a miracle when one considers the time and circumstances in which it was written. And it does encapsulate the pedigree of the underground song as it was to emerge in the work of the poets of the 1960s and 1970s. From the gypsy song comes the dream of debauchery. From the criminal song come the underground ambience and some of the actual phraseology. And from the cruel romance come the urban setting and the theme of virtue unrewarded, leading to the singer's plea for sympathy and condescension from his audience. The song has indeed "become folklore." Several variants of it have been published outside Russia.[41]

Five years after Levinton's burst of inspiration, another Leningrad poet parodied the criminal song to magnificent effect:

> When the night-time street lamps sway,
> And it's dangerous for you to walk the dark street,
>> Out of the beer-hall I come,
>> I'm expecting nobody,
> I'm incapable of falling in love again. . .
>
> One girl kissed my feet like a madwoman,
> Me and a widow drank away her house and home!
>> And my insolent laughter
>> Was always a winner,
> My young life cracked open like a nut. . .
>
> Here I sit on my prison plank bed like a king on his birthday,
> Dreaming of getting my dreary ration,
>> The raindrops knock at the window,
>> But it's all the same to me now,
> I'm ready to be the first to douse my torch. . .
>
> . . . When the night-time street lamps sway,
> And a black cat runs up the street like an imp—
>> Out of the beer-hall I come,
>> I'm expecting nobody,
> I've broken my life's record once and for all.[42]

This song was written far away from Leningrad by Gleb Gorbovsky (born 1931), one of the most talented participants in the flowering of Leningrad poetry that took place in the late 1950s.[43] He is also one of the few poets involved who has mended his rebellious ways and become an institutional figure. His "Street Lamps" ("Fonariki") instantaneously became folklore, to the author's discomfiture on one occasion:

> Gleb was sitting in a drinking joint somewhere in the Far East. Drunk, naturally. And next to him they started singing "Street Lamps." Gleb gets up: "Fellers, that song was written by me!" "Like hell it was, you bitch, THE FOLK wrote it! It's a folksong!" And the folk proceeded to smash in the sides [*boki i baki*] of the imposter poet. Gleb could never remember this incident without laughing. "That's a kind of popularity, too," he'd say.[44]

The songs of Levinton, Aleshkovsky, and Gorbovsky are examples of literature become folklore; through the operation of circumstances we happen to know the names of the authors. But these authors are not

known as performers of their own works in song form. These particular
songs exist side by side with guitar poetry and have common roots with
it, though.

*   *   *   *   *

Gypsy song and its characteristic mode of performance; the cruel
romance; and the criminal song dealing with the underworld and the
camps form the three principal components of underground song. They
are the work of poets whose names are for the most part unknown. To a
considerable extent, they exist in complementary distribution to
official song and are differentiated from it by function as much as
anything else. The same people know the whole spectrum of song and
use different elements from it on different occasions.

From the point of view of guitar poetry, the importance of the underground tradition of song is that it preserves and presents several alternative models to official song. The gypsy song offers the model of self-
contained performance, with a solo singer accompanying himself on
the guitar in a free, emotional style, taking liberties with tempo and
pitch. The cruel romance offers a range of debased literary devices, but
above all it contains a rich vein of parody and an ironic attitude toward
the sentimentalism that pervades serious song. And the criminal song
offers, at least in potential, a striking alternative ethos to the official
social code: in it, the individual asserts himself as the arbiter of his own
destiny in a world where justice is crude and swift. And in the camp
songs, there is a theme that has been excluded from official literature, a
theme centered upon suffering, deprivation, and the destruction of the
personal life of the individual.

In the literary turmoil that followed in the wake of the de-
Stalinization debate of the mid-1950s, the authors of songs, besides
expanding the middle ground in the way that was discussed earlier, saw
in underground song a set of untapped stylistic and thematic alterna-
tives and possibilities. And as we shall see, several of them used this
anonymous heritage as the main springboard for their own work.

There was more in the background than the native heritage, though.
Alongside the gypsy style, the guitar-accompanied solo style also
existed in Russia as a result of the importation of the German cabaret
song.[45] Here, the most important influence in the USSR has been the
work of Bertolt Brecht, who himself sang songs to guitar accompaniment. He was inspired to do so and learned the actual manner from

Frank Wedekind, who was probably the first European intellectual to use what had been a subliterary genre of urban entertainment for serious literary purposes. Brecht, of course, is the direct ancestor of Wolf Biermann, the outstanding contemporary German exponent of guitar-accompanied satirical song.[46] And besides the German tradition, there was the French, whose influence is attested in the use in Russian of the word *shansonn'e*. The songs and singing of Yves Montand, Georges Brassens, and others have been known and admired in the USSR since the late 1950s. Bulat Okudzhava, the pioneer Russian guitar poet, wrote an obituary notice for Brassens; much of what he said about Brassens's style and poetic significance is directly applicable to Okudzhava himself.[47] The rise to popularity of the French chansonniers in Russia was a consequence and a part of the opening up of direct cultural relations with the West in the Khrushchev period. The precise extent and nature of the non-Russian influences on the poet-singers of the 1960s, however, is a whole subject in itself.

Gypsy song, the cruel romance, and the criminal song were a strong native legacy. The foreign traditions of song that were available to the Russians combined with them in creating a rich variety of elements that could be drawn on in the creation of a new genre—guitar poetry.

The Guitar Poets

Part Two

While we're on the subject of monuments, we also need a monument to a man with a guitar.

—VLADIMIR BUKOVSKY,
To Build a Castle

4   *Magnitizdat*

THE CROP OF AMATEURS who began writing and performing songs in the late 1950s and early 1960s stayed by and large within the tolerated limits of what has here been called the middle ground. Of the major talents, Okudzhava has largely remained there, despite various trials and tribulations, and some of his work has even joined the repertoire of the official mass song. But there were some other poet-singers whose creative impulse and personality led them in the opposite direction, away from the middle ground and into the undergrowth. Chief among them were Vladimir Vysotsky and Aleksandr Galich. Significantly, their names were almost completely absent from the discussions of "author's songs" even by early critics who were trying to be objective, like Andreev and Dobrovol'sky. A comparison of what happened to Galich and Vysotsky with what happened to Okudzhava provides a very instructive lesson in the way the Soviet system has treated its creative artists in recent times. To understand the options facing the poet-singers of the 1960s as their work came into conflict with official literary policy, it is necessary to sketch in the background of the position they share with other members of the Soviet creative intelligentsia, and also to take into account the new opportunities for creative dissent that technological advance has provided.[1]

If an individual artist becomes unwilling to accept the positive and negative constraints on his freedom of expression that are inextricable from the process of publication in whatever medium in the USSR, and if he wishes actively to dissent rather than to carry on and dissemble, there are four basic ways in which he has been able to act. The first is to "choose silence" (which may be officially interpreted as an active form of dissent), either not producing anything at all or storing the work until such time, perhaps after the author's death, as publication within Russia becomes possible, or when the consequences of publication will not damage him personally. Writers call this method "working for the drawer," and it was the choice eventually made, for example, by the novelist Mikhail Bulgakov (1891–1940). The second way is to ignore the Soviet media and send work abroad. This approach became too dangerous after the novelist Boris Pilnyak (1894–1937) fell from grace for doing it unwittingly in 1929. It was then in abeyance until revived by Pasternak, Sinyavsky, and Tarsis in the exceptionally liberal conditions of the mid-1950s. The third way is to emigrate in order to pursue the creative impulse free from Soviet constraints. This device was used by Evgeny Zamyatin (1884–1937) in 1932, and then, if we set aside the emigrations in the chaotic situation during and immediately after World War II, it has become possible again—sometimes as voluntary emigration, sometimes as compulsory exile—since the early 1970s. The fourth way is to remain in the USSR, continue working, and circulate the results by private, clandestine methods.

Not all of the four ways have always been available. In the worst years of Stalinism, there was only the first. And even then it had to be camouflaged by a smokescreen of visible public activity, if the person concerned had any regard for his own physical survival and that of his relatives and associates. The fourth way has been the most frequently used during the postrevolutionary period as a whole. But the four ways are not equally available for other than political reasons. Except for the way of emigration, they are most powerfully affected by the factor of pure technological feasibility.

Of all the factors involved, the purely technological one has been the least studied while at the same time being arguably the single most powerful among them. The fact is that the various branches of the arts differ considerably with respect to the extent and nature of the technological resources they need for their expression. Because they are technologically the most demanding, film and TV are utterly at the mercy of the official monopoly in the USSR, and there is no significant dissident activity in these areas. There are only various kinds of "bending the rules," getting away with greater or lesser infractions of the limits imposed by the control mechanisms. The performing arts, similarly, are largely impracticable without considerable resources. From time to time there have been stories of various kinds of clandestine theatrical activity in the USSR, but it can leave little or no record and can operate only on a very limited scale of public access. Whether there has been a school of symphonists "writing for the drawer" in Russia in recent years remains to be seen, but none of their work could be performed, let alone recorded and published for further performance. The same goes for film. The technological requirements for the satisfactory reproduction of pictures in color mean that a dissident graphic artist in the USSR can make only one example of his product at a time.

Under these conditions, it is inevitable that dissident activity should be most strongly in evidence in those aspects of human communication where there is least mediation between artist and audience, producer and consumer. This circumstance is what gives rise to the commonplace observation that the most vital creative activity in Russia today is carried on in "pre-Gutenberg" conditions. People who have spent time with the Soviet creative intelligentsia in their native habitat would probably agree that the most vital art form now is the anecdote. It is a purely oral genre, told and retold in informal circumstances to a restricted audience, and requiring no equipment. Andrei Sinyavsky has gone so far as to attribute to the anecdote even more importance:

> The future of Russian literature, if it is destined to have a future at all, has been nourished on political jokes. . . . In its pure form, the joke demonstrates the miracle of art, deriving as it does nothing but good from the savagery and fury of dictators.[2]

And the same thing seems to be true about the song. It too thrives in adversity, becoming a purely oral art form as necessity dictates.

But the "pre-Gutenberg" idea is obviously only partly true. The USSR has not been completely insulated against technological progress. Even so relatively primitive a machine as the typewriter represents a significant departure from oral methods of preservation and transmission. Multiple identical copies can be made on it. And then multiple copies of each copy can be made. The copies are fairly durable, transmissible without direct contact with the author, and (given a certain inevitable amount of error in copying) they accurately preserve the author's text. Duplication by carbon copying on a typewriter is the classic *samizdat* vehicle. It forms the staple medium in the dissident boom that has been witnessed in Russia in the last twenty years. The number of carbon copies that can be made at one sitting using Soviet materials has been estimated differently by different people, but it cannot be above ten. Access to copying machines in Russia is very severely restricted, and duplicating machines are closely guarded. The advent of xerography has had no significant effect, because the machines are not available privately. Access to them and accounting for their use are controlled even more severely than is the case with duplicating machines.

In the case of particularly scarce *samizdat* works, it is not unknown for the pages to be split up and given to different people in turn. Sometimes "reading parties" will be organized, at which the individual pages are passed along from one person to another as they are read. But even in these circumstances reading remains essentially an individual, silent, and passive activity. And the number of copies cannot rival the capacity of the printing press.

The supply of *samizdat* is augmented by the flow of *tamizdat,* "things published over there," i.e., outside the USSR. Despite the vast increase in human traffic into and out of the USSR in the last two decades and the virtual impossibility of checking every single item of mail that comes in from abroad, it has still proved possible for the authorities to keep the inflow of *tamizdat* within the limits they are prepared to accept. This restriction is accomplished mainly by psychological blackmail rather than actual administrative measures. The incomer, particularly if he is a Soviet citizen, knows that he is liable to be searched at the border and have anything objectionable confiscated. Furthermore, he knows that the event will not go unrecorded and may have consequences for his subsequent prospects. And he knows that the possession of certain items of *tamizdat,* such as those published in Frankfurt by the anti-Soviet publishing house Posev, carries an automatic prison sentence on discovery.

But developments in electronics have brought changes in dissident activities, as in all other spheres of life. The international telephone, despite continual control that amounts to persecution, has given Russia's dissidents the means for immediate direct contact with the outside world, something quite unthinkable not much more than twenty years ago.

A vast amount of information is broadcast into the USSR by a number of foreign radio services, the principal ones being Radio Liberty, Radio Free Europe, and the BBC. Soviet jamming of them has been relatively mild in recent years—even though the Helsinki agreement was supposed to lead to the complete cessation of jamming. Radio has made a fundamental difference to the problems faced by the state's controllers of information in the USSR; since broadcasting began from outside, it has no longer been possible, as it was in Stalin's day, to seal the country off from any information that the Party-state apparatus has not sanctioned. And so *radizdat*, "publication by radio," joined the family of terms coined for the expanding numbers of potential means for dissident publicity. *Radizdat* plays a particularly important part in the cultural sphere by transmitting *samizdat* and *tamizdat* back to its country of origin.[3] The *radizdat* audience must exceed the potential readership of even the most assiduously reproduced *samizdat* carbon copy by a factor of many times.

There is also some evidence that Soviet radio hams are using private installations to broadcast uncensored material. The most striking example concerned the city of Donetsk in 1974. It was reported that more than one thousand hams had been detained since the beginning of the year.[4] And there was a case in Vilnius when one ham was sentenced to three years' imprisonment for broadcasting "anti-Soviet agitation."[5]

The third electronic device to become available, besides the telephone and radio, is the tape recorder. It has had a far more powerful impact than they on the actual generation of dissident material. The Russian for "tape recorder," borrowed from German, is *magnitofon*. This word has been truncated and compounded in Russian to form the word *magnitizdat*, "tape recorder publishing," which like *samizdat* and the others refers to both the process of production and the product, in this case dissident material recorded on magnetic tape.

The open-reel tape recorder was first marketed in the USSR on any significant scale in 1960, when 128,000 of them were manufactured. The number reached nearly a half million by 1965 and topped the million mark by the end of the decade.[6] They were, and remain, in the experience of the present writer, who first saw and heard one in 1963, very crude by Western standards. There is always at least one facility out of operation, the speed varies alarmingly, and the quality of the tapes is appallingly low. Cassette recorders have started to be manufactured and imported from the Socialist countries in recent years, and they have brought some improvement in convenience and quality. Western and Japanese machines are not on public sale in the USSR. They are available in the foreign currency shops and sometimes get into the hands of the Soviet population through illicit deals eventually going back to this source.

The things recorded on *magnitizdat* tapes are various. The Russian underground song is actually, if anything, a minority taste among people with collections of tapes. There is much more likely to be a high proportion of Western pop music and rock, recorded from the various radio stations that broadcast to the USSR from outside, and correspondingly low in quality, since they are made from long-wave broadcasts. There also will be better recordings of the same sort of music, transcribed from records brought in by foreigners or Soviet tourists; they are very much in demand. Then there might be a collection of older Russian songs, such as those of Leshchenko, which are highly prized but not officially available because of their erotic or decadent content. Besides all this music, used either as background or to dance to at parties and get-togethers, there might also be some more piquant items. One that the present author has heard is a professionally made recording of the obscene epic "Luka Mudishchev," recited to the background of Tchaikovsky's *Pathétique* symphony. *Magnitizdat* is not necessarily something politically subversive. There is a good deal in it that simply reflects the chronic shortage of consumer goods. And tape recordings are a good way in Russia as everywhere else of putting together suitable music for a party. There is also a good deal of snobbery, one-upmanship, and so on connected with the acquisition and circulation of them.

It did not take long for both authors and audience to realize that in the tape recorder they had a very potent new device for circumventing the control mechanisms. The machine had many advantages. The poet could now do more than declaim his words. He could give his voice permanence without being involved in the process of censorship, something which had not been possible in the case of the phonograph record, with its complicated and delicate manufacturing process intervening between performer and audience. With the tape recorder it became possible to make an immediate, tolerably faithful recording of voice and music, without much equipment and in private, domestic surroundings. The operation of the processes of control had driven what was most vital in Russian culture away from public places and into kitchens and living rooms. The tape recorder was the perfect facility for exploiting this domestic, "homemade" situation. Also, tapes can be copied fairly easily. All that is needed is two compatible tape recorders and a connecting lead; there is no laborious manual operation demanding a great deal of time and skill, as is the case with typewritten *samizdat*.

In addition to these advantages, the tape recorder has still others. It can be used to play to audiences of the most varied sizes, ranging from one person to as many as can be packed within earshot. It therefore creates a situation of perception that is midway between those of written literature and the performing arts.

The tape recorder also brought with it the inestimable advantage of making possible the use of music as well as words. The reading and interpretation of poetry on the page is as a rule a sophisticated, skilled, and solitary (even secretive) activity practiced by a minority of people. The number does not exceed by many the number of people actually engaged in producing the text—"Poets write for themselves and each other." Song, however, makes a much more direct and immediate impact, and it appeals to an infinitely larger audience than the one that is interested in written poetry. Melody and rhythm act together to speed the words to the listener's mind and emotions and imprint them there.

The music used by the guitar-playing poets of the 1960s in Russia was always a means to an end, however. The "homemade" quality of the whole enterprise of guitar poetry can be immediately sensed in the nature of the music. The accompaniment is never more than functional. It consists almost exclusively of simple patterns, always played on the acoustic seven-stringed guitar. These patterns are made up of the most rudimentary elements: single bass notes, roots and fifths almost without exception, on the on-beats, and simple triads on the off-beats. In this guitar style there is no influence of the blues in any shape or form. Equally, there is no organic link with traditional Russian folk music of the countryside; the undoubted links with twentieth-century urban folklore remain to be properly investigated. The guitar is a rhythmical prop and very little besides. The predominant structure is the four-line verse whose melody remains the same through the entire course of the song. Occasionally refrains and repetitions are used, but there is never any complexity that might interfere with the immediacy of the song's impact. Very seldom is strict tempo maintained. There are pauses for dramatic emphasis, scurrying accelerandi for refrains and fills. Over this primitive rhythmic and harmonic scaffolding stretches the voice. It is manifestly untrained, tonally poor, uncertain in pitch, at times employing crude recitative or ordinary speech—but always enunciating clearly. In guitar poetry the words are always more important than the music.

The homemade, markedly amateur standard of music and singing is matched on the classic *magnitizdat* tapes of the 1960s by the quality of the recordings. For the most part, these tapes were made in private by amateurs, and they are of correspondingly poor quality. It is possible to come across recordings made in actual or approximated studio conditions or taken from the public address system at concerts, but the classic article is far from good. There is usually considerable surface noise and distortion, and quite wide variations in speed. Repeated copying on different machines may render a singer's voice almost completely unrecognizable, converting a baritone into a gabbling contralto. There is usually a range of assorted clunks and pops as the microphone is shifted or bumped. And on many tapes there is persistent background noise. Some of it is extraneous, like vehicles passing in the street outside or the footsteps and voices of neighbors. Some of it, though, is an integral part of the ambience of *magnitizdat:* the creak of furniture, the chink of bottle against glass, the coughs and muttered comments from the audience in the room. Most characteristic of all is the interplay between singer and audience. There will be requests, banter, and repartee, warm or bitter laughter, pregnant silence at the conclusion of a particularly telling song followed by the bustle of tension-breaking movement and speech. Applause occurs only on recordings made in front of concert audiences, which are exceptional in *magnitizdat* as a whole.

Magnitizdat tapes started circulating on a significant scale in the early 1960s. It will never be possible to give any accurate quantitative account of the number of tapes involved in *magnitizdat* or of the numbers of people involved in the production and circulation of the tapes or making up their audience. There can be no information equivalent to the print runs of books or anything of that kind. There is no doubt that the production process has been centered on the literary intelligentsia of Moscow and Leningrad, as is the case with all dissident activity. It certainly has a stronghold in the educational elite; by the mid-1960s, as Mikhailo Mikhailov's account suggests, underground song was to be found widely among university students in Moscow. And, of course, it is cultivated and enjoyed by the political elite, too, as Aleksandr Zinoviev has indicated:

> The leadership didn't like these songs that much. But the times were such that they turned a blind eye. The children of the leadership belted out these songs at home and at their dachas with all the power their tape recorders could muster. The leaders themselves listened to them on their own, saying to themselves: "He's really laying it on thick, the bastard! But that's the truth he's gabbling! Only what's the point? You can't do anything about it anyway."

> > I have to know these laws of ours
> > Because of my position.

The more you wave your arms
The deeper you sink into the bog.

And the leader orders his spouse to serve him a bottle of cognac. And he
drinks it alone, locked up in his den.[7]

But the possession and circulation of *magnitizdat* are certainly not
restricted to the metropolitan intelligentsia. There are reports that
tapes have penetrated to the furthest corners of the USSR and found an
audience that transcends all class and social divisions.[8] But it will not
be until we have much more evidence, perhaps even now being collected by some enlightened Soviet folklorist "working for the drawer,"
that we will be able to find out even approximately how wide the
audience for *magnitizdat* has been.

The first time that the texts of *magnitizdat* songs were published, it
would seem, came when five songs by Bulat Okudzhava were included
in the second of the pioneer *samizdat* almanacs called *Syntax (Sintaksis)*, edited by Alexander Ginzburg and "published" in Moscow in
February 1960. All five of these songs have subsequently appeared in
the official Soviet press. One of them ("Len'ka Korolev"; the title is
the name of a person) even appears on the pages of the anthology
Russian Soviet Songs, 1917–1977 that was frequently cited earlier. The
three almanacs that Ginzburg managed to "publish" before his arrest
appeared in the West in 1965.[9] From this date, the penetration to the
West and publication of *magnitizdat* song texts have been uninter-
rupted. Perhaps the only possible objective indication of the scale of
the movement in its first decade is that the *Samizdat Register* maintained by Radio Liberty lists as item number 487 of *samizdat* docu-
ments that had reached the West by February 1971 "Transcriptions of
more than 750 underground and labor camp songs and poetry."[10] As we
shall see in greater detail later, Okudzhava and Galich were the first to
be published intensively outside Russia. The first collection of Okudzhava's songs appeared in 1964 and went into several editions, and
translations of his work into Western languages have been appearing
steadily since the mid-1960s. The first collection of Galich's songs was
published in 1969, after he had been the subject of considerable interest
in the Russian émigré press.

But the publication that enables the guitar poetry of the 1960s and
1970s to be seen and assessed as an entity did not appear until 1977–78.
And inevitably it came about beyond the borders of the USSR. It was a
four-volume set of texts, taken down from and accompanying thirty-
four cassette recordings made from tapes that had been brought out

during the mass exodus of Soviet Russians, the "third emigration," that took place during the 1970s. The whole thing was published by the YMCA Press in Paris under the title *Songs of the Russian Bards*.[11] This collection includes about 950 songs, by a total of twenty-four authors, including six working together in pairs. The quantitative relation between the achievements of the three great guitar poets is fairly represented in the collection. The pioneer, Okudzhava, and Aleksandr Galich have about 80 and 110 songs respectively. Vladimir Vysotsky has 295 songs. Among the others, Matveeva is represented by only 19 pieces, a reflection of her official acceptance and the consequent availability of her recordings in the USSR, but nothing like an adequate representation of her full contribution to the genre. The "second line" of true underground guitar poets is represented by Yury Kukin and Yuly Kim, with 79 and 73 songs respectively. After them come the others: Boris Almazov has 46 songs, Yury Vizbor 35, Evgeny Bachurin 31, and Aleksandr Gorodnitsky and Evgeny Klyachkin 29 each.

In order to make some assessment of the guitar song as a whole against the "spectrum of song" as described earlier, it is reasonable to begin by comparing *Songs of the Russian Bards* with the anthology *Russian Soviet Songs, 1917–1977*.

The work of Okudzhava and Matveeva appears in both collections. Indeed, Matveeva's "Red-Haired Girl" ("Ryzhaya devochka") and "The Land of Delphinia" ("Strana Del'finiya," which was cited earlier) and Okudzhava's "Len'ka Korolev," "Song of the X Paratroop Battalion" ("Pesnya desyatogo desantnogo"), and "Sentimental March" ("Sentimental'nyi marsh," alternatively known as "Nadezhda, ya vernus' togda") form a special category. They all have the curious distinction of appearing in both a definitive collection of Soviet songs and the most representative collection yet published of *magnitizdat* songs. Without making an exhaustive check of all collections and anthologies of songs published in the USSR in the last twenty years or so, it would be impossible to determine exactly how much of the contents of *Songs of the Russian Bards* had actually already been published inside the country. But it is reasonable to assume that quite a few of the songs concerned have been published in the USSR. All the Matveeva songs have been, and so have all the songs by Okudzhava. Not all the songs by the latter that appear in *Songs of the Russian Bards* have been included in collected editions of the poet's work, though, because the contents of collections are more carefully selected.

However, if we compare the contents of *Songs of the Russian Bards* with those of the Soviet anthology that was earlier cited as representative of the first phase of the guitar poetry movement, we find a considerably greater degree of overlap. Of the thirty-eight songs in the Moscow publication, eleven (some of them misattributed) can be found in *Pesni russkikh bardov*. It is also necessary to take into consideration that the Moscow publication includes the work of some songwriters who do not write their own music, as well as some who neither write nor perform their own songs. It would probably be somewhere close to the actual situation if we guessed that about one-third of the songs in *Pesni russkikh bardov* have been published in the USSR. One other consideration that must be made is that a significantly higher proportion of the contents has probably been "published" in the USSR in forms other than that of words on paper. But that, of course, must remain within the bounds of speculation. And another, more substantial, issue must also remain within the bounds of speculation: the question of what proportion of the contents of *Pesni russkikh bardov* was ever submitted formally for publication in the USSR and turned down.[12] It may safely be assumed that many of these songs would have been denied publication, at least in any topflight journal or as part of an author's book, purely on the grounds of literary quality. At a very conservative estimate, half of the contents are made up of weak, instantly forgettable stuff. The proportion would be very significantly higher if the work of Okudzhava and Galich were set aside.

It must be said in all fairness, though, that the principal aim of the anthology must have been simply to preserve for posterity as large a proportion as possible of the available texts, before the guitar poem became an irrecoverable episode in the history of modern Russian culture. And it should also be remembered that one of the most important functions of *magnitizdat* songs may be precisely to provide an outlet for inconsequentiality and triviality, impermissible within the art of Socialist Realism but profoundly needed by most people.

Given these qualifications about general quality, though, it is not difficult to point to some salient large-scale differences between the *magnitizdat* song and the official Soviet song as represented in the two anthologies. Predictably, the general tone of the two collections is strikingly different. The official anthology is dominated by the solemn, bravura, self-important mass song of the "hymn" type, with its high-flown themes and panoply of abstract nouns. The *magnitizdat* anthology, on the other hand, is subdued and melancholy, with a strong infusion of humor, mainly gentle and self-mocking; and the vocabulary is significantly more conversational than that of the official song.

A miniature piece by Yury Vizbor epitomizes the dominant tone of the *magnitizdat* song:

> It's going to be a big winter,
> Because across the river,
> Autumn is slowly dying,
> Waving its yellow hand.
>
> The dark-blue alders are weeping,
> Old Uncle Arbat is weeping,
> Soaking-wet Russia is weeping,
> Turning into fall.
>
> Destroying the snowdrifts,
> Autumn comes hard on the heels of spring. . .
> It's going to be a big winter,
> Nothing but darkness and snow.
>
> [PRB, II, 118]

The Arbat, which we will meet again in Okudzhava's work, is an old Moscow street, whose charm has been increased by the ugliness of its modern replacement. Vizbor's song would perhaps in most countries be received as a fairly innocuous mood piece about the changing seasons. But in a Russian song in modern times it is very provocative to present this kind of sadness unrelieved, without even a hint of consolation. Also, the song too readily suggests a metaphorical reading about the general situation of the country. This reading is especially inviting in view of the persistent and widespread use of weather imagery to refer to changes in Russia's political climate.

Another major difference concerns the central characters in the two categories of song. In guitar song the hero is almost without exception weak, hesitant, and perplexed. He is alienated from society, and if his relationships with any other people are discussed, it is only to point to unfulfilled love affairs. The guitar song is a refuge of the "little man"— to use one of the most hoary concepts of Russian literary history. Here he is in the work of Aleksandr Dol'sky:

> I live in my apartment, surrounded by emptiness,
> I work in a shooting gallery, taking money from the punters.
> Here comes one with a girl who's stupid and amazingly beautiful,
> He'll let off his ten shots and get gone as fast as he can.

Another one'll come in, he's had a few, medal ribbons on his chest,
He'll shoot at yesterday, he smells of onions and vodka,
And as he goes off into the misty distance he'll ask a stupid
   question:
Where'd you lose your leg? On the Stalingrad front?
So I'll tell him it wasn't at the front, it was when I was a kid . . .
And then evening will come and I'll have to find somewhere to
   go . . .

[*PRB*, I, 83]

Here we have a little group of human beings whose lives come into brief contact. They are all mean and disillusioned, and they have no sense of any kind of social cohesion or any kind of higher goals.

As might be expected, the *magnitizdat* anthology contains songs on subjects that are taboo in official literature. They include labor camps, crime, drunkenness, unhappy love involving active malevolence, and everyday life presented in an unadorned way. The *magnitizdat* song also takes impermissible views of Soviet history. Here, for example, is one of the best examples outside the work of the three great poets of a satirical *magnitizdat* song. The subject, attitudes, and treatment are all central to Soviet experience, but official literature will never be able to encompass them. The song is by Yuly Kim.

Fifty years ago my uncle's elder brother
Was taking the Winter Palace in Petrograd.
He tried hard, and took it; but meanwhile
To my grandfather was born my father.
They sang "May you live many years" to the boy,
Saying: "He'll take the place of us old men.
By the newspapers and all the signs,
You'll go far, dear lad."

Forty years ago my uncle's elder brother
Departed from the ranks for Trotskyism.
My uncle personally took his Party card away,
And said not a few bitter words.
It's thirty years now since my uncle disappeared
On account of his Trotskyite relatives.
"Who needs a family if he has the Party?"
It said in the denunciation my father wrote.

Precisely twenty years ago,
I appeared in this world.
"This young thing is dear to me," joked my dad
Among his friends, stroking his Party card.
Ten years ago there returned to Leningrad

My rehabilitated uncle.
He returned, found my dad was a deputy chief,
And quietly departed for the next world.

In that eventful year I too became a candidate member,
And I look at my daddy;
Sure, he's a fine fellow, but in my inside pocket
I've got something too . . .
He gets older with the years,
Can't fathom the new subtleties,
Calls Israel "The Yids"
And thereby plays into their hands . . .

[*PRB*, III, 62]

The satirical bite of this song can be appreciated more fully if it is read in proximity to the second verse of Lebedev-Kumach's "Song of the Motherland," which was quoted in the first chapter of this book (p. 14).

The *magnitizdat* song leaves certain official themes strictly alone. The most striking absentee is the official brand of chauvinism. Instead, one of the most famous early guitar songs expresses a gentle homesickness:

Over Canada, over Canada a low sun is setting.
I should have fallen asleep long ago, why can't I sleep?
Over Canada the sky is deep blue, with slant rain between the
   birches,
Though it's like Russia, it still isn't Russia.

Fatigue whispers to us to get warm, love plays its tricks,
The April snow teases us, the comfort of home tempts us.
But the snow's not like spring snow for me, and someone else's
   house isn't a housewarming
Though it's like making merry, it isn't making merry.

Today it's deep mud where you are, with spots of sun in the puddles.
Don't weep for your love too soon, but wait for me to come back.
Over Canada the sky is deep blue, with slant rain between the
   birches,
Though it's like Russia, it still isn't Russia.

[*PRB*, I, 67]

The dreaded birch tree strikes again. But the difference between this song and the official song is that here there is no belligerent posture. The fact that Canada is not presented as a potential aggressor that motivates a show of chauvinistic rant has been enough to keep this song under a cloud, despite its patriotic nostalgia. The author of this piece is Aleksandr Gorodnitsky, whose song about the Atlantes was cited earlier.

With regard to the themes that occur in both official songs and *magnitizdat,* it is easy to point to some salient differences in the way they are treated. The war theme, for example, is very prominent in both branches of song. A *magnitizdat* piece by Mikhail Ancharov tells about the optimistic dreams of a surviving soldier immediately after the end of hostilities. But the initial scene is set in images of a starkness that is impossible in official songs:

> The war is over, and the gurgling river
> Rolls its flat stones along;
> And dark-blue corpses stick up,
> Caught in the reeds.
>
> The wind stinks of carrion,
> Sly and thievish;
> And ocher-colored skulls
> Keep on trying to laugh.
>
> [*PRB,* II, 74]

An even more striking example of the officially impermissible treatment of the war theme is the following song by Boris Almazov:

> In station buffets, where floors aren't very clean,
> Shoving an empty bottle into their pocket,
> Old front-line soldiers die
> Of their old wounds' opening.
>
> They die, and their gray heads
> Bang down on the marble table top.
> And then their kind, sensitive commanders
> Pronounce words over their graves.
>
> Maybe there're no sirens wailing at dawn,
> Maybe no metal hurtling through the early morning;
> Soldiers get killed in wall newspapers,
> Soldiers get killed at Party meetings.
>
> [*PRB,* I, 56]

Here we have a grimly disenchanted presentation of one of the most favored aspects of the war theme in official songs: what happens to the conquering heroes in later life. We remember that in official songs their gray heads remain unbowed, since the men are always borne up by their consciousness of the ennobling valor of their experience. A couple of verses from Matusovsky's "Once a Soldier, Always a Soldier" ("Soldat—vsegda soldat," 1960) make the contrast unmistakable:

> Maybe you're no longer in the ranks,
> But under your civilian clothes
> I recognize, always and everywhere,
> A soldier's bearing.
> It's maybe a long time since
> You wore your army outfit,
> But people still say:
> Once a soldier, always a soldier.
> . . .
> A soldier doesn't take long to pack,
> Says goodbye without wasting words,
> And all his belongings
> Will fit into one sack.
> Even when he's drafted into the reserves
> He's happy to serve the fatherland;
> And that's why people say:
> Once a soldier, always a soldier . . .
>
> [*RSP,* 475]

These old soldiers not only do not die, especially not in a sordid station buffet, they don't even fade away.

Another equally unorthodox war song by Almazov begins by telling how a boy is rewarded for his good behavior by the present of a frighteningly realistic toy automatic rifle. On his way to kindergarten he fires at everything he sees, including "pigeons, shop windows, and passers-by":

> That little boy was happy
> In his foolish five years of age;
> And from the pubs the disabled ex-soldiers
> Sadly watched him go by.
>
> [*PRB,* II, 76]

Here a child is used as a negative image. And the ex-soldiers are, firstly, drinking and, secondly, do not assert that their sacrifice was worthwhile—in fact, the implication of the song is the opposite. And there is no message concerning the just war for the Motherland. These elements, natural and universal as they may be, are enough to keep Almazov's song underground in the USSR.

Even more prevalent than the war theme in both bodies of song is the subject of love. Again, it is not difficult to find in the *magnitizdat* material songs on this subject that are unthinkable in official terms because of their particularity and explicitness. Here is one by Evgenii Klyachkin:[13]

> I'll snuggle up to you under the blanket,
> You'll move away, but so what, go ahead;
> It's just that I can't do it any other way,
> Even a match can't burn on snow.
>
> It's just that you're always turning your back,
> As if you're sleeping all alone, not with me;
> I've covered myself up and I'm not looking round,
> And I'm trembling like the skin behind my knee.
>
> I know what I'm doing, but you can't understand
> My very highly associative hint . . .
> And the alarm clock won't stop ringing,
> Even the granite is pink from the hints . . .
>
> [*PRB*, II, 101]

Here is another unprepossessing love song, this time by Mikhail Ancharov. The speaker is female, a former parachutist who has left her physicist husband:

> "You'll be the number one woman in the world,
> The country will hear of your name . . ."
> Except that of the life I was promised
> I never saw a damned thing.
>
> He worked in a secret office
> Developing the country's science;
> But he was no use at all himself,
> He sweated every time he took his pants off.
>
> I can see all our boys
> Floating through the skies.
> "Mommy, mommy, look, the dandelions
> Are sending their dead petals down."
>
> They've not forgotten their Katya the parachutist;
> I shouted "Hurray!" at the top of my voice.
> Kicked the physicist in the ass,
> And cleared off, still innocent.
>
> But ruffians are pissing by the gate,
> The moonlight gleams like pee . . .
> Hello, woman's loneliness,
> That phonograph shriek every night.
>
> [*PRB*, II, 73]

Defiant infidelity on the part of a woman; her disloyalty to a hardworking and loyal servant of the country in a responsible and demanding job; and, it goes quite without saying, the naturalistic crudity of the ideas and their verbal expression—all these make this text completely unthinkable as acceptable material for the Soviet media.

A characteristically tongue-in-cheek love song by Yuly Kim conjures up a delightful impression of a Soviet official seducing a girl from the naughty capitalist West. Unlike the stereotype, he is forward and she is modest:

> You're so enchanting, so modest,
> Your shoulders and breasts are like china.
> I'm a bit scared to try and touch you,
> It's like breathing on a candle.
> When you so trustingly place
> Your fingers into my palm,
> You simply cannot imagine
> That you're putting them into the fire.
>> The moon's gone behind a cloud,
>> And then it comes out again. . .
>> Permit me to press your white hand
>> To my red heart.
>
> My feelings, my dreams, my fantasies
> Have begun to burn in my heart like a flame;
> In combat with the world bourgeoisie,
> I've earned my right to a private life.
> And I'll tell you with total frankness,
> I who've suffered in want and in struggle,
> That the cultural wealth of the bourgeoisie
> I have every right to requisition.
>> The moon's gone behind a cloud. . .
>>
>> [*PRB*, II, 119]

Everything here is beyond the permitted range of the official song: the cynical tone, the particularity, the impropriety of the man's conduct, both in itself and on the part of a Soviet official. The clichés themselves (the white hand, the knowingly banal "red" heart, the moon) also poke fun at the stereotyped accessories of official and permitted songs.

A song by Valentin Vikhorev[14] combines many unorthodox elements:

> A tram set off for the front. . .
> Mother crumpled up her hankie,
> He crushed my shoulder with his hand;
> "Stay on your feet, son."

There was paper crisscrossed on the window,
And the sore-throated rasp of sirens. . .
That winter there was a letter—
He'd been killed at Srednyaya Rogatka.

The son can't believe the news. The war ends.

Mother has another husband,
Life's life, she said.
She gave money to the church for your soul,
So don't appear in her dreams.

I'm thirty-five now,
I'm older than you, my father.
I take your granddaughter for walks
Where once the lead whistled.

It's all houses now,
It's all gardens now. . .
And your granddaughter is big enough
To pick flowers for you.

A tram set off for the front,
Twenty-five years ago.
But I've forgotten nothing.
There are flowers on your grave.

[*PRB*, III, 88]

The treatment of both the war theme and the family theme here is
incompatible with official requirements. The singer's mother should
remain faithful in widowhood to her dead soldier husband; and she
should certainly not involve the church in her actions. The son should,
indeed, not forget his father. But he should not be turned so resolutely
toward the past, which has been physically obliterated by a present of
which nothing favorable is said (or toward the future, which should be
represented by rather more positive things than a young girl who is
apparently being taught to look backward like her father). Also, there
is the grotesque image of the tram going to war, an inadmissibly unheroic reminder of just how close the Germans were to the gates of
Leningrad.

* * * * *

These few examples, which could easily be added to, have been
deliberately chosen from the work of the less-eminent poet-singers to
illustrate the way in which guitar poetry may at least to some extent be
understood as an alternative to official song. It either deals with sub-

jects the official song cannot touch or treats official subjects in an impermissible way. In this respect *magnitizdat* is clearly fulfilling one of the same functions as *samizdat* and dissident literature as a whole.

However, that is by no means the whole story. If we continue to confine our attention to the lesser lights in the movement, we see that for the most part their songs are firmly anchored in the middle ground. They neither confirm nor deny the official line. The satirical element is for the most part remarkable for its absence. A few poets are strongly satirical, outstanding among them Yuly Kim, the author of a number of texts that rank alongside the best of Vysotsky and Galich. But in contrast to the sharp particularity of Kim's satirical songs, most guitar poems have the same vagueness of reference, the same lack of particularity and specificity that we noticed in the official "mass song." There is a strong escapist element, most salient in the work of Matveeva.

Even more striking are the ways in which guitar song tacitly supports the official line. There are no songs that are antipatriotic. Just as remarkably, there are no songs in the collection that contradict the official view of motherhood. When mothers appear, they are the same grieving sponges for male guilt that are found in official song. And the love songs also tend to idolize women, to make icons of them rather than flesh-and-blood human beings. The language used in the guitar songs is certainly nearer to the colloquial end of the stylistic spectrum than is that of official song. But there is still a very noticeable absence of anything that oversteps even narrowly drawn limits of linguistic propriety. There is also a lack of evidence that the guitar poets are interested to any great extent in formal or linguistic experimentation. On all these grounds, guitar songs would not fail to meet the Party's requirement of being comprehensible to the average citizen.

It would seem, then, that the authors of guitar songs have certain assumptions in common with the people responsible for administering official culture in the USSR. To understand the guitar song purely and simply as an alternative to official culture is not possible. To some extent, it reflects a shared Russian notion of what the arts should concern themselves with and the way they should properly communicate.

These observations have been made with reference to the second rank of guitar poets. The question of whether they hold true of the three great guitar poets will be considered in the following chapters.

5   Bulat Okudzhava

BULAT OKUDZHAVA IS THE patriarch of Russian guitar poets. It was he who brought the form to prominence in Russian cultural life, and all the others have emerged from under Okudzhava's guitar in a more real sense than the nineteenth-century Russian prose writers emerged, as the famous phrase has it, from under Gogol's *Overcoat.* Okudzhava has the highest literary standing of any "bard," and he is widely recognized as a major Russian poet without qualification, a status that literary opinion has not and probably will not grant to Galich or Vysotsky. And he has survived. In fact, he is one of a very small number of modern Russian writers who have managed to establish a high reputation both inside and outside the country, and with official and unofficial opinion alike. For twenty years his work appeared extensively in *samizdat, tamizdat,* and of course *magnitizdat,* but he has remained in more or less constant good standing with the Soviet literary establishment, continues to publish and record in the USSR, and has even been allowed to make visits abroad. He has now emerged into a state of seeming inviolability, "beyond the barriers." But to account for his survival by seeing him as one of the many tokens of Soviet liberalism, a publicity exercise, is not enough.

The main facts of Okudzhava's life are well known.[1] Bulat Shalvovich Okudzhava had a Georgian father and an Armenian mother, but he was born in Moscow in 1924. Despite his manifestly non-Russian names and parentage, Okudzhava is in fact a metropolitan Russian intellectual by language, upbringing, and culture. He has described himself as "a Georgian bottled in Moscow," but that is something of a flight of fancy. Okudzhava's father was a Party official who rose to be Secretary of the Town Soviet in Nizhnii Tagil in the Urals during the

Bulat Okudzhava in the early 1960s.

1930s. He suffered the same fate as many of the Party functionaries of his level: he was arrested in 1937 during the Great Purge and shot as a German and Japanese spy, one of the most common of the absurd charges that were used as pretexts to do away with people at the time. His mother was also arrested and spent eighteen years, from 1937 to 1955, as an inmate of the GULag Archipelago. Okudzhava is the most prominent Russian writer with this kind of background, but he is by no means the only one; his close kinsman in this respect is Vasilii Aksenov. Unlike Aksenov, though, he has never used this part of his autobiography as a subject for his art. Okudzhava lived with his parents up to the time of their arrest, as they moved from assignment to assignment, from Moscow to Tbilisi, back to Moscow, then to the Urals. After the arrest of his parents he managed to remain in Moscow, finding refuge with his maternal grandmother. Then in 1939 he moved back to Tbilisi.

Okudzhava's life, therefore, began in a privileged environment. He then suddenly became an outlaw, the son of "enemies of the people," living a clandestine life. This experience is not normally regarded as a formative factor in Okudzhava's personality and literary work. It is customarily assumed to have been completely overshadowed by the next major event of his life, which was volunteering for the army in 1941—when he was still only seventeen years old—fighting through the entire war in the ranks of the infantry, and being wounded several times. If the number of references in Okudzhava's literary works is a true guide to the importance of the various facets of his biography, though, his army service certainly is the most profound of them. After he was demobilized, Okudzhava attended the university of Tbilisi, graduating in 1950. He then spent four years as a village schoolmaster near Kaluga, a town in central Russia, not far southwest of Moscow. There he was poised to begin a metropolitan literary career as soon as circumstances permitted. The prime circumstance was the rehabilitation of his parents, which happened in 1955.

Okudzhava and his mother then received the right to settle in Moscow. With an alacrity that is quite incomprehensible to people outside the system, Okudzhava became a member of the Communist Party in the same year. He was soon able to transfer from his village school to the city of Kaluga, and it was not long after, in late 1956, that he moved back to the capital, where he has remained. At first he held down a series of literary jobs, including a spell as poetry editor on the newspaper controlled by the Union of Writers, the *Literary Gazette (Literaturnaya gazeta)*.[2] He became a member of the Union of Writers in 1961, and since the following year he has been a full-time independent writer. It was at about the same time that he pioneered guitar poetry; he had been singing in private since the late 1950s, and he gave his first public recital—it was a disaster—in 1960.[3]

Okudzhava first achieved notice as a writer of prose, with a manifestly autobiographical story about his wartime experiences called "Good Luck, Schoolboy!" ("Bud' zdorov, shkolyar!"). It was published in an almanac entitled *Pages from Tarusa (Tarusskie Stranitsy)*, whose appearance was one of the most characteristic events of the Khrushchev thaw. The book, published in 1961, was edited and piloted into print by the senior liberal writer Konstantin Paustovsky (1892–1968).[4] Okudzhava's contribution was and has remained one of the most controversial items in the collection, for reasons that can easily be understood in the context of the "war theme" in official literature. Perhaps the most revealing description of the work is contained in these sneering lines from a Soviet history of literature dating from 1971. The story

> ... tells of a few days spent at the front by a youth who the day before
> had been a schoolboy, but who has been called up to fight. This kind of
> young man had already been portrayed in many works of literature ...
> which had shown the strength of the hero, the humanistic exploit of his
> selfless struggle against Fascism. The hero of Okudzhava's novella
> struggles, too, but more than anything else he is concerned with his own
> fate. When the hero says: "I don't want to die. I can say that straight out
> and not feel ashamed," he can of course be understood, but he goes on
> and on about his fear of death right through the entire work. As a result,
> the Motherland, the struggle against Fascism, and the heroism of the
> people are pushed back somewhere into the background; they become
> abstract and remote, and contrariwise the whining youth who is afraid of
> death and is in general a pretty pathetic character is given in close-up.[5]

This statement embodies the central accusation that offical criticism has continued to level at all of Okudzhava's work, not only his writings on war. His work is said to lack ideological firmness, the most salient manifestation of this defect being the absence of a positive hero. Okudzhava, for his part, has steadily defended himself as an opponent of empty heroics, big words, and abstractions that lose the individual human scale.[6] As we will see, this standpoint applies just as aptly to Okudzhava's songs as to his prose works.

Okudzhava has made many public statements about his attitude toward his army experience. As one of the relatively small number of really talented writers who actually fought their way through the war as front-line soldiers rather than as correspondents or in another similar capacity, he is continually "on call" for discussions of the subject, and there are many of them. The most recent was an interview with the journal *Theater (Teatr),* one of a series of articles and interviews devoted to the subject of literature and war. Here, Okudzhava revealed that with one of his adolescent friends he had seriously intended to run away from home to fight in the Spanish Civil War, so that, as he put it, his "second and successful attempt to take up arms against fascism" should come as no surprise. He stressed the deliberate nature of his decision. He came from a very political generation, he said, and was very serious and realistic about these things. Once he got into it, though, the effect of the war upon him as a personality had been to dispel this "youthful romanticism." It had left him not a pacifist, but with an organic hatred for war. He was not a pessimist, though, something he had often been accused of being; however, he did have plenty of objective reasons for being sad.[7] The most far-reaching statement Okudzhava has made on this subject is the following:

> For my melancholy and irony, which constitute my creative maturity, I am obliged principally to the war. . . . At the front I understood my own weakness, and became convinced that although a good deal depends on a man's strivings and his will, he still depends on objective circumstances, which compel him to suffer and deprive him of happiness, sometimes of life . . . in war I learned the great art of forgiveness and understanding. War taught me not to take delight in parades. . . . For me the war hasn't ended yet, because I can still see its victims. War helps politicians get out of their difficulties, but it destroys the thing people require more than anything else—stability in life; it threatens to break the ties that join the present with the past, ties that are the precondition of further progress.[8]

In the Soviet context, this statement is defiantly unorthodox. No adjectives of nationality or political allegiance are attached to the words *politicians* and *people,* which is more than enough to give evidence of political unreliability. But Okudzhava's war record is well known, and he is a hard man to accuse of cowardice, lack of principle, or lack of understanding.

Since "Good Luck, Schoolboy!" Okudzhava has continued to publish prose works in steady succession. In 1964 he wrote a short novel called *Zhora the Photographer (Fotograf Zhora),* which has never been published in the USSR, perhaps mainly because it first appeared abroad, in the anti-Soviet journal *Grani (Facets)* in 1969. There have been several other shorter prose works, but Okudzhava has moved toward larger forms, and in particular toward the full-blown historical novel. The first was *Poor Avrosimov (Bednyi Avrosimov)* in 1969, followed by *Merci, or The Adventures of Shipov (Mersi, ili pokhozhdeniya Shipova)* in 1971. *Poor Avrosimov* is about the Decembrist insurgent Pavel Pestel; it has also been published and performed as a play under the title *A Gulp of Freedom (Glotok svobody)*. The second novel concerns the character named in the title, who was a Tsarist police spy assigned to carry out surveillance on Leo Tolstoy. *Journey of the Dilettantes (Puteshestvie diletantov)* (1976) came next, and Okudzhava continues to devote most of his creative energy to prose,[9] having written a number of film scripts in addition to the novels.

Okudzhava's literary debut, in 1946, was as a poet, however, and he has continued to publish "normal" poems ever since. He has written more poems for reading than he has songs for singing, and even without his songs he would have a high reputation as a Soviet poet. In this respect he is unique among the three great guitar poets, but (as we have seen) he has a younger parallel in Novella Matveeva. Collections of Okudzhava's poetry have appeared steadily, though with some interruptions. His first book, called *Lyrics (Lirika)*, was published in Kaluga in 1956; it was followed by *Islands (Ostrova)* in 1959. These two books contain no texts that are identified as songs. The first book to contain Okudzhava's songs was *The Merry Drummer (Veselyi barabanshchik)* in 1964; it includes about fifteen song texts, scattered among an equal number of other poems. It was followed by *Magnanimous Month of March (Mart velikodushnyi)* in 1967. This book has a special subsection entitled "My Songs" ("Moi pesenki"), containing seventeen texts, some of them repeated from the 1964 book. The next collection, *Arbat, My Arbat (Arbat, moi Arbat)*, did not appear until 1976. This book, too, has a subsection, "My Songs," including twenty-three texts, the biggest group of Okudzhava songs published in the USSR.

In the sixties Okudzhava also published two collections in Tbilisi, mainly made up of his translations of Georgian poets. Like most other prominent Russian poets, Okudzhava has devoted a good deal of effort to translation; it was through this means, as well as editorial jobs, that he established his material base when he first moved to Moscow and became a full-time writer. Like most Soviet poet-translators, he does not have a command of the languages he translates from (mainly Georgian and Polish) but works from a line-by-line crib *(podstrochnik)* prepared by a specialist in the required language.

There were a number of reasons for the nine-year gap (1967–1976) between the publication of Okudzhava's collections in the Soviet Union. As we will see, during this period Okudzhava had almost stopped writing new songs. More important, however, difficulties had arisen as a result of the publication of his work in *samizdat* and *tamizdat,* and of its enormous, uncontrolled popularity in *magnitizdat.* In 1964 the anti-Soviet publisher Posev brought out a volume that was expanded into a two-volume collection in 1967 and has subsequently gone through many editions. Okudzhava made a record on a visit to Paris in 1968 that brought him considerable fame in Western Europe and the United States, and his songs began to be translated and published widely outside the Soviet bloc.[10]

Also, Okudzhava signed some of the most celebrated letters of protest emanating from the literary world in the heady dissident days of the 1960s, including one about the arrest of Sinyavsky and Daniel in 1966 and a letter sent by sixty-two writers to the Presidium of the XXIII Congress of the Communist Party of the RSFSR about the expulsion of Solzhenitsyn from the Union of Writers in 1969.

These signings, the foreign publications, and his fame as an underground singer brought Okudzhava's career very close to disaster. In the spring of 1972 he was hauled up before his local section of the Union of Writers and required to sign a letter to the *Literary Gazette* protesting the unauthorized publication of his work abroad and declaring his loyalty to the Party line. However, there was some consolation: Okudzhava was permitted to complain in the letter about the difficulties he was having in publishing his work in the USSR. A more serious warning was to come. In June 1972 Okudzhava was expelled from the Communist Party for "anti-Party behaviour and refusing to condemn the publication of some of his works abroad."[11] He was reinstated fairly quickly, though, and since that time he has not been subjected to really serious personal harassment by official bodies, despite continuing publication and publicity abroad. He visited the West in 1977 and again in 1981 and 1982.

Like all other Soviet writers who have some sense of personal integrity, Okudzhava has had persistent difficulty in publishing. The whole story is by no means known, but three particular instances have been documented. The first was described in the earliest serious discussion of Okudzhava's songs to appear in print, the chapter in Mikhailo Mikhailov's book about his journey to Moscow in 1964.[12] This very personal and frank account is clearly based on a private conversation between the author and Okudzhava that the poet thought either would go no further or would have no undesirable consequences in the relaxed atmosphere of those times. Mikhailov reported that *The Merry Drummer* had not been Okudzhava's own choice of title for that collection; he had originally wanted it to be called *The Midnight Trolleybus,* which of course has a much more somber ring, but the book was then banned anyway, even after the poet had protested by letter to the high Party functionary Ilichev. Mikhailov also mentioned that by 1964, the date of his writing, Okudzhava had composed about ninety songs, but that he had written none for over a year.

We also know that in 1966 the editor of the journal *Sel'skaya molodezh' (Rural Youth)* was fired for publishing some Okudzhava songs, including "The Black Cat" ("Chernyi kot"), an image that has been widely taken to refer to Stalin.[13] The third known instance of Okudzhava's problems with the censorship concerns an edition of his songs, including words and music, that was prepared for publication in the late 1960s by the Leningrad musicologist Vladimir Frumkin, who has since emigrated. The book was denied publication on the grounds that the music was incompetent. But the real reason was that the music was too competent, and popular, to be allowed to be published by an amateur composer. Frumkin tells this story as part of the introduction to an edition of Okudzhava's songs that he prepared and published more than ten years later, this time an illustrated bilingual large-format volume. It was brought out in the United States in 1980 by Ardis, the principal publisher of Russian literature outside the USSR. This edition[14] is the most authoritative publication of Okudzhava's songs, and it is also the only really worthwhile edition of any guitar poet to have been published to date. It is fitting that the first worthwhile publication should concern the first of the guitar poets. And it is a reflection on the twilight status of the genre that it has taken something like twenty years from the time many of the songs in the book were composed for them to get into print, and that the publication occurred abroad.

Besides being a composer and performer of his own songs, Okudzhava has been active for more than twenty years as a writer of commissioned songs for plays and films. For many years more of his work was recorded through this means than in his own performance. Recordings of his own performances have been available outside the

USSR since the mid-1960s, but it took another ten years before they began to be available on Soviet records. However, selections of Okudzhava's songs have been steadily available to his home audience since the late 1970s, and although nothing like his entire repertoire has been officially sanctioned, and none of the Soviet editions does anything like justice to his stature, a great many of his songs have made the transition from the underground to official recognition and have been published both abroad and in the USSR. It may well be that they constitute the largest body of work by a single author of whom that can be said. It is certainly the case by comparison with the other guitar poets. Vysotsky's work is significantly more than half underground, while Galich's is completely so; and it is difficult to see how this situation could be radically changed. Okudzhava is certainly the Russian author who has the greatest amount of work simultaneously in print in Russian both inside and outside the USSR.

Some of the reasons for this situation involve the characters and biographies of the authors concerned. It is fairly obvious that Okudzhava has been determined to make himself a life's career as a writer in Soviet Russia, and that at times he has had to pull in his sails in order to achieve this aim. By biding his time, avoiding last-ditch confrontation, keeping several kinds of literary activity going at the same time, and refusing to be intimidated, he has achieved remarkable results. His enormous popularity has also undoubtedly helped to keep him from persecution, as was the case with Vysotsky, too. Okudzhava has been a popular, even beloved, figure since the early 1960s. The tape recorder made it possible for his work to reach all corners of the country long before he was allowed official recordings and publications. But these are external matters; it is the songs themselves that hold the ultimate key to Okudzhava's status.

Okudzhava was the pioneer guitar poet, and as such he established some of the genre's essential features. Chief among them is the close interplay between text, tune, and voice. The three elements combine to individualize each song and stamp it as belonging to one particular poet. The guitar poets have avoided using one another's repertoire. Whether this individualization is necessarily also a mark of ephemerality is a different matter, though.[15] The tape recorder has brought the songs to a wider audience than the book-reading one, and there is nothing to say that it will not be an enduring audience. Besides individualization, Okudzhava introduced, and bore most of the critical brunt of introducing, the "amateur" ethos. Okudzhava freely admits, even boasts, that he has a mediocre guitar technique and an untrained voice. These things are an essential part of the style, and they function to differentiate it from the official professional song and as a token of sincerity, even when they are highly cultivated—as they are in the case of Galich and Vysotsky, both professionaly trained actors. With Okudzhava, though, they are not cultivated. His is the amateur voice par excellence. He sounds like somebody singing to himself. He has a voice that continually threatens not to be able to manage its owner's own melodies; his pitching is precarious, and his tone is unsound, almost querulous. Here he is on his own, though the tentative, retiring approach is an essential part of his persona as a songwriter. But in terms of melody he is also on his own; unlike Galich and Vysotsky, he does not use a limited set of interchangeable motifs but creates genuine melodies for each song. He is one of the great musical primitives in this respect.[16]

The second edition of Okudzhava's *65 Songs* (Ann Arbor, 1982) is the only source published so far from which it is possible to date a major body of guitar poems. And that is especially important in the case of these particular poems, because of their significance in the history of the genre. Among the sixty-five poems there is one that stands chronologically apart from the others: "Burn, Fire, Burn" ("Gori, ogon', gori"), which was Okudzhava's very first song, written when he came out of the army in 1946. There is then a long hiatus until the period 1957–62, when no less than forty-three of the songs, almost exactly two-thirds of them, were written. The eleven years 1963–73 show a dramatic recession, with only a dozen songs composed. Then comes a slight intensification, with nine songs from the period 1975–79, the latter year being the latest represented in the collection.

The implications of these dates are unmistakable. They mean that Okudzhava created the guitar poem in an intense burst of energy that coincides in time exactly with the "Khrushchev thaw," which was triggered by Khrushchev's famous "Secret Speech" at the XX Party Congress in 1956 and both culminated and terminated with the publication of Solzhenitsyn's "One Day in the Life of Ivan Denisovich" in 1962, after which the stage was set for the long winter of the Brezhnev years.[17] Unlike written and printed literature, though, sung poetry triumphantly ignored the freeze that began in Khrushchev's last year, 1963. *Magnitizdat* recordings kept Okudzhava's fame and popularity on the rise, and his work inspired others.

The title of Frumkin's edition, *65 Songs,* makes one fundamental point about Okudzhava as a guitar poet, namely, that he has been frugal and exacting in his songwriting. The collection includes all his important songs up to 1979, and the standard of them is exceptionally uniform and high. Each is a polished individual work; there is remarkably little overlap between the songs in either words or music. That does not mean that they do not exhibit a number of areas of concentration. There are three thematic foci in particular to which Okudzhava continually returns: the Moscow streets, war, and love.[18] That is not to say that his songs have "subjects" in any strict sense. As we will see, the absence of clear subject matter is one of the leading features in Okudzhava's style.

Among the dozen or so songs set in the Moscow streets are three of Okudzhava's most characteristic and successful pieces. The first of them, the most straightforward, is about the street he grew up on, "Song about the Arbat" ("Pesenka ob Arbate," 1959). It provides an excellent introduction to some of the central elements of Okudzhava's style.

> Flowing on like a river, with your odd name,
> Your asphalt transparent like river water;
> Arbat, my Arbat, you are my vocation,
> You're my joy and my disaster too.
>
> Your pedestrians are ordinary folk,
> Their heels tap as they hurry about their affairs;
> Arbat, my Arbat, you are my religion,
> Your paving lies beneath me.
>
> There's no cure at all for love of you,
> Even loving forty thousand other roads;
> Arbat, my Arbat, you are my native land,
> And I'll never get to the end of you.
>
> [65, 54][19]

The name of this street is indeed "odd" to a Russian ear. It derives from Arabic *rabad,* "suburb," and evolved because of the presence of a colony of Arab traders in the vicinity during the middle ages. Part of the song's meaning for the Russian audience, and in particular for the Muscovite, derives from the fact that next to the old Arbat, which ran higgledy-piggledy and mazed with side streets southwest from near the middle of the city, a new Arbat has been constructed, a ruler-straight six-lane highway with high-rise blocks lining it on both sides. The song implicitly asserts the superiority of the old, with its human scale and its magic, in plumb contradiction to an official ethic which is reflected in uplift songs devoted to particular places. Okudzhava's song also has a subtle melancholy that is the dominant tonality of all his work. This melancholy stems partly from the hint of personal unhappiness ("my disaster"). But it derives mainly from looking toward unknown or even unknowable dimensions—here made explicit in the song's last line— with the idea that there is always something beyond the individual's comprehension that prevents his feeling fulfilled or at ease. The song is also free from cliché, the key to the eternal freshness of Okudzhava's work. Its use of repetition is judicious, creating just the right balance between expectation and innovation.

The second Moscow song is the one Okudzhava wanted to refer to in the title of a collection, "The Last Trolleybus" ("Poslednii trolleibus," 1957):

> When I haven't the strength to overcome my troubles,
>   When despair's creeping up,
> I get on a blue trolleybus as it passes,
>   The last one, a chance one.
>
> Midnight trolleybus, sweep through the streets,
>   Make your circuits round the boulevards,
> Picking up everyone who in the night has suffered
>   Disaster, disaster.
>
> Midnight trolleybus, open your door for me!
>   For I know that this freezing midnight
> Your passengers, your crew,
>   Will come to my aid.
>
> It's not the first time I've left trouble behind
>   Riding shoulder to shoulder with them. . .
> You wouldn't think there is so much goodness
>   In silence, in silence.
>
> The midnight trolleybus sails through Moscow,
>   The roadway flows away into dawn. . .
> And the pain that pecked like a starling in my temple
>   Grows quiet.

[65, 38][20]

The troubled hero finds some relief in the city, but he does so through a private, uncommunicating act. There is the same unspecified "disaster" (*beda*) as in the Arbat song, and the mood is that same quiet melancholy. Also using a first-person speaker is a third Moscow song, "The Moscow Ant" ("Moskovskii muravei," 1956–58):

Not thirty years but three hundred—just imagine that—
Have I been walking these ancient squares and blue paving blocks;
My city bears the highest rank and title, "Moscow,"
But she comes out herself to greet every one of her guests.

I walk along her thoroughfares in the quiet of dawn,
I run along her crooked streets (forgive me, other towns). . .
For it's a Moscow ant I am, and I can never rest,
Three hundred years ago it was the same, and always will be.

I'll tell you what this city's like: it's just the same as I—
Sometimes sad and sometimes glad, but always dignified,
Is this a little girl carrying a piece of the day in her hand?
As if she's bringing lunch to me, the Moscow ant.

[65, 48]

That is about as light as the tonality of Okudzhava's songs ever becomes. It shares with the Arbat song the emphasis on historical continuity and the absence of twentieth-century accessories. The hero, as
in all three Moscow songs, is an individual, but one of the crowd, an
ordinary person without any special claim to fame or attention.

The capital appears as setting in several other songs. The famous old
thoroughfares of the center (the Volkhonka, the Neglinnaya, the Arbat
again, the Nikitsky Gate, and Smolensk Square) are imagined as pa-
trolled by "love's sentinels," "the only soldiers I acknowledge," whose
tour of duty is eternal ("Chasovye lyubvi," 1957, 36–37). There is the
famous character of the Arbat backstreets Lenka "the King," who
went off to war, did not return, but still might do so at any time,
because

> I'm sorry, but I can't imagine Moscow
> Without a king like him.
>
> [1957; 65, 41][21]

There is the phantom drummer who marches along the streets—but
can be heard only by the poet himself ("The Merry Drummer"; *Veselyi
barabanshchik,* 1960). Painters are urged to dip their brushes "into the
bustle of Arbat courtyards and the sunset," and into—

> . . . the sky blue
> Of the forgotten urban tradition;
> Carefully and lovingly, paint us
> Walking lovingly along the Tverskoi Boulevard.
>
> ["Painters" ("Zhivopistsy," 1958–61); 65, 100–101]

The only mention ever made of Okudzhava's father and his fate occurs in a song called "The Arbat Kids" ("Arbatskie rebyata," 1962):

> What did you manage to think about, my executed father,
> When I strode forward with my guitar, hysterical but alive?
> As if I were stepping down from the stage into the comfortable
>   Moscow midnight
> Where a fate is passed out free to old Arbat kids.
>
> Everything's just fine, if you ask me, and there's no cause to be
>   glum,
> Those sad commissars walk around Moscow like one man.
> And there really are no dead among the old Arbat kids,
> Just the ones who needed to have fallen asleep,
>   But the ones who didn't are not sleeping.
> Perhaps memory is a difficult duty, but Moscow has seen everything,
> And words of consolation are absurd to old Arbat kids.
>
> [1962; 65, 114–15]

Two other songs that would appear to be specifically about Moscow, "Song about Moscow at Night" ("Pesenka o nochnoi Moskve," 1966–67) and "Arbat Romance" ("Arbatskii romans," 1975), in fact contain nothing to connect them with the city, which is in keeping with the generally oblique, almost evasive attitude toward material reality in Okudzhava's writing. The city, if anything, is not the metropolis of the twentieth century, but rather its village-like core formed by the backstreets and courtyards off the older central thoroughfares, which are always referred to by their pre-Soviet names.

There is nothing that identifies Okudzhava's city as the capital of the USSR in the twentieth century. The major addition the twentieth century and Soviet power have made to the central Moscow scene is the construction of the underground railway, one of the great "achievements" of Stalin's 1930s. Okudzhava makes the Metro the pretext for a wry two-stanza parable (1956–64):

> It's never crowded in my underground,
> Because since I was a child it's been like a song
> That says, instead of a refrain:
> "Stand on the right, pass on the left!"
>
> The custom's eternal, the custom is sacred:
> The ones on the right just stand there,
> But the ones on the move must always
> Keep to the left!
>
> [65, 110–11]

The most profound of all Okudzhava's songs with a Moscow setting is one in which the themes associated with the city—the anonymous individual in the crowd, the consolations of historical awareness, the depressing brashness of the present—all come together to make the nearest thing there is in his work to a clear statement of a position. But then, characteristically, the last line opens up another vista into the unknown:

> You never can bring back the past, it's pointless to rue it.
> Every age has its own forest growing up.
> But it's a pity all the same that one can't have dinner with Pushkin,
> Even drop in to the Yar Café for fifteen minutes.
>
> Today we don't have to grope our way along the streets,
> There are cars waiting for us, and rockets to speed us into the
>   distance.
> But it's a pity all the same that there're no hansom cabs in Moscow
>   any longer,
> Not even one, and there won't ever be, more's the pity.
>
> I bow down before the unbounded sea of knowledge,
> I'm fond of my rational, highly experienced age.
> But it's a pity all the same that we still dream of idols as we did
>   before,
> And we still sometimes count ourselves slaves.
>
> Not in vain have we forged and nurtured our victories.
> We've acquired everything—a safe harbor, and light;
> But it's a pity all the same that sometimes over our victories
> Rise pedestals higher than the victories themselves.
>
> You never can bring back the past. I go out onto the street—
> And suddenly notice that right by the Nikitsky Gate
> Stands a hansom. And there's Pushkin taking a walk.
> Ah, tomorrow, probably, something will come to pass.
>
>   [1967; 65, 130–31]

As might be expected, this song does not appear on any of Okudzhava's Soviet records or in any of his published collections. Compared with the specificity of some of the dissatisfaction expressed in the songs of Galich and Vysotsky, this song would seem to be vague enough to be permissible, but it evidently is not. Its nostalgia for the past, its guarded attitude toward the achievements of the present, make it a distinctly uncomfortable piece that comes close to a direct polemic with Soviet hymns about national pride and achievements.

Okudzhava's status as a veteran gives him a unique personal authority as a writer of songs about war, but that does not obliterate the heavy weight of the massive official hymnology on the subject and give him a free hand. This pressure makes it impossible to perceive his songs on the subject in an unprejudiced way. It is not at all difficult to define the main characteristics of the Okudzhava war song: it is unheroic, understated, wry, ironic. Despite what is often thought, it is also completely lacking in historical specificity. In this respect it contrasts strongly with the war songs of Galich and Vysotsky. Okudzhava is the only front-line veteran of the three, and his songs on the subject are much milder and tentative than theirs.

Despite the impression that a superficial survey could easily give about war as a principal topic of Okudzhava's songs, there are actually only about eight specifically devoted to it. Two of them are among the poet's crowning achievements. First, there is "The Paper Soldier" ("Bumazhnyi soldat," 1959):

> But once there was a soldier boy,
> And he was bold and handsome,
> But he was just a children's toy,
> He was a paper soldier.
>
> He wanted to remake the world,
> So everyone would be happy,
> But he was hanging on a string,
> He was a paper soldier.
>
> For you he would be glad to die
> In fire and smoke twice over,
> But all you did was play with him—
> He was a paper soldier.
>
> And you would never share with him
> Your most important secrets,
> And why was that? It was because
> He was a paper soldier.
>
> And he would keep cursing his fate,
> No quiet life he wanted,
> And he kept asking: Fire, fire!
> Forgetting he was paper.
>
> Fire? I don't mind. Go on! You'll go?
> And one day he went marching.
> And then he died for nothing, for
> He was a paper soldier.

[65, 53]

Okudzhava's songs sometimes do present a clear moral—but usually one that has an oblique relationship to the ostensible subject matter.

The song about the paper soldier gives a warning about not bringing oneself harm through rash idealism; and it is also a parable about the fragility of human creatures. But there is no direct reflection of Okudzhava's own experience.

Secondly, there is the "Song of the 'American' Soldier" ("Pesnya 'amerikanskogo' soldata," 1961). The quotation marks are used because it is an open secret that the adjective within them is not part of Okudzhava's intention but a concession to the demands of official opinion. The black humor of this song is not typical of Okudzhava's style in general, and its message also is uncharacteristically straightforward:

> I'll get my greatcoat, kitbag, and helmet,
> All of them camouflage-colored,
> And off I'll stride along the humpbacked streets;
> How simple it is to be a soldier, a soldier!
>
> I'll forget all my domestic cares,
> I need no wages and no work.
> Along I go, playing with my gun,
> How simple it is to be a soldier!
>
> If anything's not right, it's not our business,
> As the saying goes, "The Motherland commanded!"
> How great to be not to blame for anything,
> Nothing but a simple soldier, a soldier!
>
> [65, 106–107]

This carefree, irresponsible "American" appears here only; and the kind of irony with which he is presented is, as we said, quite unusual in Okudzhava's work. The remaining songs about soldiers and war are more straightforward. Soldiers march off into the mist, leaving their women behind to deceive them: "A Song about Soldiers' Boots" ("Pesnya o soldatskikh sapogakh," 1956–58). There is a somber lament for the deprivations of all kinds that war brings with it in "Goodbye, Lads" ("Do svidaniya, mal'chiki," 1958). The mysterious "Forgive the Infantry" ("Prostite pekhote," 1961) opens up a much broader perspective than is offered by the infantry alone:

> Times have taught us
> To live as if bivouacked, the door open.
> Comrade Man, your duty is still tempting:
> You're always on campaign
> And there's only one thing keeps you from sleep:

> Why do we go away,
> When over the earth
>   spring
>   is storming?

> [65, 104]

The two remaining songs explicitly about the military are connected
with Okudzhava's delving into the historical past as a novelist. "Saying
Goodbye to the Cadets" ("Provody yunkerov," 1977), about the period
of World War I, is a very slight piece; and "A Battle Painting"
("Batal'noe polotno," 1973) describes what appears to be a canvas
depicting Napoleonic times. Behind a straightforward description of
the emperor's suite on the field of battle is the familiar Okudzhava turn
into the unknown:

> Somewhere under their feet and above their heads are nothing but
>   earth and sky,
> Nothing but earth and sky, earth and sky.

> [65, 140–41]

The third main thematic group comprises Okudzhava's love songs.
Again, there are only about half a dozen of them; and only a couple
belong to the very best of Okudzhava's creations. The most charming
and original of them is "Oh, Nadya, Nadenka" ("Akh, Nadya,
Nadenka," 1960), an appeal against unrequited love addressed to a
proud lady bus driver, who

> . . . wears overalls, such greasy ones,
> And an impossible beret.

The first two lines of the song contain one of Okudzhava's most evocative city scenes, achieved with just two details:

> From windows comes the scent of toasted crusts,
> Hands flicker behind curtains . . .

> [65, 87]

In its everyday immediacy and proletarian setting, "Oh, Nadya,
Nadenka" is the most Vysotsky-like of Okudzhava's love songs. But it
has a touching innocence foreign to the younger poet, an innocence
that is one of the most appealing aspects of Okudzhava's writing.

One of Okudzhava's most subtle love songs is called, unpromisingly,
"The Old Jacket" ("Staryi pidzhak," 1960).[22] It has five stanzas. A man
has been wearing the same jacket for many years, and he decides to
call the tailor in and have it remade; he jokes that this act will renew his

life. But the tailor takes him seriously and goes to work with a will. The song becomes a love song only in the last stanza:

> What he thinks is this:
> I'll only have to try my jacket on
> And I'll believe in your love again . . .
> Not likely! What a silly he is.
>
> [65, 77]

Here, Okudzhava's oblique approach and his penchant for the unexpected turn at the end of a text really pay off; he manages the elusive achievement of permanent surprise no matter how many times the text has been heard before.

A characteristic example of Okudzhava's use of compositional devices reminiscent of folklore is the love song "Along the Smolensk Road" ("Po smolenskoi doroge," 1960), which, incidentally, according to Okudzhava himself, is the only one of his songs whose melody was conceived before the words. It uses a system of triple repetitions:

> Along the Smolensk road there are forests, forests, forests,
> Along the Smolensk road there are posts, posts, posts.
> Above the Smolensk road, just like your eyes,
> Are two evening stars, the sky-blue stars of my fate.
>
> Along the Smolensk road the snow's in your face, your face,
> We keep being driven from home by cares, cares, cares.
> Perhaps if the ring of your arms were more sure
> My road would probably be a shorter one.
>
> Along the Smolensk road are forests, forests, forests,
> Along the Smolensk road the posts drone and drone,
> At the Smolensk road, like your eyes,
> Two cold sky-blue stars look down, look down.
>
> [65, 75]

This song is a very good example of the pure lyricism of Okudzhava's style. There is no narrative element; the important things are atmosphere and mood. And the mood is a melancholy one, as is almost always the case in Okudzhava's work. The exceptional feature of this song, which makes it unique in Okudzhava's repertoire and also one of a small group of texts within the guitar poem as a whole, is its setting: for once we are far away from the narrow Arbat streets, and there is an expansive landscape of trees and sky.

Perhaps the most revealing of all Okudzhava's love songs is one whose title suggests the general attitude toward sexual relations that is found in his songs as a whole: "Your Majesty, Woman" ("Vashe velichestvo, zhenshchina," 1959). It is an expression of wonder on the part of the song's first-person persona that such a divine, majestic thing as a woman would pay any attention to such an insignificant mite as himself. The first two verses of the song set a scene of gloom and discomfort; the last two express the attitude that has just been described:

> When you come to me it's like a fire.
> Smoky and hard to breathe . . .
> But please do come in.
> Why stand on the threshold?
>
> Who are you? Where are you from?
> What a pathetic person I am . . .
> I think you've just got the wrong door,
> The wrong street, city, and age.
>
> [65, 51]

This courtly, self-deprecating stance is consistent with the general attitude toward the self and the individual in Okudzhava's work. He has made himself almost embarrassingly explicit on this point:

> The theme of very many of my poem-songs is love. For a long time in this country we hardly sang about love, and in the very word "woman" there was something dubious. In protest against this falsity and puritanical sanctimoniousness, I took it upon myself for the first time in many years to sing hymns in the Russian language to woman as something sacred, to go down on my knees before her. I have to confess that my irony wouldn't work here. If I have said something in jest, then it's directed at myself as the hero of these songs, which portrayed the helplessness and failure of men. . . .
>
> [65, 51]

Whether Okudzhava always succeeds in avoiding sanctimoniousness in his love songs is a moot point. In fact, the only woman in Okudzhava's songs who gets anything but adoration is Nurse Maria:

> What was it I said to Nurse Maria
> When I embraced her?
> "You know, officers' daughters
> Never look at us soldiers."
>
> A field of clover beneath us,
> Quiet as a river,
> Waves of clover approached
> And we rocked upon them.
>
> [65, 65]

Once again there is a strong contrast with the songs of Galich and Vysotsky, both observers of women in the specific situations that Soviet society calls upon them to endure. In his treatment of women, Okudzhava is at the extreme of the romantic abstraction that is a fundamental tendency of his work. As we have seen, the official song, if anything, tends to put woman on a pedestal and sing idolatrous hymns to her, often from the point of view of a man who has betrayed her or has not been quite up to the absurdly idealistic standards he sets for himself as he goes about the nation's work and remains dutifully conscious of his responsibility to his destiny as the proletariat of the world's first socialist state. Compared with this self-image, Okudzhava's first-person male heroes are indeed backsliders and smaller-than-thou "ants." But it is not primarily in their attitude toward women that they are so remarkably different from the officially approved positive heroes that preceded them in Soviet literature, as Okudzhava is at pains to plead. In this respect they are similar to their officially approved brothers.

We can also find sentiments like the following:

> Love is that kind of thing: you can easily get lost in it,
> Get buried, spin, get lost . . .
> We all know this fatal passion,
> So there's no point in talking about it again.
>
> ["Arbatskii romans"; 65, 149]

And there is Okudzhava's precarious anthem to love as the ever-present source of hope, even in life's worst crises; it is one of many songs in which he dares to use personified abstractions in a way that modern poets have universally avoided:

> When the distant voice of trumpets suddenly starts up,
> And words, like hawks in the night, burst from burning lips,
> When melody thunders, like a passing shower; among people
> wanders
> Hope's little orchestra, conducted by Love.
>
> In the years of separation and confusion, when leaden rains
> Thrashed our backs so hard there was no pity to hope for,
> And the commanders were all hoarse . . .
> then, people were commanded by
> Hope's little orchestra, conducted by Love.
>
> [65, 127]

It may be seen from the last two quotations that the three themes we have distinguished so far—the Moscow streets, war, and love—

interpenetrate in Okudzhava's work. In fact, it is one of the most important aspects of his style that the songs are not specifically "about" certain given subjects, with reference being limited within each text to one specific area. The broad themes of the city, war, and love are only reference points that float to the surface more often than others. There is certainly no portrayal of a recognizable social order or a particular historical period, and no developed account of particular human relationships. This vagueness of reference has led many critics to categorize Okudzhava as an impressionist. In the best of the articles arguing this point, Violetta Iverni has asserted (admittedly with reference to Okudzhava's prose) that not only are there no "subjects" in Okudzhava, but there is no authorial point of view, either:

> I'm convinced that Okudzhava asserts nothing *at all;* by the nature of his talent and by his own nature he lacks any kind of tendentiousness. He is simply incapable of it. He is perhaps the most spontaneous, the most elemental of all writers who exist at the moment. And if the concept "impressionism" is capable of reflecting a combination made up of the spontaneity of the image as it arises in the author's imagination and an equally elemental, almost animal-like, organic feeling for rhythm, measure, purity of sound, and its lyric depth and fullness—then Okudzhava is an impressionist more than anyone at any time.[23]

Okudzhava himself is reported to have said:

> The work should not be tendentious, but the artist should. I certainly do have a deposit of tendentiousness inside me; it's connected with my philosophy, my position in life. I am a member of the Communist Party.[24]

Like Iverni's, this statement is too categorical when applied to Okudzhava's songs. It may be that the songs are subtle and evasive, and it may be that there is a complete discontinuity between the creative artist and the political man. But it is also certain that Okudzhava's songs do "make assertions," sometimes quite openly. Even among the few songs we have examined here, we have found Okudzhava asserting "the goodness of silence" in the trolleybus song; "Painters" is one long exhortation; "You Never Can Bring Back the Past" is full of tendentious statements about the nature of history. Admittedly metaphorical rather than explicit, but nevertheless quite transparent as a politically tendentious assertion, is the song for which the responsible editor got fired:

> Off the yard leads a doorway
> That we call the back way in,

In that doorway, like country gentry
There lives a black cat.

He hides his grin in his whiskers,
The darkness is his shield,
Other cats all sing and weep,
The black cat says nothing.

Hasn't hunted mice for ages,
He grins into his mustache,
It's us he's after, believe me,
Setting little bits of sausage.

He makes no demands or requests,
His yellow eye burns,
Everyone makes willing presents
And says thank you.

He doesn't utter a sound,
All he does is eat and drink.
If his claws touch the staircase
It's like a scratch across the throat.

And that's why it's not happy,
This house we live in. . .
We should get a light fitted,
But we can't seem to collect the cash.

[65, 89]

This statement is one of the most memorable by a Russian author about the atmosphere of the country under Stalin; its apparently throwaway final line is in fact a grim assertion of popular connivance. And in a very recent song (1983) Okudzhava has made his own comment on the arms race. It is characteristic that archaic, folkloristic images are used; the style of the original is more colloquial than is normal for Okudzhava:

The Sign

If there's a raven high above,
Things must be heading for war.
If we don't stop him circling,
If we don't stop him circling,
We'll have to go to the front.

So as there won't be war,
The raven must be killed.
So as to kill the raven,
So as to kill the raven,
A gun has to be loaded.

But if we go ahead and load the gun,
Everyone will want to shoot it,
Then as soon as the shooting starts,
Then as soon as the shooting starts,
Bullets will find holes.

Bullets pity nobody,
They don't care who they hit;
One of theirs or one of ours,
As long as they get every last one,
That's it, there's nothing left.

That's it, there's nothing left,
That's it, there's no-one left,
That's it, there's no-one left,
Except for that raven,
—And there's no-one left to shoot him,
No-one left to shoot him.

The point of view in this quietly despairing fable, as always with Okudzhava, is that of the private individual, who is doomed to act and suffer as part of a collective. The ominous raven of Russian folklore is not identified with any particular political entity; he is apparently an eternal attribute of the human situation who brings out man's worst instincts. The song presents a dilemma rather than urging a specific political course of action; but it certainly does engage a current political issue—obviously, nuclear disarmament.

So, rather than saying that Okudzhava's work is a spontaneous effusion of images, or that he avoids making statements because he feels that to do so is not a proper end of art, it is better to say that he puts together impressions of the world in order both to express subjective moods and to assert moral attitudes. Here is a very good example, the song "March Snow" ("Martovskii sneg," 1958):

In the Arbat courtyard there's gaiety and laughter.
And the pavements are already getting wet.
Weep, children! The March show is dying.
We'll give it a happy funeral.

In dark cupboards skates will rust,
Skis, forgotten, will warp in corners. . .
Weep, children! From over the white river
Very soon the grasshoppers will hurry to you.

There'll be lots of grasshoppers. Enough for everybody.
Children, you won't be playing alone. . .

Weep, children! The March snow is dying.
We'll pay it a general's honors.

Rooks will be still over its head,
The river ice will thunder into lilac crevasses. . .
But the snow woman will be left a widow . . .
Children, be good and attentive to women.

[65, 47]

The change of seasons, especially from winter to spring, is a well-worn subject in Russian writing, and Okudzhava here finds some appealing and homely images on which to focus the customary mixture of regret and exaltation. A net of repetitions holds the piece delicately together. The end of the song has the now-familiar turn into the unknown. It is keyed by a linguistic feature. Russian has *snezhnaya baba,* literally "snow woman," where English has "snowman," and the slightly derogatory *baba* leads Okudzhava into a sentEntious exhortation at the end that is completely consistent with his romantic exaltation of the sex in other songs. So the children get a fresh message instead of being instructed once more to weep.

But it remains true that Okudzhava avoids commitment to some kinds of tendentious position. There are no political positions in his work, and, most refreshingly, there are none that are tub-thumped all the way through a text in such a way as to make the moral lesson the point of the exercise.

Okudzhava's greatest achievement consists of a small number of songs which distill the essence of his nonnarrative approach. What they do is to take an image—and a great part of the achievement is that the images concerned are completely fresh and original—and sketch its emotional significance for the author's individual sensibility. Some of these songs are explicitly autobiographical, others are "objective"; some of them are sententious, others simply present the image and leave matters there. The objective and inexplicit songs are undoubtedly the finer.

However, there are no absolute boundaries between these various types. As an example, here is a completely "objective" song. Its vocabulary and phraseology, to say nothing of the pervasive triple parallelism of its structure, all relate to the conventions of the Russian folk lyric:

As for the first love—it burns the heart,
And the second comes fast after the first.

> But the third love is a key trembling in the lock,
> Key trembling in lock, suitcase in hand.
>
> As for the first war—it's nobody's fault,
> And the second is someone's fault.
> But the third war is my fault alone,
> And my fault everyone can see.
>
> As for the first deceit—it's mist at sunrise,
> And the second is reeling drunk.
> But the third deceit is blacker than night,
> Blacker than night, and more frightening than war.
>
> [65, 117]

This song acquires a completely new—and surprising—dimension when its title is put with it: "Song of My Life" ("Pesenka o moei zhizni," 1962). What autobiographical facts, from Okudzhava's life as we know it, could underlie this lyric? Does it refer to an actually experienced third love, third war, and third deceit, or is it issuing a terrible warning against them? Once again, Okudzhava is elusive and enigmatic, even when he appears to be categorical and explicit.

There are three songs which are explicitly autobiographical in their texts and which also concern the creative process. The first is almost a caricature of the extreme Romantic position in poetics, a declaration of the superiority of the unuttered word. Its first verse goes:

> I'm walking along and listening
> To what is probably the very best song
> This side of heaven,
> It's quickened inside me.

The song is described as "very unsung" *(ochen' nespetaya)*, "green as grass," and to contain a melody played by "some trumpeter yet to come." The last verse again leads away into the unknown:

> Lightly, uncommonly, merrily
> Above the crossroads whirls
> That most important song,
> The one I was unable to sing.
>
> [65, 81]

The third line of the last stanza gives this song its title, "The Important Song" ("Glavnaya pesenka," 1960). This epiphany stands at the very beginning of Okudzhava's public career as a guitar poet.

Long after the most intensive period of songwriting and performing was past, he again looked into his own creative self, but this time, ostensibly, as a historical novelist. The three verses of the resulting song tell how Okudzhava painstakingly put together a historical novel. He imagines himself to be a retired lieutenant in the process of immersing himself in the past, and he appeals to be allowed to go on writing while the red rose—the song's transparent symbol for creative imagination—goes on blooming in its brown bottle that once held imported beer. The song's refrain is a splendid notion:

> Everyone writes what he hears.
> Everyone can hear himself breathing.
> The way he breathes is the way he writes
> Without trying to do favors.
> That's how nature wanted it.
> Why—that's none of our business,
> What for is not for us to judge.
>
> [65, 160]

This song is one of the few by Okudzhava that he has "explained":

> Once, a Moscow critical journal asked me and a group of writers to put down our opinion of the nature of our creative work, the psychology of creation, what we write for, for whom, and why. Since I don't know how to write articles and didn't much like analyzing myself, I turned them down. . . . The others wrote very serious analyses of their own work. As for me, I wrote a poem and thought up some music for it. . . the result was a song . . . and I sent this song to the journal. They didn't print the poem, even though it was a direct answer to their question. . . .
>
> [65, 161]

This story turns out to be somewhat disingenuous, because Okudzhava's poem, with a dedication to Vasily Aksenov, was in fact published early in 1977.[25] It has also been released in the USSR as a song in Okudzhava's own performance.[26] What gives the piece an inescapably ironic edge in the context of Soviet literature is the fact that when Soviet writers speak about their situation, they most often use the metaphor of breathing to express their sense of the difficulties that surround them: "There's no air. . . ," "We're choking. . . ," and so on.

One of the very small number of songs that Okudzhava has written since 1980 deals even more explicitly with his attitude towards the problem of the relationship between art and "historical reality." The second stanza, with the appropriate modifications, serves as a refrain:

The Roman Empire in its period of decline
Retained the appearance of firm order.
The leader was in place, his comrades at his side,
And life was fine, to judge by the rates of pay.

The critics will say, though, that the word "comrade" isn't a Roman item,
And this mistake makes the whole song meaningless.
Maybe, maybe, maybe it isn't Roman, I don't regret it,
It doesn't bother me at all, it even uplifts me.

The young men of the Empire in its period of decline
Dreamed all the time of rolled-up greatcoats [skatki] and skirmishes [skhvatki].
Sometimes on the attack, sometimes in their trenches,
All at once they'd be in the Pamirs and then they'd be in Europe.

The critics will say, though, that a rolled-up greatcoat isn't a Roman item . . .

The peasants of the Empire in its period of decline
Ate anything they could, and got revoltingly drunk.
And for sobering up they were all partial to pickle brine,
Apparently they didn't realize there was a decline.

The critics will say, though: "Pickle brine! What next—it's not a Roman item . . .
The women of the Empire in its period of decline
Were the only ones who had a sweet time, only them, the beauties;
All paths were open before their gaze,
They worked if they wanted, or went to the forum.

The critics in chorus cry: "Ah, the forum, the forum!—now *that's* a Roman item,
Just one little word, but it does so much for the song!"
Maybe, maybe, maybe it is Roman, but what a pity,
It bothers me a bit, and brings my idea to nought.[27]

This text both exemplifies one kind of Aesopian language and makes sly fun of it at the same time; the "young men of the Empire" that leap to the Russian mind come from the north to the Pamirs (on their way to Afghanistan) and from the east into Europe, not from the south as the Romans did. And the verb that ends the refrain in the original Russian, *vozvyshaet,* rings an immediate chime with Pushkin's celebrated artistic credo:

T'my nishchikh istin mne dorozhe
Nas vozvyshayushchii obman.

> More dear to me than the multitude of poor truths
> Is deceit, which uplifts us.

Like "The Black Cat", here is another song that is highly tendentious but expressed in unemphatic, gently derisive language.

The objective songs in this final group, Okudzhava's highest achievements, vary greatly in ostensible subject matter. Here is a straightforward appeal for the "openness of soul" *(dusha naraspashku)* that is supposed to be part of the essential Russian character:

> When the snowstorm howls like a wild animal,
> Long-drawn-out and angry—
> Don't lock your door,
> Let your door be open.
>
> And if a long road lies ahead,
> A difficult one, imagine,
> Don't forget to fling your door open,
> Leave your door open.
>
> As you leave home in the silence of night,
> Decide without wasting words
> To mix in the stove the fire of pinewood
> With the fire of your soul.
>
> Let the wall be warm
> And the bench soft. . .
> Closed doors are a penny a pound,
> And a lock only costs a kopeck!
>
> [65, 71]

The nearest thing in Okudzhava's work to a Vysotsky-style narrative, but once again expressed with his usual evasiveness, mild irony, and tenderness, is the piece he at one concert introduced as "a song about how an old, sick, tired king set off to conquer another country, and what happened as a result":

> A king was preparing a campaign against another country.
> His queen had dried him a sack of rusks,
> And she'd sewn up his old cloak so carefully,
> Given him a packet of tobacco and some salt in a rag.
>
> She put her hands on the king's breast,
> And said, caressing him with her sparkling gaze:
> "Beat them really well, or you'll get called a pacifist,
> And don't forget to capture all the enemy's cakes."
>
> The king reviewed his troops in the courtyard.

Five sad soldiers, five merry ones, and a corporal.
Said the king: "We fear neither the newspapers nor the wind.
We'll beat the enemy, and come back victorious, hurrah!"

The king gives his merry soldiers jobs in the rear. The five sad ones fail to survive the campaign, the corporal marries a woman prisoner, and the army captures a whole sack of cakes. Here is how the song ends:

Orchestras, play! Songs and laughter, sound out!
Friends, it's not worth giving in to passing sadness.
There's no sense in sad soldiers' going on living,
And besides, there're never enough cakes to go round.

[65, 99]

Therein, of course, lies the essence of the Okudzhava song about war. The game is played for the whim of outsiders, who collect the glory and do not share in the suffering; the game brings out man's propensity to inflate his sense of his own importance; the little man bears the brunt, especially if he is given to melancholy; and things never turn out in the way it is boldly predicted they will. But despair is no answer, whatever the objective facts may suggest. The setting of the song is again typical—a kind of pantomime never-never-land that has some medieval trappings but absolutely nothing to do with particular countries or the specific barbarisms of twentieth-century war.

Here is an even more blasé view of the human condition:

Here's how it is in our day and age,
For every high tide there's a low one,
For every wise man there's a fool,
Everything's even, everything's fair.

But this principle doesn't suit the fools,
For you can see them at any distance.
People shout at the fools: "Fools, fools!"
And that offends them a lot.

And so the fool won't need to blush at himself,
So that each and every person should stand out,
On every wise man a label
Was hung one day.

We've seen these labels around for a long time,
They're less than a penny a pound.
And people shout at the wise ones: "Fools, fools!"
And no-one notices the fools.

[65, 95]

Again, nothing is specific, in space or time, and so nobody really needs to take offense; everyone can smile ruefully and pass on.

Okudzhava's three greatest songs have this evasive, convoluted quality to an almost maddening degree. "The Miraculous Waltz" ("Chudesnyi val's," 1961) paints a sylvan scene; it seems about to clear up its mysteries at every new line but then never quite manages to:

> In the forest, under a tree, a musician is playing a waltz.
> Playing a waltz, tenderly and passionately in turn.
> As for me, once more I'm looking at you,
> But you are looking at him, and he is looking into space.
>
> The music's been playing for an age. Our picnic's dragging on.
> The picnic where people drink and weep, love and leave.
> The musician's lips are pressed to his flute. I would press mine to you!
> But you are probably that spring that cannot save.
>
> But the musician is playing his waltz. He can see nothing.
> He stands there, his shoulders pressed to a birch tree.
> The birch twigs replace his fingers,
> And his birch eyes are stern and sad.
>
> Before him stands a pine waiting for the spring.
> But the musician grows into the ground, the sounds of the waltz flow.
> And his thin legs seem like the roots of that pine,
> In the earth they intertwine, and they can't be disentangled.
>
> The music's been playing for an age. Our love story is dragging on,
> It's been pulled into a knot, it burns but won't burn up . . .
> Come on, let's calm down! Let's all go home!
> But you're looking at him . . .
> > And the musician plays on.
> > > [65, 97]

The language, imagery, and conceptual framework of this song are of a different order of difficulty from those of any other Okudzhava song. And this song, more than any other by Okudzhava, suffers from being detached from its melody, one of the strangest and most beautiful of all the tunes of the guitar poets. Its third line begins with an abrupt change of key that turns the whole mood around, from darkness to light and reconciliation. The song is most clearly "about" the ineffability of love. There is also, without doubt, a bifurcation of the author's ego here between musician and lover. He sees himself in both roles, in the role of the artist as eternal and inextricable from natural forces, turned away from mankind and in rapt devotion to his art. But there is an absence of sequential development in the song; the connection between the appeal in the last stanza to go one's separate way has no clear connection with the argument of the rest of the piece. However, the song is without a shadow of doubt one of Okudzhava's most powerful and evocative pieces, and a text which for sheer lyric vision it would be hard to match in modern Russian poetry anywhere.

The second of the three most outstanding songs by Okudzhava is the one that has been heard outside Russia more widely than any other by him, because of its use at the conclusion of Makaveev's noted film *WR: Mysteries of the Organism*. What Okudzhava thought of that is not a matter of record. Its title seems to be the frankest acknowledgment Okudzhava has made to any literary predecessor. The song is called "The Prayer of François Villon" ("Molitva Fransua Viiona," 1964–65):

> While the earth is still turning, while the light is still bright,
> Grant Thou, O Lord, to everyone whatever he doesn't have:
> Grant Thou the wise man wisdom, grant the coward a steed,
> Grant the lucky man money . . . And don't forget about me.
>
> While the earth is still turning—for Thine is the power, O Lord!—
> Grant the power-greedy man to gorge himself on power,
> Grant the generous man respite, if only till evening comes,
> To Cain grant remorse . . . And don't forget about me.
>
> I know Thou canst do everything, I believe in Thy wisdom,
> Just as a soldier who's been killed believes he's living in paradise,
> Just as every single ear believes Thy quiet words,
> As we ourselves believe, not knowing what we do!
>
> Lord, O God of mine, my God with eyes of green!
> While the earth is still turning, itself finding that strange,
> While it still has enough time and fire,
> Grant Thou to each a little, and don't forget about me.

> [65, 121]

Once more, the text has absolutely nothing to do with contemporary Soviet reality, or with any other historically identifiable reality. Nothing about it makes a connection with the late medieval world of François Villon. Given the song's formula, it has some delightful examples of avoiding the obvious without resorting to clever paradox ("grant the coward a steed," "grant the generous man respite"). The naive selfishness of the refrain line gives the song the feel of a child's prayer. Perhaps even more important in the case of this song than of others, in translation there is no recompense for the subtle word play of the original. The phrase "Grant Cain repentance," for example, is an exquisite newly minted pun ("Kàinu dai raskàiania," which has the etymological feel of "May Cain be de-cainized"). Like "The Miraculous Waltz," the song has no narrative element and no sequential argument but works through the accumulation of parallels and repetitions. This technique is characteristic of folk art rather than the modern literary lyric; the song sounds like a charm or a spell.

Okudzhava's greatest song, though, does use the suggestion of a narrative to add to its folkloric incantational accumulation of parallel events. It is "The Blue Balloon" ("Pesenka o golubom sharike," 1957):

> Little girl crying, her balloon's flown away,
> People console her, but the balloon flies on.
>
> Young woman crying, still she has no fiancé.
> People console her, but the balloon flies on.
>
> Grown woman crying, husband's gone to another,
> People console her, but the balloon flies on.
>
> Old woman crying, she's not had much of a life.
> But the balloon's come back, and it's a blue one.
>
> [65, 32]

Here is a song with the inevitability and absolute economy of the greatest art. Okudzhava has found a striking single image whose ultimate significance remains mysterious but which nevertheless acts perfectly as a correlative of the song's action. The song defeats the predictability of a triple repetition by culminating with a fourth verse whose reversal of action and sudden addition of an epithet utterly disarm the listener. As we have seen in so many Okudzhava songs, there is a velvet sting in the tail. Rather than a conclusion, there is a new turn and a new horizon opened up, one whose terms could not be predicted from the preceding part of the text. The sadness of the first three couplets remains in the mind, but with a delicate consolation from the last. Once again, the text lacks any reference to any specific place or time. It is one of the most universal poems in the language, a masterpiece of lyric purity.

Although the song about the blue balloon is explicitly about women, it advances a view of life that is present in other songs by Okudzhava that have to do with his own experience and that of other men. To call it a cyclical view of the individual life is to make it more categorical than it ever is in the songs, but the idea of cyclical return is at its center:

Don't torment yourselves in vain, for everything has its time.
If you grow some grass, it'll be trampled by autumn.
You started your stroll from an Arbat courtyard,
And it looks as if that's where everything will return.

[65, 149]

Everything here is characteristic of Okudzhava: the fatalism, presented in a mild, understated way that manages to have a consolatory effect; the avoidance of declamatory ideas and imagery—*stroll* as a metaphor for the individual life is a typical piece of deflation. Everything will come back to where it began, changed only by the deprivations of experience. Life is a melancholy affair, but it is not tragic, nor is it absurd. Okudzhava's creative world (unlike, apparently, the historical world of his experience) does not contain the stretched extremes of passion that inform tragedy and absurdity.

These were some of the principal songs with which Okudzhava emerged as a new voice in Russian poetry and culture on the threshold of the 1960s. They have retained their popularity and their freshness for twenty years; their captivating air of sincerity has not aged into a stylistic mannerism. The guitar poets who came after Okudzhava are all in his debt for certain features of the style, but he could have no real followers. His innovations have been used by his successors for quite different ends.

6

Vladimir Vysotsky

> When a country has no God, the people need
> more than leaders. And there arises an ultra-
> respect for writers, composers, artists, be-
> cause they are creators. This esteem spills
> over to actors; actors on TV and film are
> more earthly, and closest of them all was
> Volodya, who sang the whole nation's calam-
> ity in the whole nation's language.
>
> —PAVEL LEONIDOV, *Vladimir Vysotsky*
>   *i drugie*

VLADIMIR VYSOTSKY WAS the nearest equivalent there has
ever been in the USSR to a media superstar in the West, but he was
much more besides. And he became a superstar in the context of the
Soviet system, through sheer power of talent and personality, with the
media ranged against him rather than being manipulated to his advantage. He was a genuine legend long before his life ended in 1980, when
he was only forty-two years old.

It was only after Vysotsky's death that any significant amount of
reliable information about his life became available, and that only in
the West; inside Russia there is still legend and mystery.[1] Vysotsky was
born in Moscow in 1938. His father, who has outlived him, is Jewish, a
career army officer who served with distinction in World War II, eventually retired with the rank of colonel, and took up a high executive
position with the Moscow Central Post Office. Vysotsky's parents
separated when he was one year old, and his father remarried. The boy
was brought up mainly by his mother, Nina Maksimovna, a translator

Vladimir Vysotsky in the late 1970s.

from German by profession who ran the documentation office of a Moscow scientific research institute until she retired in 1980. Mother and son spent the war in evacuation near Orenburg, and Vysotsky went to live with his father from 1947 to 1949, when the latter was serving with the Soviet army of occupation in East Germany. Fundamentally, though, Vysotsky was a Moscow child, and the main element in his upbringing was Moscow street life, followed later by the bohemian world of the trainee actor. The restless, rootless, ruthless ethos of this social context is the dominant note in Vysotsky's work—however much it may have become, as his personal situation changed, an anti-establishment metaphor. But contrary to all the rumors that flew about during his lifetime, he never served in the army and was never in prison.

In one of the very few interviews with Vysotsky ever published in the Soviet press, he stated that he had first attended a college of civil engineering when he began further education, but soon abandoned this course and went to train as an actor in the drama school of the Moscow Arts Theater.[2] He graduated in 1960, but he was not awarded a place in the troupe of the Arts Theater itself. Instead, he joined the Theater of Miniatures (*Teatr miniatyur*) and later the Pushkin Theater (*Teatr imeni Pushkina*), both central Moscow establishments. These too proved to be false starts. Vysotsky's world fell into place when he went to see the very first production by the drama company that was being put together by the eminent director Yury Lyubimov. Vysotsky applied for an audition with Lyubimov and was accepted. That was in 1964. From then until the end of his life, Vysotsky was a member of this company, universally known as the "Taganka Theater" because of its location on Taganka Square. It was his base in the capital and in the public eye.

Vysotsky said that he stayed with Lyubimov and the Taganka because of their commitment to experimentation. He was much more than a rank-and-file member of the troupe, notwithstanding the strong collective ethos normal in Soviet theaters. He soon became the star attraction and the embodiment of the Taganka approach. This approach was brash, dynamic, and athletic, a conscious antipode to the stuffy academicism of the Moscow Arts Theater.

The reputation of the company in the early years was built to a large extent on their productions of the great Brecht plays, which during the Stalin years had been considered far too colorful and challenging for production in the USSR. After his first principal part, that of the Airman in *The Good Woman of Setzuan,* Vysotsky established himself in the title role of *The Life of Galileo,* which entered the Taganka repertoire in 1967 and remains there to this day.

In his account of the postwar "literature of moral resistance" in the USSR, Grigory Svirsky mentioned the rise of the Taganka Theater as part of the revitalization of Soviet cultural life in the post-Stalin period. Svirsky described the significance of *Galileo:*

> the inquisitors [in the play], who had the same faces—fat from good living—that the Stalinist bureaucrats had, gave short shrift to dissident thought; and their methods made it look as if the inquisition, in its black medieval apparel, had taken its instructions from the Moscow City Committee of the Communist Party.[3]

For the first thirty seconds of this production, Vysotsky as Galileo had to do a handstand, a pose that struck his friend Pavel Leonidov as expressing the essence of Vysotsky's personality and attitude toward life.[4]

One of the Taganka's most characteristic early productions was Sergei Esenin's verse drama *Pugachev,* which had previously been regarded as unplayable. It is a play about the nature of revolt. The embodiment of this spirit is the runaway convict Khlopusha, who was played by

> Vysotsky, hoarse and brooding . . . the fact that it was none other fighting against his chains than freedom-loving, hard-drinking Vysotsky, gave the play an awesome, terrifying power of authenticity. . . .[5]

The last role Vysotsky created in the Taganka repertoire was that of Svidrigailov in *Crime and Punishment;* he was reported to have played the great immoralist

> in accordance with all the rules of high-society decorum, remaining the gentleman even when uttering cynical remarks and behaving abominably . . . then at one point he picked up a guitar, and was transformed before our eyes. He sang a mournful song, and in Svidrigailov's gaze was reflected something he had cherished, but forgotten long ago, something fated not to happen. He finished the song, and with guitar still in hand, he spoke of his dream of leaving for America. It was a man's dream of coming to terms with his past and starting a new life, of once more becoming pure in the eyes of God, people, and—first and foremost—himself.[6]

Vysotsky's biggest, most responsible, and most memorable stage role was that of Hamlet. The opening scene of the Taganka production was described earlier.[7] The play had its first performance in 1971. Reviews in the Soviet press were generally approving, and Vysotsky received a good deal of praise.[8] He played the part in a style stripped of romanticism and even of lyricism, with a coarse, abrasive, deintellectualized edge. This portrayal, a Hamlet of the street or even of the gutter, has been said to have been Pasternak's conception of the character in his work on the translation.[9] But for many people it was a case of self-expression by Vysotsky. And Lyubimov once privately upheld this view:

> People reproach me and say that Volodya is uncontrollable as a man and as an actor, that I don't work with him, and that he's no Hamlet or Galileo but always, in every play, Vysotsky. . . . That's true; it's because of his intensity, his charge, and his fire; he's a personality on the same level. . . . He's an uneven actor. He can be a Hamlet of genius and then a mediocre one. No, no, that's not right, it doesn't fit him. Either a genius or nothing. . . .[10]

Vysotsky was never considered to be one of the great legitimate Russian actors of his time, on a level with, for instance, Smoktunovsky. But despite his short, wiry physique and his coarse features, he was recognized early as a genuine star, with impressive presence and real charisma. He was by far the biggest box-office draw in the Soviet theater throughout the 1970s.

While his career was progressing with the Taganka company, Vysotsky was making a parallel impact in film, TV, and radio.[11] He appeared in many mediocre movies[12] and a small number of high-quality ones, playing more than twenty-five roles in his twenty-year career. One important part was the title role in *The Fourth Man (Chetvertyi)*, a spy thriller made by the eminent director Aleksandr Stolper in 1972 from a scenario by Konstantin Simonov.[13] His successes on TV included a notable Don Juan in Pushkin's *Little Tragedies*. On the screen, Vysotsky's personality projected the same magic as it did on the stage. One (perhaps legendary) testimony to this magic has been reported by Pavel Leonidov:

> . . . in the film *Two Comrades Served,* Volodya played a White Guard lieutenant in such a way that the terrified Ministry of Film immediately issued an order never to film Vysotsky in negative hero roles, because when this White Guard lieutenant, on the point of leaving his motherland, shot himself, the audiences started weeping. Soviet people feeling sorry for a White Guardsman![14]

The Vysotsky of stage and screen was the subject of intense curiosity as a personality, and there were several aspects of his private life that became the stuff of myth and legend. His turbulent character was reflected in his driving style, at one time in a big Mercedes; he had two spectacular crashes, after one of which he was clinically dead for three minutes.[15] One of these crashes led Andrei Voznesensky to write him an "optimistic requiem."[16] And it was no secret that Vysotsky was a classic Russian-style drinker, who would go off periodically on gargantuan binges. There are many stories about his being forcibly hospitalized in order to be dried out. He was said to have received the ultimate Soviet treatment for alcoholism, the insertion into the buttocks of a "torpedo" capsule that releases toxic substances, causing the bearer excruciating pain, if alcohol enters the bloodstream. There were accounts of how Lyubimov, with a critical performance looming, would spend hours in a frantic search for Vysotsky and then use all the refinements of medical technology to get him into a fit state to take the stage. Pavel Leonidov has reported Lyubimov as saying that Vysotsky's relations with the bottle reminded him of a fireman's relations with his fire, but he adds:

> I replied that I didn't understand and didn't agree, and that it was rather a matter of . . . the relations between a long drought and a tropical storm. . . .[17]

Leonidov detected the obvious deeper level to Vysotsky's drinking: it was the attempt by a pathologically tense, hyperactive personality to win some intervals of relaxation. Drink was one of the factors, perhaps the main one, that led to Vysotsky's premature death, and he was one of a considerable number of Soviet Russian creative artists who have sought this path to oblivion. The incidence of alcoholism among the "creative intelligentsia" of Soviet Russia, as indeed in the country at large, is a taboo subject,[18] and the part of Vysotsky's repertoire of songs that deals with it—a considerable part—is one of its most firmly underground elements.

The most outrageously un-Soviet and glamorous thing about Vysotsky's life was his marriage to Marina Vlady, the French film actress who was already a European superstar when she came to film in Russia in 1969. (Vysotsky was already married and the father of two sons.) The Soviet media keep quiet about the conjugal lives of public personalities in the USSR, and the resulting rumors made the Vysotsky-Vlady marriage, quite fabulous by Soviet standards, into a fairytale.

For a Soviet citizen, especially one in the public eye, to marry a person from the capitalist world (even when the person concerned is a known Communist, like Vlady) is always an act fraught with immense bureaucratic and practical difficulties. It took a number of years before the Vysotskys established the pattern that was once relished in *Paris Match*. Under the headline "Marina Vlady says 'I'm crazy about Vladimir because I only see him one day in two,'" the reporter accompanied some opulent pictures of the couple with the news that they had given the lie to the old saying "Out of sight, out of mind," and that two or three times a year this most geographically separate of couples came together with delight either in Marina's big house at Maisons-Lafitte or in Vladimir's Moscow apartment.[19] This connection eventually enabled Vysotsky, in the last few years of his life, to spend a fair amount of time away from Moscow and the Soviet environment. The Taganka company was for many years not allowed to travel outside the Communist bloc, despite pressing invitations from many parts of the world, and it gave Vysotsky some relief to have a private life line. He felt that he was an actor of international standard, and he was extremely irked by the lack of opportunity to play outside the Communist bloc, especially as Hamlet.[20]

His activity in theater and film, and his extravagant lifestyle, bestowed great glamour on Vysotsky, and even if he had done nothing else, he would have been a remarkable phenomenon in the world of Soviet culture. But while acting remained his bread and butter, it soon became a backdrop against which Vysotsky pursued his real vocation: guitar poetry. The two areas of activity were not completely detached from each other, of course. He was required to sing in his stage and film roles; the guitar-accompanied song is part of the Soviet working actor's equipment. And Vysotsky was ever more frequently commissioned to produce songs for plays and films in the same way as other established Soviet songwriters, despite his "underground" reputation. He is the author of some of the best songs on the conventional subjects of mountaineering, geological exploration, and sport.

The circumstances of exactly how and when Vysotsky became a guitar poet have been explained in several different ways. Pavel Leonidov says that Vysotsky began when he was a student in the Arts Theater school, before even Okudzhava had started as a guitar poet.[21] Ruvim Rublev says that he first heard Vysotsky sing around 1955, and at the time he was not performing any original material at all. When he was young, says Rublev, Vysotsky had happened to come by several notebooks full of genuine labor-camp and prison songs, and after he'd made a thorough study of them he started singing them for his friends, beginning actors like himself. He used to perform them at student get-togethers, and that's when they first got onto tape.[22]

Vysotsky himself once made a completely unambiguous statement about his early days:

I began writing my songs because I heard Okudzhava's. Indeed, I consider him my godfather. He gave me a nudge; by that time I'd already written a lot of poetry, and suddenly I saw that if I took an instrument and wrote a rhythmical basis for my verse, I could strengthen even more the effect it had on the audience. So I did some things to piano accompaniment and some to the accordion, and then everything somehow crystallized and simplified down to the guitar.[23]

Andrei Voznesensky describes his earliest encounter with Vysotsky in the following way:

I met him for the first time in 1965, when the Taganka put on my *Anti-Worlds*. He was just another of the Taganka people, wearing his eternally teen-age leather jacket, and in his arsenal there were only five or six songs. But there were already hints of the enormous hidden energy in him. That was long before the entire country was tossing and turning, enmeshing him, like Laocoon, in magnetic tape.[24]

Voznesensky's image is not overly fanciful. Vysotsky's fame as a creator and singer of songs was firmly established by the end of the sixties, and his reputation continued to rise throughout the seventies. As we have seen, Okudzhava faded out around 1972; Galich was forced into emigration in 1974. But Vysotsky held on, the fount of creativity seemingly inexhaustible, and the private tape recorder ensuring that his work stayed before the public.

It was inevitable that as Vysotsky's reputation as a singer and writer of unofficial songs grew greater, there would be trouble from the authorities. The attacks on him took different forms at different times. He was always subject to appropriate reprisals in the same way as any Soviet public personality, that is, denial of the opportunity to travel, denial of recording and distribution facilities, and being barred from playing certain parts. This interference is part and parcel of the professional life of all Soviet creative artists.

An early example of a public attack on Vysotsky is an article headed "What Vysotsky Is Singing About," published in 1968 by two authors, one of whom is identified as "a teacher in the consultation office of the State Institute of Culture."[25] They allege that Vysotsky used a double repertoire: a public one composed for official plays and films and a private one that he used for individual performances. In the latter, they said, he spoke "on behalf of alcoholics, soldiers in the penal battalions, criminals, people who are depraved and inadequate." He slandered Soviet reality, they said, in not speaking about World War II in heroic terms. They accused Vysotsky of "reveling in our shortcomings and making fun of what the Soviet people is right to feel proud of" (the evidence being a song actually written by Yury Vizbor[26]). Also, they alleged, Vysotsky mangled the Russian language, undermining the efforts of the education system to promote proper language etiquette. And he wrapped it all up in an attractive package which had the deadly lure of forbidden fruit and (they concluded) must be denounced and extirpated as the insidious poison it really was. The authentic voice of Soviet official humbuggery may be discerned in these charges. But it must always be remembered that they are potentially backed up by action of a most unpleasant kind from "the organs," with whose knowledge and permission they are published and often even generated for future use as ammunition. These charges are typical of what was officially said about Vysotsky as a poet-singer throughout his career.

More threatening than these allegations, though, were the ones that actually accused him of illegal conduct. Beginning in about 1968, Vysotsky regularly gave concerts of his songs, which were always massively attended. They were usually put on as technically private performances, in the sense that tickets were sold not to the public but only to the employees of the particular institution that was sponsoring the concert. This kind of activity also falls within the control system, and officials kept a tight watch on what Vysotsky was actually doing. For example, in 1968 a visit he paid to Novokuznetsk provoked a scandal. A "reader," one M. Shlifer, complained in a letter to the newspaper *Soviet Culture (Sovetskaya kul'tura)* that Vysotsky's concerts were very interesting, but that he had been giving five concerts a day, each lasting an hour and forty or even fifty minutes, and with a thousand people attending each one (and tickets still being hard to come by). The newspaper promptly investigated this allegation. It was discovered that Vysotsky in fact had given sixteen concerts in four days. This activity contravened a regulation of the Ministry of Culture; the extra concerts, the newspaper revealed, had been given "by private arrangement" with the director of the local theater. Not only that, but

Vysotsky's name did not figure on "the list of vocalists who have the right to give solo programs."[27]

What exactly happened as a result of this and similar accusations is unknown and will likely remain so. Vysotsky was probably given a reprimand at the appropriate level of the Taganka's administration and possibly even at the Ministry of Culture, and perhaps eased off for a while as a result. But he was never absent for long. Vysotsky was never persecuted and muzzled like Galich and never desisted as a result of severe warnings, like Okudzhava.

While Vysotsky was not permitted to publish or record in Russia on anything like the scale his popularity would have appeared to warrant, and the repertoire that was allowed onto records was only a narrow segment of his total output, the fact remains that he did make a number of recordings for the state monopoly company, Melodiya.[28] These performances are provided with orchestral accompaniments of quite comic crudity and do not begin to compare with the raw intensity of Vysotsky's *magnitizdat* performances. But they were made, and they were released, something that would have been unthinkable for even doctored versions of Galich's songs. In this respect, as in the case of Vysotsky the actor, there was persistent give-and-take between him and the state apparatus. How long it would have continued had Vysotsky lived is unknowable, of course; but the evidence suggests that in the late 1970s things were moving toward a crisis. He was getting more and more publicity abroad, and his conduct was becoming more and more indiscreet.

The nearest Vysotsky came to a showdown with the Soviet authorities was in connection with the *Metropol* affair in 1979. A group of writers, led by the novelist Vasily Aksenov, all authors of work that had been submitted to the Soviet press and refused publication either altogether or without substantial changes, decided that they would make a stand and demand the publication of this work in the form they wanted it. They put together an almanac, of which they made eight copies, and called it *Metropol (Metropolis)*, a triple pun: the word in the sense of "capital city"; in the sense of "underground (railway)"; and as the name of the famous hotel in the middle of Moscow, a sign that the participants were looking for somewhere to lay their heads. Twenty-three authors altogether were involved. They intended to launch their almanac at what would in the West be a straightforward publisher's party. But the café they hired for the purpose was suddenly closed, and they began to be summoned one by one to the authorities.

The almanac was sent to the United States for publication when it became clear that the Union of Writers and the "organs" were not going to be pressured into making concessions. The fate of the authors concerned has been various: exile, submission, repentance, disavowal. But if the affair may be regarded as a test case, which is certainly what the ringleaders wanted, it showed, with no room for doubt, that the system was not going to bend in response to internal pressure.[29]

Vysotsky published nineteen songs in the almanac, and another was used as an epigraph to it. The songs in *Metropol* actually have a uniquely authoritative status. They were selected and prepared for publication by the author himself, and they therefore represent a conscious statement by him about his work. None of the other publications has this authority. All the *magnitizdat* recordings are unedited, and most of them are probably unauthorized (although that admittedly gives them a different kind of positive value). The official Soviet recordings and publications have gone through the fine-grinding mill of the control system. In view of Vysotsky's death about a year after the *Metropol* affair, it is tempting to see the selection published there as his own statement about his creative career to date. The songs even appear to be, insofar as indirect evidence makes it possible to say, in chronological order of composition.

The nineteen *Metropol* songs actually do give a reasonable representation of Vysotsky's work. They certainly show his limitations and weaknesses, as well as his strengths. They begin with four of the "criminal songs" which formed the staple of his repertoire when he was beginning in the late sixties. In the first, a man serving a prison sentence writes to his faraway mates and asks them to get in touch. The famous "The One Who Was with Her Before" is an archetypal vengeance song whose central persona is a criminal who has been carved up in a gang fight after trying to get even with the man who has taken his place with his girlfriend. Then comes the uproarious "Ginger Moll" ("Ryzhaya shalava"):

Why've you gone and plucked your eyebrows, bitch?
And why've you put your blue beret on, rotten stinker?
And where d'you think you're off to in such a hurry, bag?
You can't hide it from me that you've got two tickets for our club!

You know for a fact that I'm crazy about you,
I'd be glad to spend all my time thieving for you;
But just lately it looks to me
As if you've been two-timing me a bit too often.

If it's Kolya that's involved, or even Slava,
Well, I won't object to my mates;
But if it's that Vitya from Pervaya Pereyaslavskaya Street,
I'll tear you limb from limb, so help me I will.

You red-headed bag, I'll tell you straight,
If you go on wearing that beret of yours,
I won't touch you, I'll just forget all about you,
Cover my memory in cement so nobody can dig it out.

And then when summer comes and you try to come back,
I'll grab myself such a fantastic chick
That you'll curl up with jealousy, you bitch,
You'll ask me to forgive you, but I won't give a damn.

[*M*, 191; *PRB*, III, 28–29][30]

Vysotsky used to perform this song at a breakneck tempo, making it into a tour de force of elocution, and spoofing the sexist violence of the song's surface meaning. The fourth of the criminal songs is one of the few in Vysotsky's work that has a clear autobiographical subtext: "On Bolshoi Karetnyi Row" ("Na Bol'shom Karetnom"), a lament for a misspent youth in a Moscow environment that has been left behind and then has changed out of all recognition.[31]

This little group of criminal songs is followed by a banal love song, "If I Were Rich as the Ocean King" ("Esli ia bogat, kak tsar' morskoi"), an effort best forgotten. Then comes one of Vysotsky's keynote songs, "In No-Man's-Land" ("Na neitral'noi polose"). It tells the story of a Soviet frontier soldier who goes into no-man's-land to pick some flowers for his wedding, not knowing that one of his Turkish opponents has exactly the same plan. The two men fall to the ground, overcome by the scent of the flowers. The song asks why they should not be allowed to do so. It has a moralistic, self-righteous tone that is dangerously close to the sanctimonious; its impact, such as it was, derived from the contrast with official frontier songs,[32] where the brave Soviet heroes stand firm against the sinister provocations of the unsleeping aggressors. It is the nearest thing, in Vysotsky's repertoire and maybe in the whole of Russian guitar poetry, to the pacifist anthems of the late sixties in the West.

The next song in *Metropol* is "Parody of a Bad Detective Story" ("Parodiya na plokhoi detektiv"), one of Vysotsky's best comic songs. An "un-Soviet person," calling himself "John Lancaster Peck," spends his time in Moscow secretly taking detrimental pictures of "everything we treasure and love,/ that the collective is proud of":

> The club on Nagornaya Street
> Became a public toilet.
> Our dear old Central Market
> Looked like a dirty warehouse.
> Distorted by the microfilm
> GUM was a little peasant hut,
> And I'd rather not mention
> What the Moscow Arts Theater was.
>
> [*PRB*, I, 11–12]

"Peck" enrolls a seemingly dissolute Soviet citizen as his assistant and sets him up for some preliminary tasks, promising a reward of "money, a house in Chicago, lots of women and cars." However,

> The enemy didn't realize, the fool,
> That the person he was entrusting all this to
> Was a Chekist, an intelligence major,
> And a splendid family man!
>
> [*PRB*, I, 12]

So "Peck" is brought to account. The story does indeed parody the clichés of the official Soviet spy mystery as practiced by the best-selling author Yulian Semenov. Its special appeal is created by the little touches that take it over the top (the "splendid family man," and the Arts Theater reference, especially in the mouth of a Taganka actor). Altogether, the piece is an innocent romp, sent up by Vysotsky in performance and made into something quite hilarious.

The story of John Lancaster Peck is followed by the only representative in the *Metropol* collection of the considerable number of early Vysotsky songs on the subject of sport. It is not one of the best. A boxer is being battered senseless; but his opponent, Butkeev, works so hard that he exhausts himself, and the battered pugilist wins. The most interesting thing about this song is its refrain:

> And Butkeev thought as he pummeled my jaw:
> "It's good to live, and life is good!"
>
> [*PRB*, I, 6]

This apparently innocuous quotation aroused the ire of the critics of 1968 that have just been cited; the quotation happens to be from the holy writ of Mayakovsky, and this line of his, which has become an official Soviet slogan, must not be taken in vain.

Then come two outrageous parodies of Russian folklore, "The Wild

Boar" ("O dikom vepre") and "Evil Spirits" ("Pro nechist' "), the latter a masterpiece of deromanticization and desentimentalization. The song takes some of the schoolbook characters and incidents from the traditional Russian folk tales and makes them sordid and prosaic. As a piece of pure verbal inventiveness it is one of the high points of Vysotsky's work; he revels in supernumerary rhymes and in juxtaposing conventional folk phraseology against vulgar urban slang. The stylistic and thematic virtuosity of the song is completely untranslatable. A large part of its impact derives from the contrast with the reverent official attitude toward the nation's folklore.

A third folklore skit in *Metropol* is the most explicit of them all. The title, "The Sea-Cove's Gone for Good" ("Lukomor'ya bol'she net"), refers to the most famous example in Russian poetry of the use of folklore, the introduction to Pushkin's *Ruslan and Lyudmila* ("By a sea-cove is a green oak,/A golden chain around it,/And night and day a learned cat/Walks round and round on the chain,/When he walks to the left he starts up a song,/When he walks to the right he tells a tale.") In Vysotsky's song:

> The sea-cove's gone for good,
> No trace of the oak trees.
> Oak's good for making parquet floors,
> Isn't it?
>
> [*M*, 201]

The cat is still there, though:

> The cat really does walk here,
> Walks to the right and sings,
> Walks to the left and cracks
> An anecdote!
> But that learned son of a bitch
> Flogged his gold chain to the foreign currency agency,
> And went to get relief
> From the store!
>
> [*M*, 202–203]

The virginal temptress of Russian folklore is transformed:

> And the mermaid—there's a thing!—
> Didn't keep her honor long,
> And one fine day as best she could
> Had a baby.
> The thirty-three muzhiks

> Don't acknowledge the little boy—
> Let him be for the moment
> A son of the regiment.
>
> > [*M*, 203]

The last line is a reference to a famous Soviet play, *A Son of the Regiment* by Veniamin Kaverin. "The Sea-Cove" is almost childish in the level of its humor, but once again, it has to be seen against the background of Soviet solemnity in the study of Russian folklore. In Vysotsky's performance it is a virtuoso piece, with deliberately outrageous rhymes, and sung at a breakneck tempo.

For some reason, the two last-mentioned folkloric songs are separated in the *Metropol* selection by a lyric that is among the gloomiest Vysotsky ever wrote. It has a two-line refrain:

> The Earth is covered in ice!
> The whole year round, in ice!

The rest of the song rings some changes on the theme of the first verse:

> The Earth is covered in ice!
> As if there were no spring or summer,
> The planet's clothed in something slippery,
> People fall down and hit the ice.
>
> > [*M*, 201]

The song has often been read metaphorically, of course, as a statement about the atmosphere of Russian society during the Brezhnev years. And it has also been taken as a direct confession by Vysotsky about his own sense of insecurity.

The last of the folk parodies is followed by a three-verse text whose stark refrain needs no comment:

> The people keep on complaining,
> Justice is what they want:
> "We were first in line,
> But they're already eating behind us!"
>
> > [*M*, 205]

All the songs that have been mentioned so far date from the earliest phase of Vysotsky's career; they are attested on the *magnitizdat* tapes from the late 1960s. The criminal songs and the sport songs, of which Vysotsky composed a large number, were especially characteristic of this early period. As Vysotsky moved through the seventies, the proportion of songs in which he spoke explicitly from his own point of view seemed to grow. The next song in the *Metropol* group is an example. It is a lament for Vysotsky's old friend, the writer and actor Vasily Shukshin (1929–1974), whose alcohol-accelerated death foreshadowed Vysotsky's own. The song's impact is retrospectively made very poignant by this fact; there are lines like:

> "He can't have understood omens,"
> Say the idle people in vain,
> "Death catches those of us first
> Who intend to die."

And even more ominously:

> Death picks out the very best
> And pulls them in one by one.
>
> [*M*, 206–207]

The parallels between Shukshin and Vysotsky are many. The older man had nothing like the same level of national appeal as the singer, but they were similar personalities and reacted in a similarly desperate way to the pressures of Soviet life. In particular, Egor, the hero of Shukshin's most famous story, *Kalina krasnaya* (translated as *Snowball Berry Red*), is exactly the same tough loner as the heroes of Vysotsky's criminal songs. A poem by Esenin that Egor quotes in *Kalina krasnaya,* in which Esenin identifies himself with a hunted wolf, is the direct ancestor of the first of two impassioned anthems by Vysotsky that come next in *Metropol*. It is "The Wolf Hunt":

> I'm straining my utmost, every sinew,
> But yet again, today like yesterday,
> They've surrounded me, surrounded me,
> And they're merrily herding me in to do my tricks.
>
> The shotguns are busy from behind the spruce trees,
> The hunters are hiding in their shadow,
> And the wolves go head over heels in the snow,
> Turned into living targets.

The refrain:

> The wolf hunt is on, the hunt is on!
> For gray prowlers, old ones, and cubs;
> The beaters shout, the dogs howl themselves sick,
> There's blood on the snow and the red spots of flags.

. . .
Our legs and jaws are swift.
Why, pack leader, answer us,
Do we run toward the shots as if doped,
And never try to go beyond the prohibitions?

The wolf cannot and must not do otherwise . . .
And now my time's coming to its end!
The man I'm destined for
Has smiled and lifted his gun . . .

The wolf hunt is on, the hunt is on! etc.

But I've transgressed my obedience and gone
Beyond the flags—the thirst for life was stronger!
And behind me I heard with joy
The amazed cries of the people.

I'm straining my utmost, every sinew,
But today's not the same as yesterday!
They've surrounded me, surrounded me,
But the hunters have been left empty-handed!

[*PRB*, I, 29–30]

Vysotsky wrote a sequel to "The Wolf Hunt" which is not included in *Metropol*; its title is "Hunting with Helicopters, or Where Are You, Wolves?". The wolf that got away in the earlier song is here at bay:

What can I do alone? I can do nothing.
My eyes have given out, my sense of smell is dull.
Where are you, wolves, forest beasts of yore?
Where are you, yellow-eyed tribe of mine?

I'm alive. But now I'm surrounded
By animals who never knew wolf-calls,
They're hounds, our distant relatives,
We used to think of them as our prey.

I smile at the enemy with my wolfish grin,
Baring the rotten stumps,
And on the blood-tattooed snow
Melts the sign: "We're not wolves any more!"

[*Pesni i stikhi*, 1, 310]

This is one of the most despairing of Vysotsky's later songs. "The Wolf Hunt" was followed in *Metropol* by a text that Vysotsky used to howl out in a voice more like a wolf's than he used in the song about wolves; its refrain goes:

Stoke me the bath-house smokeless [*po-belomu*],
I've had enough of this wide world [*belyi svet*]

> I'll steam myself out of my mind,
> And the hot steam will untie my tongue.
>
> [*PRB*, III, 54–55]

The hero turns out to be an ex-convict who has labored in Siberia but who retained his faith in Stalin and did not begrudge the killing work he was performing for the country and its cause, only to realize, eventually, that the cause was not worth the effort:

> The thoughts have started knocking under my skull,
> It turns out I was condemned by Them for nothing!
> So with my birch twig I'll whip out
> The inheritance of those gloomy times.

This song produced an almost frightening effect on Russian audiences; it seemed to take them by the throats and confront them with the tormenting question that they sometimes formulate for themselves as "What did we struggle for?" and to demand a despairing answer. And the personal charge that Vysotsky put into it was unmistakable. Like almost all his lyric anthems, it is expressed from the point of view of a person who has been goaded to the point of no return and feels he must do something desperate to resolve his fate.

It is aptly followed by a song in which sport is no more than the nominal subject; the hero is a racing driver, and he is the embodiment of risk, gambling with life as a pathological obsession. Characteristic of the song's tone are lines like these:

> My finish line is the horizon, the tape's the earth's end,
> I have to be first at the horizon.

The driver has to complete the course to win a wager. His enemies have set traps for him:

> I know they'll throw wrenches in my spokes,
> I can guess the way they'll cheat me,
> I know where they'll smirk and cross my path.
> And where there's a cable stretched across the road.
> . . .
>
> My finish line, the horizon, is still as far away,
> I haven't broken the tape, but I've got past the cable,
> It didn't break my neck, but from the bushes
> They're firing at my wheels.
>
> After all, it wasn't money that made me race,
> "Don't miss this chance," they said,

"Why not see if there's a limit at earth's end,
And if horizons can be pushed back?"

While I'm clocking up the miles,
I won't let anyone put a bullet in my back,
But the brakes are failing—coda!
On I go right past the horizon.

[*M*, 211]

This impassioned personal outcry—melodramatic and perhaps self-
pitying as it may be—is characteristic of the later Vysotsky.

Two songs remain of the *Metropol* collection. The first is a throwaway about a Soviet brain surgeon:

Everyone whose life wasn't bright
He turned into normal people,
But this enormous bright star
Unfortunately was a Jew.

[*M*, 212]

The text as it stands in *Metropol,* with two verses and two refrain
stanzas, looks incomplete, as if it were the beginning of a long narrative
song about what happened to this person as a result of his Jewishness.
The last song of the *Metropol* batch is one of the supreme masterpieces
of Vysotsky's last years, here called simply "A Dialogue" ("Dialog"),
but usually called in performance "Dialogue in Front of the TV":

"Ooh, Vanya, just look at them clowns,
Their mouths look as if they need bandaging,
They're so made up, aren't they, Vanya,
And they've got voices like alkies.
And that one looks like my brother,
A drunkard just like him, I'm right, aren't I,
No, go on, have a look, go on, have a look,
I'm right, Vanya!"

"Listen, Zina, hands off brother,
I don't care what he's like, he's still family.
And you're all made up yourself,
Just watch what you say to me!
Why don't you quit fretting
And get yourself down to the shop?
No? Well, I'll go myself,
Move yourself, Zina."

"Ooh, Vanya, just look at them dwarfs,
That's jersey they've got on, not cheviot.

Down at our garment factory
We'd have a job making that up.
But honest, Vanya, I'm telling you,
All your friends are such layabouts,
First thing in the morning they start drinking
That rotgut."

"My friends might not wear smart raincoats,
But they don't make their families go short.
They drink that filth to save money,
And if they do start in the morning, they pay their way.
And who are you to talk, Zina,
Once you had a boyfriend from the tire factory
And he used to drink gasoline.
Remember that, Zina?"

"Ooh, Vanya, just look, little parrots,
A-a-a-gh, it's going to make me scream, honest.
And who's that wearing that short vest?
Can I have one like that, Vanya?
Vanya, I bet you could get me one
Down at the street corner, couldn't you?
What d'you mean, give over, it's all you ever say,
It's not nice, Vanya."

"You'd be better if you kept your trap shut,
This area's got no priority any more.
And who's been writing complaints about me to work,
What d'you mean, they haven't, I've read them myself.
And besides, that vest, if you put it on,
Zina, it'd be a disgrace.
It'd take yards to make one for you,
And where's the money, Zina?"

"Ooh, Vanya, that acrobat'll be the death of me,
Just look at him twirling round, cheeky devil,
The man in charge of our club, Mr. Satikov,
Jumped about like that at work not long ago.
And Vanya, what you'll do is get back home,
Have a bite, and collapse on the bed,
Or you'll go on bawling if you're not drunk,
What're you doing, Vanya?"

"You're starting to get rude, Zina,
You're just trying to offend me.
I get so wound up during the day,
Then I get home and what do I see but you.
No wonder, is it, Zina,
I always feel like going to the shop,

That's where my mates are, Zina,
After all, I never drink on my own."

"Oh, look, there's a gymnast on now,
She can do a bit even though she's getting on . . .
Down at our milk bar, the "Swallow,"
There's a waitress who can do that."
"The only thing your friends ever do, Zina,
Is sit there knitting woolly winter hats,
People like that are so boring
They'd drive you out of your mind."

"You what, Vanya? How about Lilka Fedoseeva,
The cashier from Gorky Park?
You were after her when we had our housewarming,
I bet you think she's all right.
What's the point of arguing, Vanya,
Let's just go to Erevan for a holiday.
What d'you mean, give over, it's all you ever say,
It's not nice, Vanya."

This piece of seeming trivia needs to be understood, in the first place, against the background of the conventions of Socialist Realism, especially as manifested in song. It is clear that Vysotsky has succeeded in carrying off something that has led most Russian authors who have attempted it into portentousness, inverted snobbery, and guilt—abandoning their intelligentsia stance and actually speaking from the persona of the ordinary people of Russia. The song seems to invite contempt and condemnation for a man and wife whose mental horizons are so limited. But that is not the case. The song in fact portrays them objectively, as if to say "They may not be beautiful, but that is how they are." And it does not highhandedly and patronizingly summon them to be the vanguard of history, recall to them their revolutionary heritage, or anything that is remotely ideological. But the song does more. It implies that the people have not been ennobled by their history, and that the massive effort that has gone into indoctrinating them has been a complete failure. Astonishingly, the song was included in the posthumous Soviet collection of Vysotsky's work, probably the only item from *Metropol* that has been published in the USSR.

The other remarkable thing about this song is that it is a masterpiece of naturalistic dialogue which succeeds at the same time in being a virtuoso piece of phonetic organization. The rhyme structure of the original is ABABCCCC; the four lines at the end of each stanza, each with their single rhyme, have to use the names of the husband and wife

(Van' or Ivan, and Zin); but there is only one line in the whole song where there is any suspicion that the content has been distorted by the exigencies of the rhyme. In translation, Vysotsky's language may seem extremely prosaic. The original Russian sparkles with exuberant word play of the kind demanded by the rhyme scheme of "Dialogue in Front of the TV," and the author's performance underlines his relish as he overfulfils all norms.

While the *Metropol* songs give a balanced impression of Vysotsky's work as a whole (excluding the two extremes of publishable and completely nonpublishable), some of his very best songs are not included among them.

The criminal songs formed the central core of Vysotsky's "private" repertoire when he was in his first fame as a guitar poet. They are of several kinds. Some of them are extremely sophisticated pastiches of the underworld song, the genre that was discussed earlier as one element in the tradition of urban folk song in Russia. The subject matter is not necessarily actual criminal life, but may be simply from the low life of the city. An example is "The Lady Nark" ("Navodchitsa"), which must be one of the most outlandish love songs ever written in Russian. Vysotsky used to perform this song in a deadpan, lugubrious monotone. Once again, seen in the context of the officially approved approach to sexual relationships, the attitudes and characters of this song are outrageous.

> Today I'm going to have fun
> Arranging my Saturday;
> And if Nina doesn't play up,
> I'll arrange my whole life!
>
> "Hang on, you dope, don't you know she's a nark?
> What for?" "Don't care, I just fancy her."
> "Hang on, you dope, there's some of us getting together,
> Let's go down the pub and drown your desire."
>
> "Don't try getting at me today,
> You can stuff your booze today;
> Today Nina's making her decision,
> Today my life's being settled."
>
> "She's been around, that Nina has,
> She's lived with the whole of Ordynka Street!
> Anybody can sleep with her if they want to."
> "Makes no difference to me, I just fancy her a lot.

She said she loves me." "Come off it, that's past and gone,
I'll lay a hundred rubles to one she's putting you on."
"It's a bad sign if it's her doing the asking."
"Means nothing to me, I just fancy her a lot."

"But her voice is hoarse, and she's filthy,
She's got one black eye and her legs don't match,
She's always dressed like a charwoman."
"Be damned to that, I fancy her.

I know everybody says she's not good-looking,
But I like them better if they're like that,
What do I care if she's a nark?
It just makes me fancy her even more."

                                        [*PRB*, III, 31–32]

One of the most subtle of all Vysotsky's criminal songs, one which
goes far beyond the regular limits of the genre, is "The Anti-Semites"
("Antisemity"):

Why should I be just a common criminal?
Wouldn't it be better to join the Anti-Semites?
On their side they've got no laws, that's true,
But they have got the support and enthusiasm of millions.

Well, I decided, somebody has to get beaten up,
But I thought I'd better find out who these Semites are;
What if they turn out to be decent people,
What if I stand to make something out of them?

But my friend and teacher, the alkie at the grocer's,
Told me that these Semites are only ordinary Jews;
That's a stroke of luck, isn't it, lads?
Now I've calmed down, what is there to be scared of?

I held out for a long time, I always had
A respectful attitude toward Albert Einstein;
I hope folk will forgive me if I ask
What should be done about Abraham Lincoln?

Among them is Kapler, who suffered at Stalin's hands,
And Charlie Chaplin, I've always liked him,
My mate Rabinovich, the victims of Fascism,
And even the founding father of Marxism.

That same mate told me once after we'd done a little job
That they drink the blood of Christian babies,
And the lads told me once down at the pub
That once, long ago, they crucified God.

They have to have blood, they once got worked up
And tortured an elephant at the zoo;
I know for sure that they stole from the people
All the grain from last year's harvest.

Along the railway line from Kursk to Kazan
They've built themselves second homes, and they live there like
   gods;
I'm ready for anything, for punchups and violence,
I beat up the Yids so's to save Mother Russia.

[PRB, III, 10–11]

The reactions that this song produces in a Russian audience are complicated. It spells out some of the most notorious elements in gut Russian anti-Semitism but appears to defuse them by passing them off as the views of a simple-minded clod of the criminal classes. An extremely delicate balance is achieved between the wholehearted realistic representation of *lumpen* attitudes and the temptation to recognize and agree with these attitudes in their more sophisticated forms. The last line of the song paraphrases the slogan of official anti-Semitism in the prerevolutionary period, a slogan still very much alive in the Russian folk memory.

There is another group of Vysotsky songs that exudes a guileless lunacy which is very rare indeed in Russian humor. It is true that behind them it is possible to identify all sorts of digs at Soviet attitudes, but nevertheless they have an immediate and very pure appeal. Perhaps the best of this group is the following:

The Yogi

What are the claims to fame of Indian culture?
Well, there's Shiva, who's got lots of arms and fangs;
There's an actor that we've heard of, Raj Kapur,
And that strange caste, the yogis, and the tale.

People say that at one time yogis could do it
Even if they'd not taken a damn thing in their mouth for a year,
But these days they're breaking records,
Eating everything and drinking all year round.

I know that yogis have a lot of secrets,
I'd like to have a tête-to-tête with one.
Even poison has no effect on yogis,
Against poisons they have immunity.

An hour under water, and he doesn't breathe once,
Doesn't take offense at one word, or two.

And if he feels he's an old man, suddenly
He'll say "Stop!" and rightaway he's a corpse.

And us? —Well, we're no worse than many,
We too can go without a night's sleep.
There's a lot of yogis wandering around here,
Though I admit they're very hard to spot.

Yogis can do many many tricks.
Lately there was one who suddenly lay down.
Two whole days went flashing by (Shame!)
He just went on lying there, fast asleep.

I once asked a yogi who'd had a bit to drink
(He was eating razor blades and nails like sausage)—
"Listen, friend, reveal yourself to me, honest to God
I'll take the secret with me to my grave."

The answer to my question was simple,
But he and I had a terrible argument.
I could just reveal what his answer was,
But the yogi told me to keep the secret, that's all.

[PRB, I, 13]

The *Metropol* selection, by definition given the purposes for which the collection was put together, contains none of the songs by Vysotsky that were published or recorded in the USSR. But at least one of these ranks with his very best work, even in the adulterated version released on record. It is called "A.M. P.T." ("Utrennyaya gimnastika"):

Breathe in deeply, stretch those arms out,
Take it easy (-three-and-four-and-)
Bright and breezy, grace of movement, sculptured pose,
It's what strengthens you all over,
Gets you sober in the morning,
(If you're still alive)—yes! It's gym-
-nastics!

If you're home in your apartment,
On the floor! (-and-three-and-four-and-)
Carry out the movements in the proper way;
Do away with outside things,
Keep your mind on what's to come,
Breathe in deeply until you're in-
-capable!

Lately there's a worldwide growth of
Cholera germs (-and-three-and-four-and-)
More and still more people keep on falling ill;

> If you're fragile—in your coffin!
> If you want to keep your health up,
> Folks, the thing you really need is rub-
> -bing down!
>
> If you're getting tired already
> (Sit down, stand up, sit down, stand up)
> No need to fear the Arctic or the Antarctic;
> Chief Academician Joffe
> Proved that brandy and that coffee
> Will do instead of physioprophy-
> -laxis!
>
> Right, cut out that conversation,
> Knees-bend, knees-bend 'til you're dropping,
> And no need for gloominess or furrowed brows;
> If you're feeling very bad,
> Rub down with what comes to hand,
> Have recourse to hydropro-
> -cedures!
>
> Bad news causes us no bother,
> Running on the spot's our answer,
> Even a beginner is a winner;
> It's just great—a field of runners
> With no winners and no laggers,
> Running on the spot is the pan-
> -pacifier!
>
> > > > > > > [*PRB*, IV, 76–77]

The butt of the joke is the morning keep-fit broadcast which goes out over the main Soviet radio network. Its ballet-class piano and Butlin-redcoat instructor arouse derisive mockery in most Russians, but Vysotsky's comment is in a class of its own. This song, sung by the author to the accompaniment of an elephantine thirties-style dance orchestra, has been released on one of Vysotsky's Soviet records. Clearly, there is nothing here that goes very deep; there is even a dollop of uplift at the end.

One of the very few songs of Vysotsky's that stands as an indisputable masterpiece is "The Song of Serezhka Fomin" ("Pesenka pro Serezhku Fomina"). Not a single word in it could be omitted or changed without doing damage:

> I grew up same as other backstreet kids,
> We used to drink vodka and sing songs at night;
> But we never had much time for Serezhka Fomin
> Because he was always serious.

Once we were round at Serezhka Fomin's place,
That's where we usually got together,
And that war had broken out
We learned from Molotov's famous speech.

At the recruiting center they said: "Old man!
Your place of work means you get exemption";
I turned it down, but Serezhka Fomin
Was got off by his old man, a professor.

I'm spilling my blood for you, my country,
But all the same my heart is full of distress.
I'm spilling my blood for Serezhka Fomin,
And he just sits there without a care in the world.

But at last the war finished.
It was like getting a ton weight off our shoulders.
I bump into Serezhka Fomin—
And he's a Hero of the Soviet Union.

[*PRB*, IV, 24]

This song is a classic ballad. It is understated, stylistically perfect, constructed with judicious parallelism, tautly economical but with just the right amount of repetition to make the effect inevitable (in performance the last couplet of each verse is repeated), and it tells a story that unfolds in an inexorable way to the final punch line and then needs no further comment. In the *magnitizdat* recordings it is invariably followed by a troubled silence from the audience. The song is a negation of the official war song, because it points to privilege and social injustice, when the events of 1941–45 are officially proclaimed to have welded Soviet society together in their just common cause. The hero, the "I" of the song, is exactly that ordinary man doing his duty who is a cliché hero of Soviet war mythology, as we have seen. But Vysotsky's hero is contemptuous rather than indulging himself in resentment and bitterness—another reason why the song's dry economy is so effective. This song is entirely Soviet in its data, a-Soviet in the mental horizon of the hero, and anti-Soviet in its implications. It is saved from being actionably anti-Soviet by retaining a positive view of the Russian people, or at least by not denigrating their "achievements." But it is not alone in this respect among Vysotsky's songs, as we have seen even in the *Metropol* group, which errs on the side of caution. But why was the author of items like these allowed to remain not only free but in the public eye?

One clear—if superficial—reason why Vysotsky was permitted to survive is that quite a number of his songs actually promote the official line of the time they were composed, especially some songs he wrote making fun of the Chinese during their cultural revolution. These songs portray the Chinese as nasty, destructive little boys going through an adolescent revolutionary tantrum. Here is an example, this time with a sporting subject:

> The professionals get loads of salary,
> They don't care if they spit their teeth out on the ice;
> They're paid superdough, thousands and thousands,
> Even if they lose and even if they draw.
>
> These players are crafty, they go for the body,
> Thump opponents in the teeth and don't give a damn;
> But they wind up getting their own legs done in,
> And get a walking stick instead of a hockey stick.
>
> To the professionals, those desperate fellows,
> The game's a lottery, a matter of luck.
> They play their marker like a bull plays the matador,
> Though you'd have thought it should be the other way around.
>
> There lies the marker as if he was dead,
> So what? That's his lookout, let him lie;
> Don't mess it up, Bull, God wants the puck in the net,
> God's up there in the stands and he won't let you off.
> . . .
> The professionals get paid through all sorts of channels
> Big amounts, little amounts, into the bank;
> But our Russian lads stay on the same money
> And they've still gone ahead five times already.
>
> So let them get on with their big-league intriguing,
> And let them call hockey "the Canadian game";
> It's our turn now, we're looking forward to next time;
> But as for our footballers . . . let's hope they improve.
>
> [*PRB*, II, 7]

This song was written during the epic Moscow series of 1972 that led to a Soviet defeat at the hands of the visiting Canadians. The entire country held its breath during the series, and national pride was painfully at stake. The tone of Vysotsky's song is exactly in tune with the Soviet official myth about the unscrupulous professionalism of the Canadians and the clean sporting amateurism of the Russians.

This particular song is explicit in this respect, but the vast majority of Vysotsky's songs about international politics, World War II, and the various professions are on the same level. The reason these songs are unsuitable for transmission is their form, not their content. Vysotsky succeeds in expressing popular attitudes that correspond in principle with official ones (usually involving that endemic Russian chauvinism which is so offensive to foreigners)—but he does so in a style which is incompatible with the linguistic decorum of the media.

For this and other reasons, Vysotsky managed to carry on despite the kind of public attacks that have intimidated or led to the arrest or silencing by other means of most other Soviet authors who have been subjected to them. There was a sort of unholy conspiracy between him and the Soviet official world. The Party and state apparatus by implication acknowledged him as the most authentic voice of their historical time and their country, someone who was perhaps unruly, disrespectful, and even downright subversive at times, but nevertheless someone who spoke to them in their own language and about their own life. It is in this important respect that Vysotsky was the unofficial bard of the official world instead of being (like Galich) a force alien to it, something it felt threatened by and needed to destroy.[33]

Vysotsky, of course, was perfectly well aware of this situation. He even wrote a song about it:

> The time for introductions and preludes is gone,
> Everything's fine—straight up, no fooling.
> I get invitations from big people
> To come and sing them "The Wolf Hunt."
> . . .
> He's listened right through to the last note;
> Furious because the last words are missing,
> He picks up the phone and says "Get me
> The author of 'The Hunt' in my office tomorrow."
>
> I didn't take any Dutch courage,
> And, forcing back the stammers,
> Standing in the doorway, I bawled out "The Hunt"
> From beginning to end.
> . . .
> And he heard me out benevolently
> And even clapped at the end.
>
> Taking a bottle from his bookshelf
> And making it ring against the glass,
> He burst out: "But that's about me,
> About all of us, what've wolves got to do with it?"
>
> That's it, now something's bound to happen,
> For three years I've had five calls a day;

I get invitations from big people
To come and sing them "The Wolf Hunt."

[*PRB*, IV, 1]

The feeling that he was being played with and used by the official world must have been one of the main factors that contributed to Vysotsky's permanent anxiety and tension, his feeling of always being at the end of his tether. This strain is the keynote of all Vysotsky's "personal" songs. In this respect he is the polar opposite of Okudzhava; and he is very different too from Galich, in whose work there is occasionally real anger, but always with a softening note of self-doubt. Vysotsky is extroverted, bombastic, maximalist, violently intense.

The most succinct expression of this attitude is the song that was used as an epigraph to the *Metropol* collection, one which Vysotsky often saved up as the final encore at his concerts. ("Fed up to the throat" is the equivalent of English "fed up to the back teeth.")

I'm fed up to the throat, up to the chin.
Even songs are starting to make me tired.
If only I could sink to the bottom, like a submarine,
So nothing could get my bearings!

My friend gave me a glass of vodka,
And told me things would get better.
My friend introduced me to Vera when I was drunk,
"Vera will help, and the vodka will save you."

But neither Vera nor the vodka helped.
The vodka gave me a hangover, and what was there to take from
    Vera?
I'd like to sink to the bottom, like a submarine,
And not send any messages!

I'm fed up to the throat, up to the gullet,
Oh! I'm sick of singing and playing.
I'd like to sink to the bottom
So nothing could get my bearings!

[*PRB*, I, 6]

Naturally, this hysterical intensity is subject to diminishing returns. A dozen songs by Vysotsky are as much as anyone can take at any one time without being overwhelmed. Undeniably, Vysotsky is limited. The number of contemplative lyrics in his work is very small. He is not often subtle; in fact, most of the time he is gloriously, exultantly vulgar. But there is always delight in his humor, such a bright, pure spot on the dismal map of Russian literature in the Brezhnev age.

And Vysotsky's prodigious inventiveness works against him, too. Over a period of fifteen years, perhaps a little longer, he wrote something like five hundred texts, something like three per month, in addition to all his other activities. Inevitably, by no means all of them stand the test of time, to say the very least. There are no songs by Vysotsky that have the bland grayness of official song, but many of them are trivial, many are facile, and many of them are virtually interchangeable. In this respect, too, Vysotsky stands at the opposite extreme from Okudzhava, the author of a small number of highly individualized, carefully wrought pieces. Vysotsky was a prodigal inventor of words, just as he was a prodigal personality.

Nobody could continue for long at Vysotsky's intensity without blowing up. The drinking bouts provided temporary oblivion from time to time, but the old driving devil quickly returned. And the inevitable happened: Vysotsky died, of heart failure, on 25 July 1980, in Moscow.

The initial paralyzed disbelief was followed by displays of public feeling that had not been seen in Russia, some said with ghoulish irony, since the death of Stalin in 1953.[34] For the Russians, the event even eclipsed the Olympic Games, which were being held in Moscow at the time. Vysotsky died on a Friday morning. As soon as the news began to spread, a crowd started to form near the Taganka Theater and continued to stand there until, on Monday, people without special invitations were allowed into the theater to pay their last respects to his body, which had been taken there on Saturday. Behind closed doors, in the theater, there was a funeral service with the choir of the Bolshoi Theater, recordings of Vysotsky's voice, and various addresses, all "choreographed" by Lyubimov. The funeral on 29 July was an even bigger demonstration of popular feeling. Vysotsky was adjudged insufficiently eminent to rate a place in the cemetery of the Novodovichii Monastery, where leaders in all walks of life are interred (except for the very highest, who rate the Kremlin Wall). He was assigned to the more homely Vagankovo Cemetery, whose biggest claim to fame is the grave of Sergei Esenin. For Vysotsky's interment, there was a massive police presence; access to the graveside was strictly controlled; people were required to present their flowers to the police, to be placed by them on the grave later. The grave has already become a place of pilgrimage, with anonymous visitors keeping the flowers renewed.

It will never be known whether or not Vysotsky would have gone on to experience increasingly sharp confrontation with the official world, perhaps eventually being forced to decide whether to remain in the

USSR or become an involuntary émigré. At all events, with his death (as is often the case with underground or semiofficial Soviet writers), publication of his work in the USSR became easier. Two poems were published in the annual almanac *Poetry Day (Den' poezii)* in 1981,[35] and a batch more, with a preface by Andrei Voznesensky that has been cited several times here, in a well-regarded journal early in 1982.[36] To the amazement of the reading public, a whole volume of lyrics was published later the same year.[37] And that was not only after the *Metropol* scandal; more and more work by Vysotsky had been being published outside the USSR in the previous two years,[38] and his work had been increasingly discussed there as an anti-Soviet phenomenon.[39] He had even given concerts abroad, including one phenomenally high-charged occasion in New York before a largely Russian émigré audience. Fortunately, a recording was made of it, and it had been released before Vysotsky's death.[40]

The most moving tribute to Vysotsky has been that of his fellow guitar poet Bulat Okudzhava:

> I thought I would make up a song about Volodya Vysotsky . . .
> Yet another who will not come back from the campaign.
> He sinned, people say, doused his candle before it was time,
> He lived as best he could, and nature knows none who sin not.
>
> Separation's not for long, just a second, and then
> We too will set off along his hot trail.
> May his hoarse baritone circle over Moscow,
> And with him we'll laugh and with him we'll weep.
>
> I wanted to make up a song about Volodya Vysotsky,
> But my hand trembled, and the tune didn't fit the line.
> A white Moscow stork has flown up into the white sky,
> A black Moscow stork has come down to the black earth.[41]

The folkloric image at the end, with its plainly religious significance, is quintessential Okudzhava, and the understated, mournful tone of the whole piece is a deliberate contrast to the subject's melodramatic, declamatory manner.

The tributes to Vysotsky by his fellow Russian intellectuals contain warm personal sentiments,[42] but there is a curious hesitancy in some of them about his stature in the context of Russian culture. And that seems to have been a source of anxiety for Vysotsky himself, another element that added to the strains he was continually subjected to by the official world. He was the most widely popular of the guitar poets and, indeed, probably one of the most popular personalities ever in the USSR as a whole, ranking with soccer and ice hockey stars in a dimension beyond anything that is usually reached by people from the arts. But this glory and fame did not satisfy Vysotsky himself. The problem is implicit in the words of Vladimir Maksimov, the exiled novelist and editor, in an interview soon after Vysotsky's death:

> About Vysotsky . . . sad that it was so early . . . terrible. I always respected him as an actor and loved his songs, but he does not seem to me to be a literary phenomenon. He is rather a sociocultural phenomenon, perhaps. . . . A witness to the age, a representative of the age . . . he had a very accurate feeling for it. But literature? I don't know. To be honest, I don't think so. . . .[43]

Okudzhava once expressed a similar kind of reservation about Vysotsky's stature and accomplishments when asked to comment on his death and that of Shukshin:

> Shukshin was a very talented *maitre*. Nothing more! Vysotsky is a much more significant revelation, although in his verse he did not achieve the same perfection (I mean artistic perfection) as Vasily Shukshin did in prose. But Volodya was approaching a higher mastery, he was moving, in the sphere of form as well, toward ever higher art.[44]

Against this statement we may set Andrei Voznesensky's words about one of Vysotsky's most passionate personal anthems, "Persnickety Ponies" ("Koni priveredlivye"):

> . . . that is a great song and great poetry, where the voice tosses the guitar away, wipes the cynical grin of everyday life from its lips . . . and gives itself up to the very highest spirit of poetry, the elemental force and truth of suffering—in it we hear not a chansonnier, but the destiny of a poet.[45]

Voznesensky was even more explicit in his poem of tribute:

> Don't call him a bard.
> He was a poet by nature.[46]

But even Voznesensky is guarded; the implication is that Vysotsky was a poet by nature, but that what he actually produced was not poetry or literature. The last stanza of his poem seems to make the distinction explicit:

> Scribes will remain scribes
> in their corrupt, chalky papers.
> Singers will remain singers
> in the million-strong sigh of the people.[47]

However, there is ambiguity here, too: *scribe (pisets)* is a derogatory term for a mediocre writer, while *singer (pevets)* has for centuries been a high literary word for *poet* (English *bard,* perhaps), and Voznesensky's use means that as well as, literally, "singer."

To ask whether or not Vysotsky was "a real poet" is actually in the last analysis irrelevant. But it is a question that tortured Vysotsky himself, and it comes from deep inside the Russian cultural tradition. So does the most striking of all the posthumous tributes paid to him, this one in an anonymous editorial:

> He became Russia's favorite son because he didn't needle her, didn't tell her how to live, didn't give lectures on morals, but gave a real scale of values which are valid for use in the appalling circumstances she finds herself in now. Every person according to his age and almost according to his profession received from Vysotsky support and a point of reference from which he could assess what's good and what's bad.[48]

In other words, Russian literature (official or unofficial) that is not didactic in intent still needs to offer lessons for life in order to attain the highest popularity. But there can be no doubt whatsoever that of Vysotsky's massive repertoire, it is the songs furthest away from high literature that are the greatest—songs like "Serezhka Fomin," "The Anti-Semites," "Dialogue in Front of the TV," "The Lady Nark," and "The Yogi." All of them are "objective" in the sense of using a persona that is distinct from the author's own; all of them are humorous, covering the whole spectrum from nonsense ("The Yogi") to the black irony of "Serezhka Fomin." And they deal with everyday life. They portray this life as brutish, untouched by official ideology, and centered on laughter, violence, alcohol, and sex. They are informed by a clear-eyed understanding of, and compassion for, ordinary people that are absolutely beyond the reach of officially approved literature and art. That is social realism of a very high artistic order, and it exposes the crippling sham of the dogma of Socialist Realism.

But what kind of moral guidance can possibly be found in Vysotsky's songs? That the personal lyrics express the gloom and alarm of people at the current state of the country is indubitable; this famous folk-style ballad is a true anthem for the Brezhnev years:

> Why is the house quiet and plunged in gloom,
> Standing at the windswept edge of town,
> All its windows looking out on gloom,
> And its doors on the high road?

Ah, I'm so tired, but I've unharnessed the horses,
Hey, anyone there alive, come out and help!
Nobody there, just a shadow in the doorway,
And the carrion crow's circling lower . . .

[*PRB*, II, 12–13]

But it is not so much as a barometer of the national mood that Vysotsky was important. What matters more is the system of ethics that underlies the criminal songs and the songs of everyday life. They proclaim the irrelevance of official ideology and present an alternative— unedifying but nevertheless preferable. This alternative is based on the individual rather than the collective, and it is a system in which justice is personal and swift, retribution is a principle of the highest value, and there is no intermediacy between the wrongdoer and the victim. This code provides a stark alternative to Soviet goals, and it is not difficult to see its attraction in a society where the individual feels himself utterly at the mercy of a soulless machine. And Vysotsky himself embodied this sense of escape from the grinding might of the state.

Whether Vysotsky was a phenomenon whose significance will not outlast his epoch—the late sixties and the seventies—cannot be predicted. He certainly spoke for a generation, and his songs may grow old with this generation. But it is quite certain that, in contrast to the official "People's Artists" of the Soviet state in his time, Vysotsky was the genuine thing: an artist of the people and for the people, whose life and work became folklore during their creator's own lifetime.

Aleksandr Galich in the early 1970s.

7 Aleksandr Galich

GALICH WAS THE PEN NAME used by Aleksandr Arkad'evich Ginzburg (1919–1977) throughout his unique literary career, and it is practically the only thing that all four phases of this career have in common.[1]

Galich entered Soviet literature at an extraordinarily early age. He had spent his childhood in various towns in the south of Russia. His family eventually settled in Moscow in the mid-1920s. An uncle who taught at Moscow University provided a contact with the literary intelligentsia of the capital. Galich actually made his debut in print with a poem that was published in the newspaper of the Communist Party youth organization, *Komsomol'skaya pravda,* in 1935. His promise as a poet was endorsed by one of the most senior Soviet poets of the time, Eduard Bagritsky, and Galich seemed set to make his way into literature via the hierarchy of literary circles and youth organizations. But he was also stage-struck, and he was torn between writing and acting. Eventually he opted for acting. He was successful in a fiercely competitive audition for what became Stanislavsky's last teaching venture, and studied under the great director for four years. When Stanislavsky died in 1938, his studio disintegrated, and Galich became a member of the Arbuzov-Pluchek troupe. This troupe was an experimental organization dedicated to the collective development of plays, and it succeeded in staging the remarkable "Komsomol drama" *City of the Dawn;* but its next effort was terminated by the German invasion in 1941. Galich volunteered for the army, but he was turned down on medical grounds. He spent the war traveling extensively as a forces entertainer. The first phase of his career thus contained a false start as a poet, then training and a blighted career as a professional actor, and finally an intensive spell of practical experience as an entertainer. In retrospect, the contribution to his guitar poetry made by these layers of experience can be seen to have been considerable. It was also significant that Galich added to his metropolitan upbringing the experience of years spent wandering in provincial Russia.

The second phase of Galich's career began after the war and was the longest of the four; it lasted some twenty years, its final years overlapped by the third phase. During this period Galich was a Soviet writer, specializing in plays and film scripts. His success was built on a vaudeville that he cowrote in 1948, *Taimyr' Calling (Vas vyzyvaet Taimyr')*. It stayed on the boards for many years and made Galich a reputation and a good deal of money. He continued to turn out dramas and screenplays into the mid-sixties, and became a trusted and well-rewarded member of the Soviet literary establishment. Throughout this period, Galich seems to have accepted the restrictions on creative freedom imposed by the extremely taxing controls under which the Soviet theater worked at the time. He even had some success as a writer of official mass songs. One of them was a "mommy song," "Goodbye, Mommy, Don't Be Sad" ("Do svidan'ya, mama, ne goryui"), and it had music by one of the most eminent Soviet composers, V. I. Solov'ev-Sedoi. Another had music by the absolute master of mass song tunes, Matvei Blanter; it was called "Oh, Northern Sea" ("Oi ty, severnoe more").

Galich's career as an official Soviet writer was at its peak in the late 1950s. In the handbooks of the time he is treated, if not as an outstanding writer, then as a solid second-ranker. The 1961 *Theatrical Encyclopedia* lists his credits, and adds: "The central theme of G.'s work is the romance of the struggle and creative labor of Soviet youth."[2] And the *Concise Literary Encyclopedia* states: "Galich's comedies are characterized by romantic elevation, lyricism, and humor."[3] One of his friends described the Galich of the late 1950s as

> . . . one of the top dozen Moscow scriptwriters and dramatists. . . . Sasha was a member of every possible union, society, committee, section. He had awards, diplomas, and so on. Sasha was enchanting, witty, and handsome; he loved elegant foreign-looking clothes; he used to travel abroad. He was a fine piano player, a king at billiards, and a first-rate preference and poker player. Sasha lived well, had no lack of money, and had a magnificent apartment in the writers' building near Aeroflotovskaya underground station, and in it I saw quite a few antiques.[4]

In 1962 this respected and apparently well-adjusted Soviet writer began creating and performing songs that stood no chance of publication—as he must have known, given his extensive experience in dealing with the business of literature. The steps that led to his renunciation of his orthodox career cannot all be established. There was no single irrevocable decision to dissent, but an erratic progress from acceptance into rejection. The event about which we know most is the banning of Galich's play *Matrosskaya tishina* (the title is the name of a Moscow street.)

The reason we know about this incident is that Galich constructed a book around it, a powerful and complex work that uses the text of the play as a basis for telling as much of the story of Galich's life as he ever cared to reveal publicly. The play traces the history of a Russian Jewish family through three generations. Its message is that Jews in the USSR should integrate with the Russians and other nationalities in serving the supranational cause of Communism, particularly as manifested in the armed struggle against Fascism. Galich had written the play soon after the war, and then shelved it, obviously because of the virulent official anti-Semitism of Stalin's later years. He took it out again in the more relaxed atmosphere of the late 1950s,

> . . . after the XX Congress of the Party and Khrushchev's unmasking of Stalin's crimes. . . . Once more we started believing! Once more like sheep we bleated with joy and rushed out into the nice green grass—which turned out to be a stinking bog![5]

The play went into production in the new Sovremennik Theater. It went through all the stages of preparation, right up to the dress rehearsal, but was then banned for public performance. Galich called his account of the process *The Dress Rehearsal (General'naya repetitsiya)*. The reason for the ban, as Galich elicited when he was granted an interview at Party headquarters, was that it was not considered permissible to portray a Jew as a hero of the war. The Party functionary dealing with the case explained to Galich that although the Jews had perhaps suffered at the hands of the Fascists, they had not, like the Russians and others, distinguished themselves in fighting back.

This cynical rejection really rankled with Galich. Apart from the ideological issues, his self-respect as a working Soviet author was involved; he had thought himself a master of the system, in tune with current developments. The setback with his play happened in 1958, during the relaxation—always precarious—that led up to the publication of Solzhenitsyn's "One Day in the Life of Ivan Denisovich" in 1962. Galich decided that he must find a new medium of expression. And the medium he found was the guitar-accompanied song.

As we have seen, the period when Galich's playwriting career foundered was precisely the time that Okudzhava was beginning to make a mark as the pioneer of guitar poetry. And Galich, as a member of the inner circle of the Moscow literary intelligentsia, could not possibly have avoided coming across Okudzhava's songs when they first appeared. But Galich himself was no novice at guitar-accompanied song. As he tells us in one of the retrospective passages of *The Dress Rehearsal,* he had spent a good deal of time during the war entertaining the troops with guitar-accompanied songs and ballads, often making them up on the spot to refer to people in the audience. And he had a wealth of experience as a performer to call on. In this respect, the analogy between Galich and Vysotsky is very strong, and their professional polish as actors sets them apart from the marked amateurism of Okudzhava's singing and playing.

It is reliably reported that Galich wrote his first song, and thereby began the third phase of his creative career, in the "Ivan Denisovich" year, 1962. One remarkable thing about Galich as a creative artist was that when he turned to song, he was reborn. For nothing that he wrote as an orthodox Soviet writer has any lasting merit. It is the most dismal hackwork. That is not generally true of other established Soviet writers who have become dissidents. They have usually been the authors of at least one outstanding literary work; Viktor Nekrasov and Vladimir Maksimov come to mind. In Galich's case there is a startling discontinuity between the levels of his orthodox and his dissident work. It is obviously true that his years of experience in writing dialogue and developing characters in dramatic situations had a profound influence on his technical competence as a writer of songs. But the satirical core of the songs and the personal charge that lies behind it have no equivalent, nor could they have, in the work he had written for Soviet consumption.

The result of Galich's turn to song was that in the course of a decade he lost everything he had acquired as a privileged official writer and became instead a persecuted dissident. The change was not abrupt. Until at least 1967 he was still getting work into the Soviet media. And, as we will see, the tensions of his double life were one of the most powerful stimuli behind his songs. On the one hand, he retained his perquisites as a Soviet writer in good standing; on the other, *magnitiz-dat* was ensuring that his songs became an ever more prominent component of the swelling tide of unofficial literature.

The pivotal year was 1968. The Sinyavsky/Daniel trial in 1966, the Six-Day War of 1967—whose effect on Galich as the author of *Matrosskaya tishina* was particularly strong—and finally, the Soviet invasion of Czechoslovakia in 1968; along with all Soviet intellectuals, Galich was racked by these events. His songs of the time seldom discuss them in a direct way, but they form one of the most powerful testimonies to the crisis of conscience that these events engendered. In 1968, before the invasion, Galich had his greatest triumph as a guitar poet. It came at the now-legendary "Festival of Bards," which took place in March of that year before an audience of twenty-five hundred people. The location was the Siberian new city of Akademgorodok, which is populated almost entirely by research workers from the nearby scientific institutes. Galich later wrote:

> As I now realize, it was my first and my last open concert, with tickets even being sold for it. I had just finished performing my "Pasternak in Memoriam," and behold, after the final words, something improbable happened—the audience, . . . rose to its feet and for a whole moment stood in silence, before breaking out in tumultuous applause.[6]

In addition to the provocations of which this was the greatest, Galich's work was beginning to be published abroad. A *samizdat* collection of his songs was pirated by the anti-Soviet publisher Posev in 1969. This book is simply entitled *Pesni (Songs)*. It contains only about forty items, but they include most of the greatest songs Galich was to create. The evidence of these texts was more than enough to damn Galich not just as a Soviet writer but as a Soviet citizen, too. We do not know if Galich was given the usual opportunity to recant and publish a "confession" admitting his fault, condemning the foreign publication, and protesting his loyalty. As we have seen, Okudzhava took this opportunity when it was offered, albeit in oblique fashion, and survived. But for Galich, there was by the end of the 1960s no way back into Soviet literature.

The full panoply of Galich's achievement as a writer of songs was enshrined in a volume published in West Germany while Galich was still in Moscow, but this time with the author's consent and cooperation. It appeared in 1972 and is called *Generation of the Doomed (Pokolenie obrechennykh)*. It contains about one hundred shorter pieces and two long composite poems, "Stalin" and "Kaddish." The shorter songs, though, are themselves relatively long when compared with Okudzhava's work; and Galich tended to increase their weight even more by combining them into groups or cycles on related themes. Roughly speaking, the shorter songs divide into two kinds. The first, and generally less impressive, kind consists of lyrical statements that express a first-person point of view. The second, the kind of song in which Galich is unsurpassed, consists of satirical "songs of everyday life" (*bytovye pesni*), which are dramatic and narrative in design. These songs have a strong element of the grotesque, and they are often conducted on more than one narrative plane at the same time. The feature that sets them off most strongly from the work of all the other guitar poets is their extensive presentation of character.

A characteristic example of the Galich "song of everyday life" is "In His Image and Likeness" ("Po obrazu i podobiyu"), which has a sardonic epigraph: ". . . or, as it said over the gates of Buchenwald, *Jedem das Seine*, 'To Each his Own.' " The refrain of the song contains a characteristic play on words, juxtaposing the name "Bach" against the Russian word for "God," *Bog,* which is pronounced with almost exactly the same terminal consonant as "Bach" and therefore differs from it only by a single vowel sound.

> The day's beginning and the day's business,
> But this accursed mass hasn't let me sleep,
> I've a pain in my back, and my side aches,
> The house stinks of endless laundry. . .
>   "Good morning, Bach," says God,
>   "Good morning, God," says Bach,
>   "Good morning!"
>
> And over our heads, every single morning,
> Like crows over a burnt-out place,
> The loudspeakers rant, the loudspeakers rant,
> "Good morning, get up, comrades!"
>
> And then, still asleep, we ride the underground,
> The train, the tram, and the bus,
> And turning their guts inside out, the loudspeakers
> Roar about victories and valor.
>
> When I'm half asleep, there comes a time
> When in a fit of despair I could
> Smash those loudspeakers, strike them down,
> And get to hear the beauty of silence. . .

With your wife nagging, be so good as to try
To write a modulation from C major into B minor.
From family squabbles, from debts and spats
There's nowhere to go and things won't work.
   "Don't be sad, Bach," says God,
    "I'll try, God," says Bach,
      "I'll try!"

Granny's had a stroke, the wife's ailing,
There isn't enough of this, there isn't enough of that,
We have to have medicine, we need the hospital,
Only who the hell knows when there'll be a place,

And in my break I get called to the Party office,
The chief's hopping about in there,
"Since that's how things are, we'll help you out,
We'll make you a ten-ruble grant."

The cashier spit-fingers the notes one by one,
And splits a bandit grin,
I'll buy a half-liter, I'll buy some validol,
200 grams of cheese, 200 grams of sausage. . .

That cutting wind is foretelling winter,
The doors of St. Thomas's chapel let in drafts,
And the organ is singing that the sum of it all
Is eternal dream, decay, and dust!   ·
   "Don't you blaspheme, Bach," says God,
    "But listen here, God," says Bach,
      "You listen here!"

That bitch next door's really having a ball,
Girlies howling and jackals cackling,
I'll open my half-liter, slice my cheese,
Give the wife some validol on a sugar lump,

I'll pour my first, and then another,
And have a bite of cheese and sausage,
And about how I'm the most heroic hero
I'll hear on the radio with pleasure.

And I'll stoke up my war-trophy pipe,
Make fun of my mooing granny,
And pour another, and then another,
And pop in next door for some extra. . .

He takes off his camisole, pulls off his wig,
The kids in the nursery whisper—the old man's back,
Well, he's past forty, no little age,
There's a blue tinge like dust round his lips.

"Goodnight, Bach," says God,
"Goodnight, God," says Bach,
"Goodnight!"

[*KV,* 238–40]⁷

Here we have a narrative told in a low, naturalistic style, with a good deal of direct speech and interior monologue. It is "a day in the life" of a lowly Soviet citizen. What this citizen does illustrates the central thrust of Galich's satire. The people are engaged mind and body in a sordid struggle with *byt,* "the daily grind". They are surrounded by the ghastly trumpetings of official propaganda, which has absolutely no connection with the reality of their lives. Meanwhile, in a double narrative plane that gives the song that element of the grotesque so often found in Galich, there are Johann Sebastian Bach, God, and the world of eighteenth-century art. Bach too is weighed down by the cares of the daily grind. But in his agony he communicates with the eternal, whereas the Soviet citizen just escapes into drunken oblivion.

The enormous range of characters in Galich's songs has led Efim Etkind to speak of them as a "human comedy," a "model of our society," a small-scale but comparably wide-ranging parallel to Balzac's panorama of nineteenth-century French life, and their inherent dramatism stimulated Andrei Sinyavsky's reference to "Galich's theater."⁸ The songs do in fact range over the entire spectrum of Soviet society. What is particularly remarkable about them is that they pay just as much attention, if not more, to the controllers, the establishment, of this society as to the victims of it. A whole range of Party functionaries, from Stalin himself down to the retired hit men of the security organs, and the loyal chauffeur of a local Party official, tell their stories. There is an especially remarkable gallery of women characters; and although in the grand tradition of Russian literature they are cast mainly as victims of the sociosexual process, they do include such formidable creatures as Comrade Paramonova, a Party functionary of substantial rank.

The most memorable single character created by Galich is Klim Petrovich Kolomiitsev, "workshop foreman, holder of many decorations, member of the Bureau of the Party committee, and deputy of the town soviet." Klim Petrovich is surely one of the most convincing proletarians ever to appear in Russian literature. He is portrayed in a total of six songs, several of them very long even for Galich. In all except one of them, Klim is the sole narrator. His language is for the most part the raw, pithy argot of the urban working class, grossly coarse and grotesquely interspersed with the parroted clichés Klim has acquired along with his Party responsibilities. But although he is used to expose and ridicule the hollowness of official propaganda, Klim is not himself entirely a figure of fun. He is an honest, if rather dim, specimen. He has a strong sense of his own worth, and he is a responsible foreman. He also has no illusions about the Soviet system. When he tries to get his whole section rewarded for its exemplary production, instead of simply reaping medals and material privileges for himself, he is fobbed off by the bureaucratic apparatus—because his factory manufactures barbed wire, and to announce record production in this area would damage the USSR's international reputation. Klim Petrovich's response to this appeal to his Party consciousness is a disgusted binge. He is made a fool of again by the bureaucrats when one day they pick him up on short notice to give a speech at a Party meeting "in defense of peace." In routine fashion, he is handed the text of "his" speech in the car on the way to the meeting, and he proceeds to read it in his usual dogged way, until he is brought up short by the following heartfelt appeal to his audience:

> "The Israeli warmongers," said I—
> "Are known the whole world over!
> As a mother and a woman," said I—
> "I demand they be called to account!"
>
> [KV, 380]

In horror, Klim realizes that he has been handed the wrong speech. However, there is no sign of any reaction from the audience, which as usual is taking no notice of the proceedings, so Klim finishes his assignment and is warmly congratulated by the Party boss.

In another song, Klim is sent on a trade union delegation to Algeria. The delegation makes the usual round of propaganda appearances. Klim gets fed up and exhausted, and he desires some real Russian food to put him back on his feet. But his wife has been able to pack him only some tins of fish in brine *(salaka),* all there was in the shops when he left. It leaves him gasping with thirst. Klim in his disgust utters the ultimate profanity:

> I'm not *baldy,* do your mother! I'm not *eternal,*
> I could drop dead from that there salaka!
>
> [KV, 391]

A disrespectful reference to Lenin's most salient physical characteristic is coupled with a typically semiliterate distortion of an official epithet (*vechnyy,* "eternal," for *bessmertnyy,* "immortal"); and interposed is a euphemistic version of the most common Russian obscenity. Something of the shocking impact of this single line on a Soviet audience can be imagined if it is set in the context of the normal tone of public reference to Lenin, such as Oshanin's "Lenin Is Always with Thee," a song that was cited earlier. Anyway, Klim decides he has to have some real food, so he goes to the local shop and buys what he thinks the salesgirl tells him is a tin of meat, bitterly resenting having to dole out his precious foreign currency for this purpose. But the tin turns out to contain not only fish but that same Soviet salaka in brine that he had brought with him from Russia. His reaction is spluttering indignation:

> We're helping them, the vermin,
> And it's us who suffer for it!
>
> All that foreign life of theirs is a mess!
> It's even worse (beg pardon!) than ours is!
>
> [*KV,* 392]

The only Klim Petrovich song not narrated by the hero himself is called "The Lament of Darya Kolomiitseva concerning the Drunkenness of Her Husband, Klim Petrovich." Mrs. Kolomiitsev gets disgusted with her husband's extended drinking one hot summer, and resolves to reform him. So one Sunday, she sets out on the table the grandest feast she can assemble, including the dreaded bottle of vodka. But she substitutes kerosene for the vodka. Then she dotingly encourages Klim to take a big glassful.

> He drank it down to the last drop,
> And wiped his nose, that's all.
> Fished out a mushroom with his finger,
> Gave me a bleary look,
> Munched the mushroom, and said:
> "No, I really don't like boletus!"
>
> [*KV,* 389]

The way Klim Petrovich combines this unreformed patriarchal outlook and lifestyle with his Party membership and his chauvinism is something that rang all too true with the Russian audience, who took Klim to their hearts.

In Galich's songs, a good deal of attention is paid to the depiction of sexual relationships in Soviet society. Here we find an uncompromising antithesis of what the official song has to say on the subject. We have met the attitudes held by the narrator of "In His Image and Likeness" already. The Party official Comrade Paramonova, who was mentioned earlier, appears in Galich's most famous husband-and-wife satire, "The Red Triangle." While his wife is abroad on official business, Comrade Paramonova's lowly husband, the anonymous narrator of the song, has an affair with a young girl. But someone sends his wife an anonymous tipoff, and when she gets back, she storms off indignantly and has him hauled up at a Party meeting to be censured for immoral conduct. The circumstances of the meeting take us into the very thick of Soviet society:

> Well, all right, so I go to the meeting,
> It was the first of the month, as I remember,
> Of course, I made sure to get a sick note
> And a statement from the clinic (they were nervous).
>
> I see Paramonova in a nice new scarf,
> When she saw me she turned all red,
> The first business was "Freedom for Africa!"
> I came later, under "A.O.B."
>
> During Ghana everyone went to the buffet for sausages,
> I'd have got a kilo myself, only I was a bit short,
> When they called me, I melted from bashfulness,
> But they shouted from the hall, "Let's have the details!"
>
>> Everything on the line!
>> Everything right on the line!
>
> O dear, what is there to say, what is there to ask?
> I stand here before you as if I was naked,
> Yes, I did have fun with Auntie Pasha's niece,
> Took her to the Pekin Hotel and Sokolniki Park.
>
> And in my moral profile, I said,
> Is the rotten influence of the West,
> But after all, I said, we don't live on a cloud,
> And it's all really smoke without fire, I said.
>
> I tried to milk their pity, tried to win them over,
> Read my statement saying I'm a mental case.
> Well, they congratulated me on my resurrection,
> And hit me with a severe reprimand, entered in my Party card.
>
> [*KV*, 174–75]

He then tries desperately to make up with Comrade Paramonova, but she will have nothing to do with him. The Trade Union intervenes and urges them to make up. The official persuasion softens Paramonova's determination, and they leave the office together:

> We set off arm in arm to the Pekin Hotel,
> She drank wine and I drank vodka,
> Toasting our exemplary Soviet family!
>
> [*KV*, 176]

The penultimate line of this stanza may be cited as a tiny example of what gives Galich's songs their limpet grip on Soviet reality. In Russian, the line is: "Ona vypila 'dyurso', a ya 'pertsovuyu'." The two nouns in it are not generic, as they were in the translation just offered; they are highly specific. Comrade Paramonova chooses *dyurso*, high-quality Soviet wine she feels to be rather refined but not pretentious and foreign (the name derives from the place of manufacture, a town near Novorossiisk.) Her husband needs his jolt, and as a Russian male is bound to choose vodka, but on this occasion he adds a little spice by having *pertsovka*, "pepper vodka." Galich uses the adjectival form *pertsovaya*, "peppered," the word on the label of the bottle. It is this word that rhymes with the last one in the main part of the song, *obraztsovuyu*, "exemplary." It is details such as these, which thickly stud the texts of Galich's songs, that make their full meaning evade a non-Soviet audience, even a Russian one. It goes without saying that they make Galich impossible to translate without either extensive annotation or much watering-down with paraphrase, which always has to be in the direction of the general, thereby losing that specificity which is the leading stylistic feature of the songs. And we recall from our discussion of the official song that this specificity is directly antithetical to the misty vagueness in which official songs shroud the unacceptable face of Soviet reality.

The pattern set in "The Red Triangle" of a weak, cringing man and a formidable, powerful woman is common in Galich's love stories. None of them have any conventional idealism, none are uplifting. There are several examples of sexual exploitation for social advancement, another feature of Soviet society that is an official un-subject. The most outspoken one of this kind is "Tonechka." It is narrated by a man who takes up with Tonechka, the daughter of a highly placed, privileged official. His former girlfriend makes no secret of her contempt for his opportunism. He moves in with Tonechka and proceeds to enjoy the sweet delights of Soviet high life:

> Even my trousers have zippers on now,
> And there's as much wine as you can drink,
> And we have an eight-by-ten toilet . . .

> Daddy comes home about midnight,
> All the minions stand to attention!
> I serve him a shot of vodka,
> And tell him a joke about the Yids . . .
>
> [*KV*, 180–81]

But his former girl is unrepentant; she now works as a ticket girl in a suburban cinema. She has neither sold out nor forgiven, remaining scornfully defiant. Her opposite is the heroine of the ghoulishly ironic "A Jolly Conversation" ("Veselyi razgovor"), who works as a cashier in a shop. The supervisor, Zvantsev, makes a pass at her, but she refuses him. She waits until Mr. Right comes along in the person of Alesha, who "although he's bald and a Jew, he's a decent sort." He goes off to the war and is killed, leaving her still working behind her cash register, raising their daughter alone. Zvantsev renews his advances, and when she refuses him again, he frames her; she is sentenced for embezzlement and does time in labor camp. Her daughter turns twenty. She is often in the shop, and when Zvantsev turns his attention to her, she accepts it and they get married. Soon her mother is a grandmother, and still working behind her cash register. This tale of a blighted life is a classic Galich. The contrast with the official "mommy song" is patent; and as we remember, Galich had first-hand knowledge of the official variety.

Another classic female victim is the eponymous heroine of "The General's Daughter." Born in Leningrad, she is now stuck in the back of beyond, in Karaganda, the chief coal-mining area of the GULag, where she has been exiled along with her formerly privileged parents when they fell from grace. Every month, when his wife is having her period, her "cavalier" comes to visit, and she cooks and cleans for him. He works as a pirate taxi driver, and the general's daughter took up with him because he had a picture postcard of Leningrad on his dashboard. While she chops onion for his vodka as he sleeps (in a detail of appalling cruelty, Galich has him take his wallet with him when he goes to the toilet), she reflects on her life:

> At least he has pity on me,
> At least he comes here, at least he breathes!
>
> [*KV*, 115]

Her horizons and her hopes are limited to the mass of practical things she has to get through the next day. She has heard there is to be a delivery of sardines to the depot, and "people say they're from

Leningrad." She will make sure she gets some, and she will even give a few to her rival, the wife, "so she won't think I'm greedy." The song, as so frequently in Galich's work, has a refrain, which recurs with slight variations after every third stanza:

> Oh, Karaganda, you Karaganda!
> If a woman's proud here, she's good for nothing!
> O Lord, give us this day our daily bread,
> Think what Russia's like, it's no worse here!
> Ka-ra-gan-da!

[KV, 116]

This sordid state of oppression is not only woman's lot, though. In "Guignol Farce," a man is driven to suicide by the pressure of providing for his six children. He has applied for a loan from the "Mutual Help," but has been refused because "every ruble is needed to catch up with America." The refrain of this song is also plaintive:

> There's this to buy, and there's that to buy,
> You can only drink water on this money,
> As for cheese for your tea, or a bit of sausage,
> It's twenty kopecks here and twenty there,
> And where can you get them?

[KV, 242]

The oppressive, gloomy tone of "The General's Daughter," "Guignol Farce," and others like them among the genre songs is alleviated by the humor of the great satirical songs. "The Red Triangle" is one of them; its sordid story is narrated by the two-timing husband with a comic mixture of self-pity and abject terror before his wife, the dreadful Comrade Paramonova. Rivaling "The Red Triangle" is another worm's-eye view of Soviet society, with a similarly petty hero, "The Ballad of Surplus Value." A Soviet citizen is left a fortune by his auntie in capitalist "Fingalia." He goes on an almighty farewell binge, borrowing freely from his friends and insulting his bosses. But there is a revolution in Fingalia, and all private property is nationalized. The solemn broadcast congratulations of the Soviet government are followed in the song by the would-be millionaire's spluttering curses at the untimely operation of "Karl Marx's party tricks."

This shameless send-up of official teaching is matched by certain songs in which Galich takes the subjects of official mass songs and completely stands them on their heads. One outstanding example of such a song is "The Mistake." It uses exactly the same metrical structure and the same system of repetitions as Konstantin Vanshenkin's song "Alesha" (1967), about "a Russian soldier in Bulgaria." He is a statue on a monument, standing immovable above a foreign city in all kinds of weather, on eternal guard.[9] In Galich's song, which was probably written as an immediate response to Vanshenkin's, a platoon of Russian infantry, killed in action near Narva in 1943 and lying in their frozen graves "two by two, just as we marched," hears a bugle call. They get up ready for action, for they know that if Russia is calling her dead, the situation is desperate and they must respond. But they discover that it is a false alarm. The call was a hunting horn, merrily sounding as the sportsmen pursue their pleasure across the place the infantrymen are buried. The song is said to refer to an incident during Fidel Castro's visit to the USSR at the invitation of Nikita Khrushchev in 1962. Galich's "The Mistake" is a perfect example of the underground song as a negation of the official mass song, in this case of the song on the theme of World War II, which, as we have seen, is one of its staple subjects. Galich's exposure of the cynical exploitation of the people by the Soviet authorities, and their willingness to sacrifice themselves for what they think is a noble Russian cause, make "The Mistake" one of his most powerful songs, received in *magnitizdat* recitals with heart-searching silence.

Galich is also the author of one song on the GULag theme that instantly became a classic of underground folklore, "Clouds." For a number of years, nobody would believe that its author could possibly be anyone but a returned veteran of the camps:

> The clouds float by, the clouds,
> Without hurrying, like in a film.
> I'm eating chicken *tabaka,*
> And I've sunk a load of cognac.

> The clouds float off to Abakan,
> Unhurried they float.
> They're warm, I bet, those clouds,
> But I've been frozen through forever!

> Like a horseshoe I froze into the sleigh tracks,
> Into the ice I was chipping with my pick!
> After all, not for nothing
> I blew away twenty years in those camps.

> I still have that snow crust before my eyes!
> I still have the din of frisking in my ears!
> Hey, bring me a pineapple
> And another 200 g. of cognac!

The clouds float by, the clouds,
Floating to Kolyma, that dear old place,
And they don't need a lawyer,
An amnesty's neither here nor there.

Me too, I live a first-rate life!
Twenty years I swapped for one day!
And I sit in this bar like a lord,
I've even got some teeth left!

The clouds float off to the east,
They've no pension, no worries. . .
Me, on the 4th I get a money order,
And another on the 23rd.

And on those days, just like me,
Half the country sits in the bars!
And in our memory off to those places
Float the clouds, the clouds. . .

[*KV,* 80]

Meanwhile, in another corner of Galich's world, the former custodians of these victims are also living out their lives. They too are enjoying their pensions. They are quite unrepentant, and even frankly nostalgic for the old days of Stalin's terror, when things were much more clear-cut than they have become since. The song called "Incantation" ("Zaklinanie"), which belongs to the same cycle as "Clouds," relates the thoughts of one of "Stalin's eagles" as he whiles away his time by the Black Sea:

He picked up his personal pension,
Popped into the "Float" for a bit,
It smelled of shellfish and mold,
And the ceiling was stained with urine,

The *shashlyk* made him belch like a candle flame,
And the *sulguni* stank of cod. . .
He'd much rather sit by a nice little river
Than over this vasty deep.

O you sea, sea, sea, Black Sea,
What a twisty-twiny thing you are!
You don't abide by the rules,
First you're Cain and then you're Abel!

Lord, have mercy upon me, have mercy!

And along the beach, where couples should go at evening,
He wandered alone, thoughtful and glum.

This black, trashy, villainous thing
Permits itself far too much!

The waves roll in, the infernal rogues,
They'd rather not understand the regime!
If he weren't in retirement now
He'd certainly show them what's what!

> Oh you sea, sea, sea, Black Sea,
> Pity you're not under investigation or convicted,
> I'd have you charged and off to Inta,
> You'd not be black, you'd turn white!

> Lord, have mercy upon me, have mercy!

And in his hotel, a strange and terrible
Dream he dreamed as he dozed,
Where the Black Sea under escort
Was driven by stages to Inta.

And blessed among the blessed in Christ,
As he smoked his "Lighthouse"-brand fag,
He watched his brave army guard lads
Herd the natural element into a camp hut.

> O you sea, sea, sea, Black Sea,
> Now I've got you tamed and under law!
> We've been taught this kind of chemistry—
> How to deal with natural elements!

> Lord, have mercy upon me, have mercy!

So he lay there with a beatific smile,
The smile even parted his cheekbones. . .
But it must have been the final clue
For Death, that smile.

And he got up neither next day nor next evening;
The floorman went for the doctor,
And the floormaid lit a candle for the Lord
Over the happy hitman. . .

> And there sounded the sea, sea, sea, Black Sea,
> That free sea, tamed by no-one,
> And it behaved not according to the rules,
> It was Cain and Abel, too!

> Lord, have mercy upon me, one last time!

[*KV,* 96–97]

(*Sulguni* or *suluguni* is a Caucasian delicacy, deep-fried cheese; Inta is one of the main centers of the GULag archipelago.) The juxtaposition of linguistic registers in this song recalls what we saw in "In His Image and Likeness." The sadistic spite of the retired goon's mental processes, expressed in subliterary colloquialisms, is interspersed with the Church Slavonic of the Orthodox liturgy. The contrast between the two was emphasized in Galich's performance of the song; the liturgical line was a mixture of sigh and prayer, as if the author-performer were asking forgiveness for his own song, while the goon's thoughts were delivered in a menacing side-of-mouth hiss.

The most profound songs by Galich about the victors and victims of the Stalin years are those in which the two categories of citizen are shown interacting. A poignant song of this kind is the long, typically multilinear "Fame Is the Spur" ("Zhelanie slavy"). It juxtaposes in a cancer ward two pensioners, one of whom was earlier guarded by the other in a labor camp. They pass the time together, and find themselves locked in mutual dependence:

> The warder and the former "number so-and-so,"
> Now we can't make it without each other.
> We'd like to die at the same time.
> The hospital's asleep; silence, all in order.
> Then he said, rising on his elbow:
> "Pity I didn't finish you off in Vyatka, you bitch,
> Real sly bastards, you prisoners . . ."
> He fell back, made funny gurgling noises,
> And then the warder passed away,
> And his hospital cot sailed off
> Into those seas that have no end or beginning!
> I covered him up with his sheet . . .
> The snow keeps on falling over Moscow,
> And my dear son, over that same snow,
> Takes the warder's daughter for a walk . . .
>
> [*KV*, 101]

This situation is one of several in Galich's songs about Soviet society that embody one of the central points he has to make about the Stalin period. He sees the essence of the phenomenon as a process of mutual connivance in oppression. He asserts that the Soviet people is responsible for its own history and in fact supported Stalinism. This interpretation, of course, runs directly counter to the message of Khrushchev's "Secret Speech," which portrayed Stalinism as a perversion of Party authority that led to the slaughter of innocent citizens, especially regrettable being the victims who were Party members. It also runs directly counter to the mainstream of dissident political thought, which is inclined to see Stalinism as the mature expression of Lenin's policies, but imposed on an innocent population. For Galich of the 1960s, the official theory is simply an easy way out, a facile justification for the continuation of the Party's self-assumed right to control the political process. And in his song "The Night Watch" ("Nochnoi dozor"), Galich gave one of the most graphic warnings that nothing had essentially changed, and that the return of Stalinism is therefore an ever-present danger. It is conveyed through a nightmare vision in which the thousands of discarded statues of "The Genius of All Times and Peoples" come to life and make a moonlit march on Red Square, there to review a parade of monsters. Then morning comes, and

> The bronze statues go back where they came from,
> But the alabaster ones lie hidden away.
> Maybe they're crippled for the time being,
> But even their dust retains its shape,
> These alabaster ones just need some human flesh,
> And once more they'll acquire their greatness!
>   And the drums will beat!
>   The drums will beat,
>   Beat, beat, beat!
>
> [KV, 44]

Typically, the last line, which recurs throughout the song, echoes one of Stalin's most famous slogans, proclaiming that the security organs would "beat, beat, and beat again" the class enemy.

Galich's "Poem about Stalin" ("Poema o Staline") is his most complex single work. The complete text has six "chapters," some of which Galich occasionally sang as independent songs in their own right. The first chapter contains the most grotesque juxtaposition of any that Galich conceived, when he makes Stalin appear at the Nativity and turn its events into a saturnalia reminiscent of the Soviet 1930s. The leader stands over the crib and turns his pock-marked face toward the Infant:

> "So this is the one, that same
> Pathetic orphan of the earth
> Who will vie with me
> In blood and hosannas . . ."
>
> [KV, 270]

The second chapter consists entirely of Stalin's imprecation against the Jews and against Christ; its culmination is chilling:

You are not the son of God, but the son of man,
If You could exclaim "Thou shalt not kill!"
Fisher of men, You went out in the morning
With a pitiful net of easy words,
And after two thousand years,
Show me how rich Your haul has been!
Weak-hearted and a bit simple,
You trusted both God and Caesar,
I won't repeat Your mistakes,
Not a single one will I repeat!
Not one blasphemer will be found in the world
Who would lift a lance against me!
If I should die—which might happen—
My kingdom will be eternal!

[*KV,* 272]

But when we next see Stalin, he has his reign of terror behind him, and he has eliminated all opposition—including those imaginary opponents who were his closest friends and associates. He is utterly alone. He cannot sleep. He is tormented by incipient remorse, and by the ghosts of his victims, but he is still dementedly convinced that his suspicions were well founded. Suddenly, church bells ring out, and he is struck down by a revelation; he tries to remember the Lord's Prayer, but cannot. And he dies, pleading with the Christian God for remission and forgiveness. His voice trails away on the word *forgive.*

After this threefold portrayal of Stalin, in his primal determination, his full unmitigated evil, and his imagined pathetic end, he does not appear again in person. Instead, the fourth chapter switches to his victims, and we have the dissolute "Conversation at Night in a Restaurant Car," stylistically one of the most overt examples of the use of gypsy song in guitar poetry. Here, a survivor of the camps drunkenly relates how one day his camp commandant, "The Godfather" *(kum)*, addressed the massed convicts:

"There's been," he said, "the main congress
Of our famous Party.
About China and Laos
There were discussions.
Then arose the special problem
Of the Father and Genius."
The Godfather ate up his cucumber
And concluded, in torment:
"It turns out that the Father
Wasn't a father, but a bastard . . ."

[*KV,* 276]

The convicts hew down a massive statue of Stalin. An amnesty is promulgated. But the survivor's tale falls away into disjointed exclamations as *delirium tremens* takes hold. He imagines himself attacked by demons that fly in through the carriage window. This picture of the degeneration resulting from the leader's policies, and the confusion and disorientation that followed Khrushchev's revision of them, is one of the most striking that Galich ever created.

The author himself appears, and the element of drunkenness is continued from the preceding chapter, in the fifth part, called "A Chapter Written While Heavily under the Influence, and Being an Authorial Digression." It contains a good deal of the self-deprecation that permeates Galich's first-person songs. But it also repeats a message that forms, as we shall see, the central thesis of Galich's active conclusions from the Stalin experience:

> There's no need to be afraid, fellows!
> It's a delusion: "No thoroughfare"
> And "No entry without written permission."
> The only thing you need to fear
> Is the person who says "I know what's necessary!"
> Drive him away! Don't trust him!
> He's telling stories! He doesn't know what's necessary!
>
> [*KV,* 280]

The breast-beating tone of the fifth chapter, which had been alleviated by the laconic and highly colloquial formulations that the author's supposed drunkenness causes, appears without any mitigation in the sixth and final chapter of "Stalin." It is the chapter that Galich most frequently detached from the main body of the poem and performed as an independent song. It brings the work full circle by going back to the biblical setting of the first chapter and again intercutting it with Stalin's Russia. The modern parts concern an interrogation. It drags on and on; the victim grows a beard like a prophet as the interrogator, himself with a heart condition and with no appetite for his work, grimly goes on with his assignment. Eventually, there is the inevitable confession and sentence to exile, and the interrogator is rewarded with a month's holiday.

> Later, all sorts of crapinations happened.
> The frowning interrogator draws his pension in Moscow,
> And a note with a seal confirming rehabilitation
> Was dispatched to the prophet's widow in Kalinin.
>
> [*KV,* 281]

But the modern story is dominated by the biblical, which presents the most extreme image Galich ever found to project his guilt at the suffering of women. The Virgin Mary is seen, as in Catholic mythology, as the cynosure of all human suffering, and she bears her burden with dignified, silent forbearance:

> The Madonna walked through Judea,
> Ever lighter, thinner, more delicate,
> Grew her body with every step . . .
> And around her Judea made its noise
> Not wishing to remember its dead.
> But shadows were laid on that clay,
> And shadows lurked in every step,
> The shadows of all butyrkas and treblinkas,
> Of all betrayals, treasons, and crucifixions . . .
>
> Ave Maria!
> [*KV*, 281]

It is quite clear, in this long song, that the power of Galich's art diminishes as its focus moves away from his own society and his own times. Equally, it diminishes as he moves away from the dramatic presentation of character in the character's own words—as is the case here with Stalin—toward his own subjective, external description of it, as is the case with the Madonna. The vitality of the language, the sureness and economy of the style, are at their most powerful when Galich puts thoughts and words into the heads and mouths of his compatriots and contemporaries.

The "Poem about Stalin" is rivaled only by Galich's own "Kaddish" in the whole of Russian guitar poetry as an extended, multipart work. Despite the attempts Galich makes to bring together the six parts, he is by no means completely successful. The poem contains examples of both the best and the worst features of his earlier work. Among the triumphs are his most daring exercise in the grotesque—the juxtaposition of Stalin and the infant Christ. The restaurant car monologue is one of Galich's most convincing portrayals of a rank-and-file victim of the Stalin system. And the second chapter, consisting entirely of Stalin's own words, is the most powerful presentation in Russian literature so far of the vaunting evil of the dictator's personality.

The world of Galich's songs about Soviet society, as we have seen, is populated by a "doomed generation" whose members have experienced the hell on earth of the Stalin years. They cannot get the results out of their systems. What is more, they are either oblivious to their true condition or they actually prefer it to a condition of conscious responsibility. Within Galich's world, in direct contradiction to official socialist myth, the individual is alone, pitted against his fellows in a wolflike struggle. There is cynical exploitation of one person by another. Society is divided into an elite, who have possessions and influence, and an oppressed mass, which has only its misery. Both sides are sordid. And there is no escape from this world, except perhaps through suicide (as in "Guignol Farce"), alcohol (a constant palliative for the male characters), and a few refuges glimpsed in dreams.

In all of Galich's work, the only woman to escape is the heroine of his very first song. Lenochka Potapova is a sergeant in the Moscow police force. She is on traffic duty one day, and she has the temerity to halt a column of official cars coming from the airport. In the leading car, a "handsome Ethiopian" rises on his "cream-colored cushion" and throws her a chrysanthemum. The next day she is summoned to the unholy of unholies, the Central Committee of the Communist Party of the Soviet Union. The committee members are giving a reception for the Ethiopian. He is bored stiff while the dignitaries pay court to him as a potential ally for Soviet colonial expansion, but he comes to life when:

> All in tulle and velvet
> Lenochka entered the hall,
> Everyone gasped out loud
> When she entered.
> And the handsome royal himself,
> Achmet Ali-Pasha,
> Exclaimed: "Well, hello!"
> When she came in.
> And soon our Lenochka
> Was known by the whole wide world.
> This lass from Ostankino
> Was known by the whole wide world.
> When Prince Achmet did his dad in
> And became Shah himself,
> Sharina L. Potapova
> Was known by the whole wide world.
>
> [*KV,* 186]

Galich never returned to the light-hearted tone of this fantasy tribute to all the Russian girls who have discovered that "abroad" is the only way out. More typical is the resigned pessimism of the refuge glimpsed in a first-person song:

> They say there are some islands somewhere,
> Where on the shore grows the grass of oblivion,

It cures pride, and grief, and baseness, and sickness,
That's the kind of islands there are on earth!
. . .
They say there are some islands somewhere,
Where twice two doesn't always make four,
Count as much as you like, it's all a mist,
Only what suits your heart is right, that alone.
That's the kind of islands there are on earth!

They say there are some islands,
Where untruth is not truth,
Where there's no idleness, no poverty,
And no pale of settlement, nor ever was.
That's the kind of islands I've imagined!

[*KV*, 67]

The oppression of human beings by social forces is a venerable and central theme of Russian literature, of course. The distinctive contribution to it made in Galich's satirical songs of the 1960s derives from a complete absence, on the part of the author, of any sentimentalization or idealization. His ordinary people are not made noble or spiritually regenerate by their degradation, and there is no humanitarian message to be gleaned from their plight. For Galich, in strong contrast to his great contemporary Solzhenitsyn, it is certainly possible to crush the humanity out of a human being, leaving behind a sordid animal. It is in this respect that Galich's earlier songs convey a message that is incompatible with the ideals of both Communism and Christianity.

But Galich does not depict oppression from the point of view of a moral superior. On the contrary, the power of the songs comes to a large extent from his awareness of his own complicity in the network of guilt. This awareness is not, of course, stated explicitly in the genre songs, such as most of those that have been discussed so far. It underlies them, and is manifest in Galich's performance. It comes out in full force only in Galich's first-person songs. Here, he bears witness without any sense of self-righteousness or moral superiority, and he persistently expresses doubt as to his own fitness for his role as satirical exposer and truth teller. One graphic example of this stance is the frame story of "Fame Is the Spur." In it, Galich presents his real self as a singer of *magnitizdat* songs, and puts into song the actual circumstances of a recital. The beginning of the song goes:

Unconnected with art,
Not admitted into the temple,
I sing to snacks

> And a bottle of vodka.
> Why should I get worked up
> At the brink of disaster?
> Just pour out the first drink
> And I'll give you a song!

The singer introduces a new song; it is the story of the two cancer patients. He comes to the end of it.

> . . . My voice dies away as if in cotton wool,
> But the strings ring on.
> For decency's sake
> Everybody's quiet for half a minute.
> . . .
> Unfamiliar faces
> Soaked in drunken despair . . .
> I tremble with shame,
> A twitch in my temple . . .
>
> . . . There I sit, twanging my guitar,
> Guffaws, din, cackling, ringing . . .
> And the next-door informer behind the wall
> Hides his tape machine in its drawer . . .
>
> [*KV,* 101–102]

The powerful dose of self-contempt behind these lines is the hallmark of Galich's first-person songs. He feels that what he is doing is sordid and unworthy. Underlying everything is the sense of guilt induced by the application to himself of the doctrine of individual responsibility that he has announced in the genre songs. He himself has not acted in the way he has subsequently understood to be right. He has not suffered. His descriptions of humiliation and deprivation are consciously vicarious; he himself has spent many years as one of the "haves," the privileged elite.

But there is more to it than that. He has failed to act even after making the decision to dissent. This self-reproach reaches its climax in Galich's "Petersburg Romance," which was written in August 1968, actually on the day *before* the Soviet invasion of Czechoslovakia.[10] Using the events of the Decembrist rising of 1825 as the explicit subject, Galich laments his failure to act in the face of a historical imperative:

> And then came the fatal morning.
> It seemed not at all disgraceful,

> So wise it seemed, so discerning,
> To say that one wasn't available.
>
> [*KV,* 28]

But Galich is not muzzled by this burden of personal unworthiness. He asserts that it does not invalidate the right, even the duty, of the individual to speak out about what he sees to be wrong:

> It's the chosen alone who may judge?
> I'm not chosen, but I shall judge!
>
> ["Untitled" ("Bez nazvaniya"; *KV,* 54)]

The submission to regimentation, even out of the apparently noble motive of a sense of personal unworthiness, is a recipe for disaster:

> If everyone marches in step
> The bridge will come tumbling down.
>
> ["The Law of Nature"
> ("Zakon prirody"; *KV,* 31)]

It is a crime to forgive and forget, to turn the other cheek:

> Nonresistance of the conscience—
> The most convenient of eccentricities.
>
> ["The Train" ("Poezd"; *KV,* 61)]

> People will forgive me out of indifference.
> I shan't forgive them, the indifferent ones!
>
> ["Dozing Off and Waking Up"
> ("Zasypaya i prosypayas' "; *KV,* 65)]

Both the satirical genre songs and the first-person songs that Galich created in the 1960s present an unmitigated panorama of disaster, failure, and guilt. There is just one note of consolation. It resides in the efficacy and permanence of the poetic word. Galich created a whole series of songs in memory of the literary victims of Russia's past, and their subjects and dedications read like a martyrology. They include Solomon Mikhoels (1890–1948; "The Train"); Frida Vigdorova (1915–1965; "Friends Keep Going Away"); Varlaam Shalamov (1907–1980; "Everything Happens at the Wrong Time"); Boris Pasternak (1890–1960) in the poem explicitly dedicated to him; Anna Akhmatova (1889–1966; "August Once More"); Mikhail Zoshchenko (1895–1958; "The Hills of Manchuria"); Daniil Kharms (1906–1942; "The Tobacco Legend"); and Osip Mandel'shtam (1891–1938; "The Return to Ithaca"). There are several more. These songs bear witness to the heroic feat of the people concerned in wresting some lasting achievement from their unequal struggle with the oppressive might of the Soviet system. And by implication they claim association on the part of Galich. However, Galich usually portrays himself in the explicitly autobiographical songs as old, broken-down, tired and ill, second-rate. But he dares to claim personal immortality.

> So, for the sake of this single line
> That time throws me as a tip,
> To the merry generous world
> One fine day I bid goodbye.
>
> I made my dear ones prematurely aged,
> Strode past the limit with my songs,
> Made people who love me weep,
> And wouldn't heed their weeping.
>
> But these whispers of mine
> Will ring out until Judgment Day . . .
> ["Some Day a Clapped-Out Historian"
> ("Kogda-nibud' doshlyi istorik"; *KV,* 77)]

The ultimate declaration of this faith is a song that could well stand as an epitaph to the entire heroic dissident cause of the 1960s. It is called "We're No Worse Than Horace." This complex song portrays two kinds of dissent. On the one hand there is a passive kind that is manifested in covert, fashionable unorthodoxy, saying "boo" to authority only when it's not looking. On the other hand, there is genuine dissidence, carried on by a small number of people who are prepared to take the consequences. They set up no grand monuments, and they are under constant surveillance. But Galich declares his faith in the effectiveness of their activity:

> Untruth ranges round from one area to another,
> Pooling experience with neighboring Untruth;
> But what is sung *sotto voce* thunders out,
> What's read in a whisper rings forth,
>
> There're no stalls, no boxes, no balcony,
> No claque going crazy in fits,
> There's just a "Yauza"-type tape recorder,
> That's all! But it's enough!
> [*KV,* 170]

This declaration is one of the statements that made Galich the principal artistic spokesman for the dissidents of the 1960s.[11] The faith that

motivated them all was that some progress could actually be achieved
in Soviet Russia through moral resistance and bearing witness, however humble and insignificant the means might seem when compared
with the mighty state apparatus against which they set themselves. For
them, and for the Galich of the 1960s, the main lesson of the Stalinist
past was that silence is connivance. Galich's "Goldminers' Waltz"
("Staratel'skii val'sok"), probably his most famous single song, encapsulates this attitude. He decreed that it should stand first in any edition
of his work.

> We've called ourselves adults for a long time now,
> And we pay no tribute to childishness,
> We don't long to get away into the far distance
> Searching for treasure on a fabulous island.
> Or into the desert, or to the cold pole,
> Or to get into a lugger and . . . beggar off.
> But insofar as silence is gold,
> We are prospectors, no question of it.
>
> Keep quiet, and you'll join the rich!
> Keep quiet, keep quiet, keep quiet!
>
> Believing neither heart nor intellect,
> Hiding our eyes for safety's sake,
> How many times we kept silent in different ways,
> But not *against,* of course, but *for!*
> Where are the squealers and the moaners now?
> They've made their noise and come to an early end . . .
> And the silent ones have become the bosses,
> Because silence is gold.
>
> Keep quiet, and you'll join the number ones!
> Keep quiet, keep quiet, keep quiet!
>
> And now, when we've moved into first place,
> We're itching to make speeches,
> But under all these verbal pearls
> Silence shows through like a stain.
> So let others cry out from despair,
> From insult, from pain, from hunger!
> *We* know there's more profit in silence,
> Because silence is gold!
>
> It's so easy to join the rich,
> It's so easy to join the number ones,
> It's so easy to join the—executioners:
> Keep quiet, keep quiet, keep quiet!

[*KV,* 25–26]

With songs like this one attaining ever wider notoriety through the uncontrollable labyrinths of *magnitizdat,* it was inevitable that the wrath of Party and state would come down on Galich's head. When the blow eventually did fall, it was with exemplary severity.[12] On 29 December 1971, Galich was expelled from the Union of Soviet Writers. Shortly afterward, in an associated decision, he was expelled from the Union of Cinematographic Workers. The consequences of expulsion for a Soviet writer are far-reaching. They include probable deprivation of earnings, loss of the privileged access to material goods that is essential in order to live a half-decent life in Soviet conditions, and the implication that future publication of work will be difficult, if not impossible. That had happened to several writers before Galich, the most famous path-breaker of the post-Stalin period being Boris Pasternak in 1958. But Galich was also expelled from membership in the Literary Fund *(Litfond),* which meant that in future he would not be able to collect payments for his works. Solzhenitsyn's is the only other widely known case of expulsion from the *Litfond.* It meant that the authorities anathematized Galich and condemned him to starvation if he wished to remain a writer inside Russia.

The reasons given for expelling Galich from the Union of Writers were two: not disavowing the publication of his works abroad, and encouraging Soviet Jews to emigrate to Israel, "crimes incompatible with the high calling of Soviet writer."[13] The evidence for the second of these charges was a number of songs which explicitly deal with the problems faced by Soviet Jews in the period after the Six-Day War. The most substantial of them is the long poem "Kaddish," which is about Janusz Korczak, the outstanding pedagogue, a Polish Jew who met a martyr's death at the hand of the Nazis during World War II. The poem abounds in implied parallels between the situation of the Jews in Russia and Eastern Europe under Hitler and their present situation under Communism. Among the other songs on Jewish subjects is one that became a kind of anthem for the early members of the Third Emigration, which was beginning just as Galich was expelled from his union memberships. "Song of Exodus" ("Pesnya iskhoda") is dated 20 December 1971:

> You're leaving? Well, leave, then,
> Through customs and clouds.
> From farewell handshakes
> My hand's grown thin!

The final, defiant stanza of the song goes:

> Here I stay . . . is that so strange?
> My habitual wave of the hand!
> Leave, then! But I'm staying.
> I shall stay on this soil.
> Someone, despising his fatigue,
> Must guard the peace of the dead!
>
> [*KV*, 47–49]

The dead that Galich mentions in the body of the song are the Jewish victims of World War II and the victims of the GULag. There is an even more provocative song from the point of view of the Soviet authorities, "Warning" ("Predosterezhenie"), which counsels Jews not to take part in Soviet social life, because they will always be suspected, discriminated against, and kept away from high responsibility. Here, Galich has turned full circle from his aborted play. And the message of "Warning" was nothing short of an act of high treason in the eyes of the Soviet official world. The direct political advocacy in this song, and the others on Jewish themes, has no equivalent in the work of other guitar poets, and it is this element that motivated the severity with which Galich was treated when he was called to account.

The last phase of the third period of Galich's creative life lasted for over two years from the time of his expulsion from Soviet literature. He continued to live in Moscow. He took an ever more visible part in the civil rights movement, signing several open letters of protest about the maltreatment of literary intellectuals. And he continued to sing his songs at private gatherings. He also continued to write. It was in 1973 that he wrote *The Dress Rehearsal,* making it a settling of accounts with his past as a Soviet citizen and writer.

Among the songs written during this period of limbo are some that retain the authentic ring of the old Galich. One of them, "A Confession of Love" ("Priznanie v lyubvi"), is his ultimate expression of guilty remorse for the plight of woman in Soviet society. The song sketches a scene in a typical packed Moscow bus. Strap-hanging in the crowd, an elderly woman falls into a reverie about her life—two sons killed in the war, husband frozen to death in the camps, daughter in the hospital with cancer, and son-in-law a drunk—and she forgets to buy a ticket. She is publicly reviled by a "conscientious" Soviet citizen:

> We're in the lead in history,
> With gales lashing our heads,

> And there are still people
> Who want everything for nothing!
>
> [*KV,* 312]

She dissolves into helpless, despairing tears. The framing commentary of this song is significant. There can be no comparison between the circumstances Galich depicts as bringing about the woman's despair and those affecting the lives of women in official songs; but the attitude of the author is a similar reverent compassion:

> I love you, your eyes, lips, and hair,
> You tired people grown old before your time,
> You wretched people who newspaper columns
> Praise with shameless fanfares every single day.
>
> [*KV,* 313]

The last stanza of the song summons people to forget the official call to be "vigilant"—the Stalinist euphemism encouraging mutual denunciation—and instead to be "trusting," and leave vigilance to the security forces.

The masterpiece of the limbo period is a vignette inspired by Galich's coming across a peculiar machine outside the sanatorium for actors of the Bolshoi Theater just outside Moscow. It was a wooden post, with numbers crudely painted down it, and a string going over a wheel at the top. One end of the string carried a counterbalancing weight and dangled by the post, while the other disappeared into the ground. When Galich asked the janitor what this thing was, he learned that it was a "shitometer" *(govnomer)*. On the unseen end of the string was a float resting on top of the contents of the cesspool; as the level rose, the string ran out and the weight made an indication against the numbers. The caretaker would then know when to call in the sanitation men to come and empty the cesspool. Galich called his poem on the subject "Landscape" ("Peizazh"):

> Everything was overcast and gray,
> The forest stood as if dead,
> With only the shitometer weight
> Barely nodding its head.

> Not all's in vain in this world
> (Though it's not worth a cent!)
> For as long as weights exist
> And you can *see* the level of the shit!
>
> [*KV,* 314–15]

The image of the shitometer, of course, stands not only for Galich himself as a satirical witness but for the entire civic tradition in Russian literature. The poem (Galich spoke this piece rather than singing it) expresses that faith in the value of the poetic word which had provided the redeeming streak of optimism in the work of the underground, dissident third period of Galich's creative life.

Through 1972 and 1973, Galich's material position, and his health, got steadily worse. Eventually he was forced to betray the statement he had made in "Song of Exodus" and apply to leave the country. When he knew finally that it was only a matter of time before he left, probably forever, he began a set of songs in which he tried to cauterize the wounds of nostalgia before he actually experienced the sensation itself. He explained later that it was like a mother deliberately taking her child into a house where there is measles, so that the child will be infected and then be done with the disease. Thus began the fourth and final phase of Galich's creative life, the émigré phase.

In the limbo period between expulsion from his union memberships and expulsion from the country, Galich wrote about twenty-five new songs. They include the two satirical pieces that have just been cited. But the sentimentality present in the first-person frame of "A Confession of Love" comes more and more to set the general tone of the work. The pitiless views behind the songs of the 1960s, their black picture of unmitigated human disaster, are softened. The most overt sign that Galich's views had actually changed was that at some time in 1972 he was received into the Orthodox Church. The sense of spiritual reconciliation and peace that this step brought with it is adumbrated in some of the songs he wrote in the limbo period, such as "Psalm" ("Psalom"). This song tells of how the author in his youth created himself a false god, a god made from words, who commanded "Go forth and kill!" He was replaced by a god made from fear, whose whispered command was the same. This notion is a renunciation of Galich's former creative personality, of course. It does not actually announce the acceptance of the new God, but it makes the point clear with the use of a capital letter in the last stanza:

> Once more, sadly and sternly
> I leave the house in the morning—
> Searching for the good God,
> And—oh! may God help me!

[*KV,* 329]

The most poignant song of the limbo period, a song that was used as the title for two books, was "When I Return" ("Kogda ya vernus' "). It was also used as the epigraph for all the work of the fourth period. Here, the religious element is explicit:

> When I return,
> I will go to that one and only house,
> Where the sky cannot rival the sky-blue cupola,
> And the smell of incense, like orphanage bread,
> Will strike into me and ripple in my heart—
> When I return,
> Oh, when I return!

The confidence of the constantly repeated line in this song is undermined by its modified use as a coda: "But when will I return?" (KV, 299).

Galich left Russia in the summer of 1974. He spent a year based in Oslo, where he had connections dating back to his visit as a Soviet filmmaker. It was in Oslo that he made his only recording under studio conditions, resulting in the album called *A Whispered Cry*.[14] The high technical quality of this recording only emphasizes a drop in artistic quality compared with the homemade *magnitizdat* recordings of the late 1960s. Some of the songs are provided with an accompanying trio, and the vulgarity reaches its height with a realistic train effect from the drummer in the song dedicated to Solomon Mikhoels. The evidence of this record, and of the one Vysotsky made in France, strongly suggests that solo guitar accompaniment is the only possible vehicle for guitar song. Okudzhava has never agreed to record with anything else but his own guitar, and his recordings are the purer for this restraint.

Galich also began giving concerts as soon as he arrived in the West. And he began making broadcasts over Radio Liberty. In the autumn of 1974, under the title "Aleksandr Galich Talks and Sings," he began a series of recitals of his own songs, interspersed with commentary on them and on current affairs. Paradoxically, through this means he was undoubtedly reaching a wider audience at any given time than he could ever have hoped to reach as an underground poet inside the USSR. And he became associated with the board of the new journal *Continent* (*Kontinent*), which has gone on to become the most successful and prestigious literary-political organ of the new émigrés. About a year after he left Russia, Galich accepted a staff post with Radio Liberty. He first worked in Munich and then in late 1976 transferred to Paris, where he became director of the organization's cultural section. In Paris, of course, he was at the heart of the European component of the emigration. He continued to travel widely, making two tours to Israel and one to the United States, and many appearances throughout western Europe.

The fourth and final phase of Galich's creative life was cut short by his accidental death. He gave what was to be his last concert on 3 December 1977, as part of the Venice Biennale, which was dedicated that year to the dissident culture of Eastern Europe. After the conference, Galich returned to Paris. On 15 December he came back from work to his apartment and, without even taking off his overcoat, went to plug in his new tape recorder (or radio receiver, according to some accounts). There was a short circuit, and he was electrocuted. There have been all sorts of rumors about the "real" cause of his death, with the security services on both sides of the ideological divide being suspected and accused, but the inquest conducted by the French police reached a verdict of accidental death. Galich was buried in the Russian Orthodox cemetery in Paris along with generations of other Russian exiles.

When Galich came to the West, he was confident that his creative gift would survive the loss of his native linguistic environment, the wellspring of his greatest songs. He was in his mid-50s, he said:

> I'm not a boy, I'm someone who's lived. During these years I've accumulated and worked up so much, that I hope God will grant me the time to finish, here in the West, everything I began or intended to write in the Soviet Union.[15]

And he emphasized the positive role he thought that he, along with the other new émigrés, could play:

> Russia, the spirit of the Russian people, has so to speak sent us forth into other countries, with a single purpose—to preserve our spiritual culture, to take it into the world, to nurture it, and, if we have the strength, to increase it.[16]

But he was concerned with more than such a conservation of cultural values. Galich considered that he could break through the language barrier and get his message through to foreign audiences. After all, his preferred medium was song, which had the additional, international, element of music; and he possessed the training of a professional actor and had a considerable amount of experience as a performer. Galich did indeed receive an enthusiastic response on occasion from foreign audiences, working in the usual way for foreign poets, having a translation read in the appropriate language before he performed the song. But it was clear that the intimate immediacy of *magnitizdat* and the clandestine Moscow performances had been irrecoverably lost. Galich himself once admitted his awareness of this loss:

> My appearances in Italy have convinced me that with a good interpreter it is possible to appear in front of an audience that doesn't understand Russian. There's nothing you can compare with the joy you feel when you're in contact with Russians, though. . . . Consequently, I long very much for my Russian audience.[17]

Galich also made the attempt to turn his attention to Western society and comment on it in song from the point of view of the post-Soviet Russian émigré. This endeavor produced the cycle "The Wild West" ("Dikii zapad"), which is made up of nine songs. Here, Galich gave poetic expression to that indignant scorn for Western liberalism, its indifference to the Communist threat, and its flirting with Communism itself, that has been expressed frequently and forcefully by the editors and contributors to *Continent*. In "An Old Song" ("Staraya pesnya"), Galich complains about a lack of orientation. In Russia, it had been clear which side any individual was on:

> We knew for sure
> On which days
> It was our disaster and their honor.
> For we were we,
> And they were they,
> And the others, well, they didn't matter!

However, in the West:

> But, here,
> Amid this flaming darkness,
> Where even shadows live in shadow,
> We're at a loss sometimes—
> Where are we?
> And from which side are *they* coming?

The result is a feeling of abandoned isolation:

> There we stand,
> Open to all the winds
> From all four sides, you could say!

[*KV*, 359–60]

Galich's impatience with what he saw as the spinelessness of Western society, and its fatal inclination toward compromise, is expressed in the title song of the cycle. The song has the subtitle "A Letter to Moscow, Sent by Hand":

> Don't drop tears on your letters,
> Our hearts are breaking as it is!
> We're living in the Wild West,
> And it sure is pretty wild!
>
> But it isn't a cowboy wildness.
> There's another game going on here:
> They prefer to drink Polish vodka
> With their Moscow caviar.
>
> Here, in the West,
> Which has been sold out
> And crucified for a bet,
> In their Parises and their Londons
> Like devils
> There are savages!
> . . .
> Stupified by Sartres
> Of all sizes and breeds!
>
> Out of idleness, out of weakness,
> What they like best is noise!
> They want another Bastille
> So they can go off and storm it!
>
> It's stupid to argue with them,
> They're only shadows!

$$[KV, 374-75]$$

There is very little evidence on which to essay judgments about what would have become of Galich as a guitar poet had accidental death not cut short his life. There is the possibility that he would have turned the cutting edge of his satirical talent against Western society in a more substantial and successful way than he does in "The Wild West." It would be stupid not to understand the passionate anxiety felt upon contemplating open societies by those people who have passed through Stalinism and the rigors of dissidence and exile. But Galich's denigration of what he saw as the West's inability to recognize the paramount danger from the East is expressed mainly in abstract fulmination. Unlike the satires about Soviet society he had composed in the sixties, these songs lack the authentic speaking voice, and they lack the depth of understanding of the societies and their inmates which form their targets. But most of all they lack the moral basis of the earlier songs.

This basis was Galich's sense of guilt. In the USSR after his anathematization and before his exile, and in the West in emigration, he was speaking from a position of moral rectitude, of reconciliation with his own personality; and it led him, with damaging results for his art, to preach and teach. Galich's great guitar songs were the satires, written and sung about his fellow citizens and in their own voices. His own personality was shielded, but the songs were fueled by his personal sense of guilt at his morally ambiguous position as a privileged beneficiary of Soviet society. The spiritual peace and the moral resolution that he acquired when he became an outcast seem to have fatally diverted him from the expression of his truest talent, which was for dramatic satire.

But nothing can take away from his achievement as a guitar poet inside Soviet Russia. He took the genre that Okudzhava had developed as a new outlet for the expression of the lyric sensibility in Russian and turned it into a mighty weapon of social and political criticism. The most telling tribute to Galich's power is the complete official suppression of his work in the USSR. When Vysotsky died, many words were written and spoken publicly about guitar poetry and the "bards": Galich's name was never mentioned.[18]

Of all the guitar poets, Galich was the most intimately tied to Soviet society and culture. His language, his characters, the situations and framework of ideas found in his songs, are all reflections of the unique society of which he was the coeval and which he understood so profoundly. As a modern Russian satirist he ranks with Zoshchenko, and he has no equal among satirists of the post-Stalin era. As a master of the grotesque he ranks alongside Bulgakov. His achievement was to speak to his contemporaries with sufficient power to overcome and make nonsense of the denial of publication that was imposed by the controllers of the media. And there is no doubt whatsoever that this power will suffice to keep Galich's songs at the forefront of the Russian cultural consciousness, whether or not they are ever published in their native country.

8 Guitar Poetry as Literary Genre

Guitar Poetry as Literary Genre

IT WAS ASSERTED IN THE introduction to this book that there is no hard and fast distinction between guitar poetry and "normal" Russian literary poetry. This statement is as true in the realm of style as in any other. Guitar poetry has no single specific style of its own. The songs of Galich, for example, have more in common with his own poetry for reading, and those of Okudzhava with his, than the songs of either have in common with each other. And the style of Okudzhava's songs has more in common with that of some published Soviet songs than it does with the unofficial poetry of Joseph Brodsky. There are important similarities between the style of some guitar songs, especially those of Galich and Vysotsky, and that of some dissident literature in other genres—especially the satirical prose of Erofeev, Terz, and Voinovich. This similarity is in part a natural reflection of their shared function as a deliberate antithesis of the characteristic styles of official literature. In style, as in all other respects, guitar poetry is a part of contemporary Russian literature, and it has common characteristics with different areas of that literature according to function.

But guitar poetry as a genre does exhibit some characteristic stylistic tendencies. The most salient among them reflect the universal tendencies of sung texts.[1] The use of repetition and refrain is prominent. These devices are used with far greater frequency in sung texts than in poetry meant to be read on the page. The reasons are not far to seek. The words of songs are intended for aural perception; the listener has no control over the order and manner in which the material is presented. The author therefore tends to use additional emphasis, in the form of repetition, for his main points. He may also consider providing a refrain, which may serve to mark the structure of the text in an aurally perceptible way, fulfilling the same function as white space on the page between the stanzas of a poem for reading. It may also provide a resting period to allow the listener a break in concentration, a moment of relaxation. These elementary functions of repetition and refrain operate just as strongly, it seems, when the song is composed in the sure knowledge that it will be recorded, providing the listener with the possibility of going back and controlling the presentation of the material.

Of course, the music may and probably will differentiate refrains and repetitions. But the resulting variety within unity is lost when the text is set down on the page and lacks its musical accompaniment. That is perhaps the most severe shortcoming that song texts incur when they are divorced from their music. They may well come to seem unnecessarily repetitive, annoyingly insistent, unsubtle. In this respect, guitar poetry shares a common fate with all sung verse.

The use of repetition and refrain increases the general level of phonetic patterning in the text. This enriched patterning may be further heightened by the use of standard phonetic devices of poetry such as assonance and alliteration. But there are considerable differences between the styles of the individual guitar poets in this respect. Okudzhava is generally sparing in his use of phonetic enrichment, aiming at a mellifluous sound texture based on the careful organization of vowels and the avoidance of large clusters of consonants. Galich is the most studied and inventive of the great guitar poets in this regard, pulling off virtuoso feats of echo and pun. Vysotsky's style, as in several other respects, is at the opposite extreme from Okudzhava's; he is often excessive and slapdash, indulging in strings of rhymes for their own sake. But these excesses are rescued in performance by the author's own mocking recognition of his outrageousness.

Nothing can make up for the loss of the author's own performance when guitar poetry is divorced from his voice and set down on the page. The author's performance is an essential part of the song's semantics. A small number of guitar songs, as with songs of other kinds, have left their authors behind and assumed an anonymous existence as folklore. They exist in the memories and performance of thousands of people. Sung by someone other than the author, they are still capable of making a profound impression in the right circumstances. But that impression is never as strong as it is when the author's own guitar-accompanied voice comes directly from his lips or through the speaker of a tape recorder. Here we have a fundamental difference between guitar poetry and what Mark Booth calls "song poetry":

> What the modern reader most wants to find in poetry is the poet's personal encounter with reality, fixed with subtle rightness in a unique construction of language. It should be clear that songs almost never answer to this expectation.[2]

But Russian guitar poems do answer to this expectation, most adequately when they are experienced in the poet's own performance. In this respect, they lean toward the condition of poetry rather than the condition of song.

However, it would be absurd to suggest that the absence of the author's voice destroys the artistic effect of a guitar song. The best examples of the genre still stand up to examination and analysis on the page, just as much as any other kind of song does.

The versification of Russian guitar poetry has the same elaborate, highly regulated feel for the anglophone reader as Russian poetry does in general. And it is true that guitar poetry does employ syllabotonic lines, rhyme, and invariant stanza forms, just like most Russian poetry. But the versification of guitar poetry has some distinguishing features apart from the use of refrain and repetition that was mentioned earlier.[3] As a whole, guitar poetry tends to use polymetric structures more than poetry for reading, that is, the use of more than one metrical design in the course of the text. And there is a more even distribution between the four major groups of meters (iambic, trochaic, ternary, and non-classical) than is the case with poetry for reading; in particular, the iambic tetrameter and pentameter, and the three-ictus *dol'nik*, which are very prominent in Russian poetry, are much less frequently used in guitar poetry.

Within these general properties of guitar poetry, each of the three great guitar poets has molded himself a distinctive selection from the repertoire of Russian metrical resources. Okudzhava is the most conservative. He has a repertoire that is certainly wide and varied but not all that sharply distinct from the repertoire used by modern Russian poets in general. However, one feature of his versification sets it off quite sharply from that of Vysotsky and especially Galich: Okudzhava, like most poets writing for reading, tends to use a single metrical design throughout the whole length of a song. This simplicity is compensated for by the relative complexity of Okudzhava's melodies compared with those of Vysotsky and Galich. The latter favor polymetrical structures and less adventurous melodies. In Vysotsky's work, it is common for two contrasting metrical designs to appear in alternation, one often being a refrain. In Galich's work, however, structures of considerable complexity appear, sometimes consisting of three and even four contrasting metrical designs. Combined with the changing melodies that accompany the changing metrical designs, the effect is one of great richness and variety, an effect that is completely lost in translation.

The origins of the versification of Russian guitar poetry can only be guessed at in the present state of knowledge. One thing that is certain, though, is that it derives directly neither from the Russian folk tradition nor from the tradition of high literary poetry. It is certainly possible to find in the work of the guitar poets some isolated examples of meters that are based on folklore. The use of folk-based meters, though, is relatively rare in guitar poetry as a whole. It is probable, although it remains to be demonstrated in detail, that the characteristic forms of Russian guitar poetry derive, as do a great number of the metrically innovative forms in Russian poetry, from foreign sources. Prominent among them would be the translations into Russian of such ballad-inclined poets as Béranger and Kipling.

Low and High Styles

Stylistic range is one respect in which unofficial Russian literature is most clearly differentiated from official literature. Generally speaking, techniques that have become commonplace in modern anglophone literature have been regarded as unacceptable by the controllers of publication in the Russian language, both inside and outside the country. Noticeable absentees from modern Russian literature have been the absurd and the erotic, the twin literary spearheads of subversive anarchy. The Russian literary prints have always been concerned with various kinds of high seriousness and the promotion of whatever particular point of view their ideological masters have demanded from them.

Published Russian literature exhibits constraints at both stylistic extremes, high and low. At the low end of the scale, a very large area of normal spoken Russian is considered unprintable, both in the USSR and outside it.[4] The attitudes that keep this language out of print are probably shared rather than imposed, because it is a fact that when Russian writers are working "for the drawer" or outside the limitations imposed by Soviet standards of propriety, they do not as a rule take advantage of their freedom to use "unprintable" words. These archaic standards of propriety have meant that it is still relatively easy for a writer to shock by using language that is normally considered unprintable. And a number of underground and émigré dissident writers, most prominently Eduard Limonov, Yuz Aleshkovsky, and Venedikt Erofeev, have exploited the possibilities of breaking the convention. The scandal caused by Limonov's novel *It's Me, Eddie! (Eto ya, Edichka!)* showed how intense were the passions that could still be aroused by foul language and explicit description—even among the Russian émigré community, surrounded as it is by the unrestrained pornography of Western societies.

The guitar poets have gone nowhere near the lengths Limonov went to in this book. They have evidently considered, along with the vast majority of dissident writers, that there is simply so much to be said plainly that cannot be said in official literature that an expansion of stylistic limits is unnecessary. Certainly, there is no guitar poet who has attacked official canons primarily in terms of style rather than content.

However, that is not by any means to say that the guitar poets have been indifferent to the effect of official stylistic restraints. The opposite is the case. They have felt in general that the language of official literature has become so stereotyped as to be literally meaningless, and that it is part of their task to find fresh means of expression. What they have done in this connection is to concentrate more than anything else on the colloquial end of the stylistic spectrum, attempting to capture the flavor of informal spoken Russian, but without dipping to any great extent into the subliterary range.

The point may be graphically illustrated by reference to one of the classic *magnitizdat* tapes made by Galich around 1969. The audience, to judge from the background noises on the tape, is quite small, a dozen people at most. They are in someone's flat, and the atmosphere is convivial. There are sounds of drinks being poured. At one point a car goes past and almost brings the proceedings to a halt. Galich sings his most classic dissident songs, with no holds barred as regards content. They include "Guignol Farce" ("Fars-gin'ol") and "The Ballad of Surplus Value" ("Ballada o pribavochnoi stoimosti"). When he introduces the former song, Galich says: ". . . there's this song . . . please excuse me for the first word . . . it's called 'Guignol Farce'." The first line of the song goes: "Vse zasrantsy, vse nakhlebniki, . . ." The word that Galich apologizes for is in fact the first noun in the line, *zasrantsy,* a noun formed from the unprintable verb *srat'*, "to shit." The singular form, *zasranets,* is equivalent to one of the many parallel English derivatives such as "shithead." The Russian word is not permissible in polite mixed company, and it is certainly not printable. But it is by no stretch of the imagination obscene, or even seriously objectionable. The fact that Galich feels the need to apologize for the word in a private gathering shows the power of the norms that operate in Russian speech etiquette, especially for someone of Galich's generation. It shows that these norms are still very strong even for someone who has cast off the official restraints and is writing without taking account of the control system.

On the same tape, Galich sings "The Ballad of Surplus Value." The song includes the line "Posylayu nachal'stvo ya v zadnitsu." Galich pronounces the last of these words in a primly distorted way. But there is an audible intake of breath from several people in the small audience. The word *zadnitsa* means, according to the *Oxford Russian-English Dictionary,* "arse, buttocks," and it is marked as stylistically vulgar. The line means literally "I send the bosses into (my) ass," i.e., tell them where they can get off. It is an innocuous enough everyday phrase; but it is quite unprintable in Russian. And again, the tape makes plain the author's own embarrassment and his audience's surprise.

Further examples of this kind of sailing close to the wind could be quoted from Galich's work. But there are not many of them. And there are absolutely no cases of outright obscenity.

The same is true of Vysotsky's songs. Among them, and especially in the criminal songs, it is possible to find some striking curses, perhaps the most expressive of them being "Ya zh te nogi oblomayu, v Boga dushu mat'!" (*PRB,* III, 28)—"I'll smash your legs, into God soul mother!" The first phrase here is a standard Russian threat, and printable. The second is a fairly common colloquial phrase whose elements are printable individually and in this combination, but which also occur in unprintable phrases. The effect is to suggest violent blasphemous obscenity without actually articulating an authentic unprintable phrase. The use of euphemism is normal in Vysotsky's low-life songs, and characteristic of the linguistic procedures of dissident Russian literature. In his performance of these songs, Vysotsky sometimes interjects words that verge on the unprintable. The most common one is *blya,* an abbreviation of *blyad',* "whore," one of the most frequently used curses in Russian. On a slightly higher stylistic level, but still extremely dubious from the point of view of printability, come lines like Vysotsky's "No kto-to tam odnazhdy skurvilsya, ssuchilsya" (*PRB,* III, 28). The two words at the end of this line are verbs formed from nouns, respectively *kurva,* "whore," and *suka,* "bitch," the former always unprintable, the latter unprintable when used as a curse. The phrase actually means "Then someone went and turned informer." But it is the following line of the song which is a greater infringement of linguistic propriety. It uses not obscenities but thieves' cant: "Shepnul, navel,—i ya sgorel." It means literally "(He) whispered, directed, and I burned up," which means to say that the person concerned informed, put the police on the right track, and the speaker was arrested. This kind of undecorous language, with its unacceptable implication that there is a criminal class in the USSR, is as thoroughly frowned on by official opinion as is actual obscenity.

This type of language is used most consistently in Vysotsky's criminal songs, where it contributes to stylization and relates to tradition. Of the three great guitar poets, it is Galich whose language is at the same time the most "realistic" and the most unremittingly colloquial. This fact has been recognized by all Russians who have commented on his work. For example, Nataliya Rubenshtein cites the following stanza, which comes from Galich's "Ballad about the General's Daughter" ("Ballada pro general'skuyu doch' "):

> On suchek iz gulevykh shoferov,
> On baryga, i kalymshchik, i zhmot,
> On na torgovoi daet,—bud' zdorov,
> Gde za rup', a gde kakuyu prizhmet.[5]

Nataliya Rubenshtein cites this particular stanza to make the point that it is completely untranslatable, and would need pages of commentary to explain the sociological reality behind it. But by no means all Russian native speakers would understand it at first hearing. The reason is that every single element in it belongs to subliterary contemporary Russian slang. It combines ellipsis (the second couplet) and cant vocabulary (the second line) in a baffling way. The words are used as much to give an impression of spoken language as for their literal meaning; and their effect is to make a very sharp break with public linguistic etiquette.

It is characteristic of Galich's work that the quatrain about the taxi driver is direct speech, used by one of the characters in the song from which it comes. The use of polyphony, a multiplicity of voices, is one special characteristic of Galich's work. It reaches an extreme in one of his greatest songs, "Composition No. 27, or Trolleybus Abstraction" ("Kompozitsiya No. 27, ili trolleibusnaya abstraktsiya"). The stanzas of this song consist of three parts: four lines of direct speech, purportedly overheard in a packed Moscow trolleybus; four lines of blasé comment from the author; and finally a couplet that cites a Soviet advertising slogan:

> "He didn't get there fair and square, he crept,"
> "He got them a vacuum and a carpet from TsUM,"
> "And she said to him, 'You swine, you swine!' "
> "They were doing annual stocktaking just then."
>> Outside, rain and then snow,
>> Rain then snow, tears then laughter.
>> One man's slaughter is another's execution,
>> Some fall in love, others are disgraced.
>>> "Use the services of Aeroflot!
>>> Save time!" and tra-la-la!

This passage mixes linguistic registers in a way that is kept out of official literature because it is not edifying. It falls below the standards of public linguistic etiquette (or, as Galich would have maintained, it is not dead enough to be printed in the USSR). And, of course, it lacks the "ideological awareness" demanded of official literature. In English it seems rather banal, but in its own linguistic context it is, while grotesque, startlingly fresh and realistic. Galich in particular (and guitar poetry in general) in this respect was trying to substantiate the stylistic breakthrough that was attempted in the post-Stalin period, an attempt at innovation that inevitably ran into the sand in official literature.

Still, the fact remains that Galich, Vysotsky in his criminal songs, and to a large extent Kim in his satires almost always do remain within the bounds of publicly sanctioned linguistic propriety. Departures from it remain rare. In the case of Okudzhava, there is absolutely nothing in his songs that would in principle be unprintable in the USSR. What makes his language distinctive is, as was suggested in an earlier chapter, the fact that he completely avoids the clichés of officially sanctioned literature.

The other stylistic extreme, the high end of the register and the textual "difficulty" associated with it, has also been censored out of Soviet literature. It is not compatible with the didactic aims of Socialist Realism. Like the low end of the stylistic spectrum, however, high-style difficulty is not found to any great extent in unofficial literature either, and therefore it must be considered to be a shared assumption on the part of both official and dissident authors. Unofficial literature, too, is written to be understood by the widest possible public, and it therefore does its best to be comprehensible, to make an immediate impact, and not to be limited in its audience to those who have the education and leisure to spend time on study. This point was made with maximal force by Aleksandr Galich in one of the interviews he gave soon after he was forced to leave the USSR. He described poetry as "a cry for help," and argued that it would be pointless for anyone to cry for help in incomprehensible language.[6] In guitar poetry, as in dissident literature in general, the message, the "what," is primary.

Guitar Poetry and Light Verse

Russian guitar poetry, then, tends to use elaborate versification and colloquial vocabulary. Its texts are seldom difficult or obscure. And also, guitar songs, especially those of Vysotsky and Galich, tend to tell stories. For the anglophone student of poetry—and indeed, for some Russians—these characteristics consign guitar poetry to the category of "light verse," something distinct from, and inferior to, serious literary poetry. Indeed, the three categories proposed in W. H. Auden's definition of light verse would neatly take in all the work of the Russian guitar poets:

> (1) Poetry written for performance, to be spoken or sung before an audience. . . .
> (2) Poetry intended to be read, but having for its subject-matter the everyday social life of its period or the experiences of the poet as an ordinary human being. . . .
> (3) Such nonsense poetry as, through its properties and technique, has a general appeal. . . .[7]

In a discussion of light verse that takes Auden's as a point of departure, Kingsley Amis disagrees with much that Auden had said in this preface. But he adds one notion that encapsulates the reason why much Russian poetry in general, and especially guitar poetry, sounds like light verse to the anglophone audience: "Light verse makes stringent demands on the author's technique. It prefers forms incompatible with decent seriousness: jogging rhythms, elaborate rhymes. . . ."[8] Auden maintained that "light verse can be serious," but that this seriousness had been beyond the reach of English poets since the Romantic Revival. Since that time, he asserted, "it has only been in trivial matters that poets have felt in sufficient intimacy with their audience to be able to forget themselves and their singing robes."[9] Amis, while not entirely accepting this assertion, did agree that light verse could exist only by reference to a serious tradition running side by side with it, since light verse is "altogether literary, artificial, and impure."[10]

These observations, by two eminent English poets, admirably point up a cardinal difference between the Russian and English poetic traditions. The fact is that for a Russian, a poem needs to be "light" in the Auden sense, and also to meet Amis's "stringent technical demands" in order to qualify as a serious poem and avoid being light in the sense of trivial. There is in Russian no significant tradition of "light" poetry which exists by reference to a more serious tradition; in the minds of Russians, a poem is either serious or not a poem.[11] But the fundamental reason for this situation is connected, in a grotesquely paradoxical way, with Auden's definition of the social conditions necessary for the existence of a poetic tradition with no split between "light" and "serious": "Poetry which is at the same time light and adult can only be written in a society which is both integrated and free."[12] When he wrote this statement in the late 1930s, Auden undoubtedly had in mind some form of Communist society of the future. The situation of Russian literature in the Soviet period, though, suggests that the conditions Auden hoped for can also come about in a society that is integrated by servitude. Official Soviet opinion would accept Auden's contention without reservation, and claim that the literature of Socialist Realism exemplifies the result—a literature that is accessible and serious at the same time. But events have shown that it is in fact the dissident stream in modern Russian literature that exemplifies this condition. It speaks to an unfree people about the problems their enforced integration has brought upon them.

There is another barrier that distorts the perception of Russian guitar poetry by non-Russians: while the connections between poetry and song have been intimate and enduring through European literary history, during the twentieth century the gap between them has tended to widen. In most countries it has widened to the point of their becoming completely separate. Melody is now thought either to detract from the artistic purity of the text or to distract the audience from its message. Even more, there has been a widening gap and eventual severance between poet and singer, who in ancient cultures were not distinguished from each other. The poet has become more and more the remote artist who communicates with his audience through the medium of the printed word studied in isolation by a silent reader. The success or failure of the communication might not necessarily worry the poet very much at all. And the singer has moved further and further away from the author of his words and also, with the exception of opera, away from what is accepted as art and is instead relegated to the status of entertainment. Rock music, in which the author and singer are usually the same person, does not command serious attention as literature.

In Russia, however, the oral element in literary culture, including singing, has not been subjected to quite the same devaluation and specialization. It is a commonplace that in the tradition of modern Russian poetry, the most authentic mode in which the text can be communicated and perceived is felt to be the poet's own voice, speaking aloud to an audience that is physically present. And the prevalent Russian fashion in the declamation of poetry borders closely upon song. It employs a range of pitch and an emotional intensity that strike anglophones as melodramatic to the point of comicality. From this kind of declamation it is only a short step to the deliberately unmelodic singing style of the guitar poet.

The idea of Philip Larkin or Robert Lowell's singing their poems to their own guitar accompaniment is ludicrous. Conversely, most literate anglophones would consider that because Bob Dylan, say, sings his words to a guitar, he cannot be a serious poet. But for a Russian poet, to sing is not absurd or demeaning at all. If anything, it represents a legitimate recapturing of a device that properly belongs within the resources of his art. The Russian poet who chooses this unsophisticated medium to ensure that his unsophisticated message gets across effectively may seem naive or dull to the foreign audience, which looks at him from the dazzling context of the contemporary Western media, through which all styles of all ages are available simultaneously. But for his countrymen, he is a serious poet, and his message matters.

Conclusions

Guitar poetry, which is poetry sung by the author to his own guitar accompaniment, emerged in Russia in the late 1950s and was a prominent feature of Russian cultural life for some twenty years. Its impact and popularity were made through *magnitizdat,* publication and circulation by tape recorder. Russian guitar poetry has no equivalent in the contemporary cultures of other nations, though there certainly have been individual poets, such as Georges Brassens and Wolf Biermann, whose work is close to it in technique and spirit. Guitar poetry in Russia, though, belongs to the country's serious literary tradition. And in no other country is *magnitizdat* as important as it is in the USSR.

The pioneer Russian guitar poet was Bulat Okudzhava. When he began, he was not working in an established poetic mode. Rather, his songs brought together elements from different traditions and married them in a new synthesis. Although almost all the Russian poets for two hundred years had written songs, they had not as a rule performed them or composed their own music. Meanwhile, guitar-accompanied solo song had also been a feature of Russian cultural life since the eighteenth century. It was first associated with gypsy song, but eventually it became a popular kind of informal entertainment in a wide variety of social contexts. Okudzhava was the first poet to take this style, add elements from urban folklore, and use the resulting medium for serious poetic expression. Guitar poetry provides a good example of how a subliterary demotic form may be picked up and elevated to serve at the forefront of literary development. Many elements of its verbal style exist in Russian spoken poetry, though; the style of guitar poetry is not specific and exclusive.

Guitar poetry was not a development that came from outside the mainstream of the Russian literary process. It was initially created by members of that same metropolitan intelligentsia which is at the forefront of all Russian cultural life, and for their consumption. All three of the great guitar poets were brought up on the streets of Moscow. All three of them were near the center of cultural life before they emerged as guitar poets. And for all three of them, guitar poetry was preceded and accompanied by other forms of creative activity—Okudzhava as poet and novelist, Galich as dramatist, Vysotsky as actor. This situation also reflects the novelty of guitar poetry as a cultural phenomenon; it was not and never became an established and sufficient basis for professional literary existence.

That it did not become so is also a strong indication of the dissident, unofficial status of guitar poetry in the USSR. However, no absolute distinction can be drawn between the content of guitar poetry and that of officially accepted songs and poetry. Rather, there is between them a substantial "middle ground" where they overlap. This overlap involves both themes and style. Several themes in particular can be found here. Both official and dissident song tends to idealize woman, and to be patriotic. And songs not written for publication do not as a rule break the stylistic taboos that hold in official Soviet literature.

But guitar poetry in the main and at its most characteristic is an expression of dissent from officially promoted and accepted forms, themes, and style. As such, it has a good deal in common with other kinds of dissident Russian literature. Like them, it deals with forbidden subjects, opposes official themes and attitudes both implicitly and explicitly, uses language that is too frank and realistic to be tolerated in the media, and is a haven for irresponsible humor.

The precondition for the rise to popularity of guitar poetry was the tape recorder in private hands. It has been the only genre in which technological developments have been exploited by creative artists themselves to bypass and overcome the official monopoly on the public media in the USSR. The existence of private tape recorders meant that the guitar song was outside official control and could not be suppressed. For the first time in the long history of Russian dissident song, there was a medium that gave the author's message permanence. With *magnitizdat,* dissident song moved out of folklore and into literature.

The success of guitar poetry has fed to a considerable extent on the failure of official song to capture the hearts, minds, and memories of Soviet citizens, partly because of the fact that normal people naturally resent and resist anything that is forced down their throats. And under Soviet conditions, media saturation has been achieved more completely than by any other official ideology in modern history. But the ideological control of official song has made it incapable of satisfying the requirements that seem essential if any work of art is to become genuinely popular: that it provide either a credible representation of people's actual lives or a tempting alternative to them. Official Soviet song, like Soviet literature, cannot deal with everyday life as it actually is for most Russian people, because reality contradicts officially enforced claims about what the Bolshevik Revolution has meant for the people. And the mythological alternative that official ideology promotes, the promise of a radiant future for all mankind, commands no suspension of disbelief.

Guitar poetry does not suffer from these shortcomings. It can speak in natural language about everyday life as people know it to be; it has done so mainly in the work of Galich and Vysotsky. And it can provide myths that promise a palatable escape from everyday life; that it has done mainly in the work of Okudzhava and to a lesser extent that of Vysotsky. These two functions come together in providing a sense of consolation. On the one hand, people are assured that their problems are understood by others and not faced by them alone as individuals; and on the other, they are assured that man is capable of inventing an escape from the dictatorship of immediate reality. Guitar poetry has provided this consolation. And like other forms of dissident literature, it has also testified to the great historical experience of the Russian people, and to their private experience, in a way whose authenticity is beyond the reach of official art.

The three outstanding individuals who chose and developed guitar poetry as their medium of expression have each made a distinct contribution above and beyond the general achievement of the genre as a whole. In the last analysis, there are in the works of the great guitar poets three contrasting interpretations of the nature and purpose of human life. For Vysotsky, human life is hard and unjust, but it is knowable and susceptible to change through man's own efforts, even if only by a despairing individual act of revenge. For Okudzhava, life is sad most of the time, illuminated occasionally by the example of certain charismatic individuals and by the glow of certain ideals, chief among them being love. But in the last analysis life is unknowable, leaving humans baffled in their attempts to encompass it. Finally, for Galich, as for Vysotsky, life may be understood and manipulated. But the manipulation is performed by forces of evil. And in the last analysis life is absurd, especially when viewed in the light of man's solemn moralizing about it.

The work of the three great guitar poets also offers an instructive case study in the relationships between experience and expression in verbal art. All three poets write about war. But the only one of them who actually experienced it, Okudzhava, deals with the subject in a much more abstract, detached fashion than the others; their impressions were second-hand, deriving from service in the rear (Galich) and the stories of a father and uncle (Vysotsky) who both had outstanding combat records. Galich, who wrote about the GULag primarily as a debt of honor to a beloved cousin who spent many years in the camps, but had no personal knowledge of them, created some of the most powerful artistic treatments of the phenomenon. Vysotsky's criminal underworld, whose authenticity in language and morals has been repeatedly endorsed, seems to have been based on an extrapolation from the poet's experience of Moscow's intellectual bohemia.

The three great guitar poets also had contrasting individual styles within the framework of the genre's communal features. Okudzhava was a wistful lyricist and melodist whose agnostic attitude toward the "accursed questions" was expressed through gentle, evocative, and genuinely fresh images. Vysotsky was the spokesman for urban *homo sovieticus,* using the language of the backstreets to tell anecdotes and to howl out the pain of his self-destructive personality. Galich was a suave teller of black satirical stories, a dramatic and narrative poet whose attitudes were projected through dozens of fictional personae. Together, their work forms a major strand in Russian dissident literature of the post-Stalin era. Individually, their fates exemplify contrasting resolutions of the conflict between the creative individual and the Soviet authorities during this period. Okudzhava adjusted, survived, and has been increasingly accepted; Vysotsky drove himself to destruction in a tormenting dilemma between revolt and accommodation; and Galich was persecuted and driven out, his work anathematized in his native country.

Guitar poetry was at its peak in the late 1960s and early 1970s. At this time, the three great poet-singers were all composing and performing inside Russia. Each one had built up a repertoire of songs sufficient to define himself as a distinct creative individual. And then disintegration set in. Okudzhava faded out as a writer of songs in the wake of his brush with the Party in 1972. Galich was forced into emigration in 1974, and by that time he had virtually exhausted himself as a creative writer. Vysotsky grew more desperate and despairing. He continued to write and sing songs at the furious pace characteristic of everything he did until death caught up with him in 1980. His death meant that the great active era of guitar poetry had come to an end. But the tapes of *mag-*

nitizdat have survived and will continue to preserve the authentic contemporary record of this remarkable poetic form.

There are no signs that a second generation of guitar poets is ready to carry on the work of the original masters. Instead, if anything, the next generation of dissident singers in the USSR has turned away from the forms and themes of guitar poetry and is looking to Western rock music as a source of inspiration.[1] All in all, it seems likely that guitar poetry will move into history along with the people who created and received it with such alacrity in the 1960s and 1970s.

Notes

Introduction

1. So far as he is aware, the present writer developed the term *guitar poetry* during the course of work on this book; it had no existing equivalent among the Russian terms used to refer to the genre or its practitioners.

2. Yury Mal'tsev, "Menestreli," in *Vol'naya russkaya literatura, 1955–1975* (Frankfurt/M, 1976), pp. 302–25; Grigory Svirsky, "Magnitofonnaya revolyutsiya," in *Na lobnom meste: Literatura nravstvennogo soprotivleniya (1946–1976 gg.)* (London, 1979), pp. 463–89.

3. The most comprehensive study of recent Russian literature is Deming Brown's *Soviet Russian Literature since Stalin* (Cambridge, 1978). It excludes émigré Russian literature but admits everything that has "emerged" from Soviet society, wherever published. Brown allots one chapter to "underground" literature as a whole (pp. 352–72), of which guitar poetry gets two pages (pp. 365–67). In the revised and enlarged edition of E. J. Brown's standard *Russian Literature since the Revolution* (Cambridge, Mass. and London, 1982), Okudzhava appears almost exclusively as a prose writer, Vysotsky as the contributor of one item to the almanac *Metropol,* and Galich is not mentioned at all.

4. The only substantial studies in English specifically devoted to guitar poetry are G. S. Smith, "Modern Russian Underground Song: An Introductory Survey," *Journal of Russian Studies* 28 (1974): 3–12, and Gene Sosin, "Magnitizdat: Uncensored Songs of Dissent," in *Dissent in the USSR,* ed. Rudolf L. Tökés (Baltimore and London, 1975), pp. 276–309.

5. This assertion does not mean that the music of guitar poetry can be dismissed as a mere appendage to the words. The actual subtleties within Galich's seeming musical monotony are valuably discussed in Vladimir Frumkin, "Ne tol'ko slovo: vslushivayas' v Galicha," *Obozrenie* 8 (1984), in press. I am grateful to Professor Frumkin for the opportunity to read this article in manuscript.

6. The two classic collections, both compiled and introduced by Professor I. N. Rozanov, Russia's greatest authority on sung poetry, are *Pesni russkikh poetov (XVIII-pervaya polovina XIX veka)* (Leningrad, 1936) and *Russkie pesni XIX veka* (Moscow, 1944). There is no satisfactory equivalent for the modern period. V. E. Gusev's revision of Rozanov's collections, *Pesni i romansy russkikh poetov* (Moscow-Leningrad, 1963), is cautious in the extreme.

7. One striking anticipation of the modern Russian guitar poets is the case of the actor Nikolai Grigor'evich Tsyganov (1797–1833), author of many songs, including the immortal "Red Sarafan" (the *sarafan* is a traditional Russian peasant woman's dress.) A recent Soviet commentator, A. V. Sidel'nikova, writes: "N. G. Tsyganov did not write down his songs, but performed them to

guitar accompaniment among his friends, and it was evidently through them that they broke through into oral existence. . . . Tsyganov . . . never saw the first printed edition of his works" ("N. G. Tsyganov i ego pesennoe tvorchestvo," *Uchenye zapiski moskovskogo gosudarstvennogo pedagogicheskogo instituta,* vol. 455, 1971, pp. 143–59).

1. Song in State Service

1. Anon., "Sovetskaya pesnya," *Pravda,* 12 September 1975, p. 1.

2. *Russkie sovetskie pesni, 1917–1977,* comp. N. Kryukov and Ya. Shvedov (Moscow, 1977), pp. 164–65.

3. As quoted in Harold Swayze, *The Political Control of Soviet Literature, 1946–1959* (Cambridge, Mass., 1962), p. 113. The second paragraph was slightly modified at the V Congress of Soviet Writers in 1954.

4. The evolution of the official theory is illustrated in C. Vaughan James, *Soviet Socialist Realism: Origins and Theory* (London, 1973). Its practical significance is examined in Abram Terts (Andrei Sinyavsky), "Chto takoe sotsialisticheskii realizm," in *Fantasticheskii mir Abrama Tertsa* (London, 1967), pp. 399–446; translated as Abram Tertz, *On Socialist Realism* (New York, 1960). Katerina Clark's *The Soviet Novel: History as Ritual* (Chicago and London, 1981) provides an illuminating discussion of the origins and nature of Socialist Realism and its reflection in the orthodox Soviet novel from the 1930s to the present day.

5. Geoffrey Hosking, *Beyond Socialist Realism* (London, 1980); Deming Brown, "The Literary Situation," in his *Russian Literature since Stalin* (Cambridge, 1978), pp. 1–22.

6. The best available discussion of the system is contained in *The Soviet Censorship,* ed. Martin Dewhirst and Robert Farrell (Metuchen, N.J., 1973); also helpful are the relevant sections of Ronald Hingley, *Russian Writers and Soviet Society, 1917–1978* (London, 1978), and Andrei Sinyavsky, "Samizdat and the Rebirth of Literature," *Index on Censorship* 9, no. 4 (1980): 8–13.

7. *Russkie sovetskie pesni, 1917–1977.* This book will be referred to hereafter as *RSP.*

8. Robert Rothstein, "The Quiet Rehabilitation of the Brick Factory: Early Soviet Popular Music and Its Critics," *Slavic and East European Journal* 39, no. 3 (1980): 374–85.

9. The best available treatment of the subject is Vladimir Frumkin's regrettably brief "Tekhnologiya ubezhdeniya: zametki o politicheskoi pesne," *Obozrenie* 5 (July 1983): 17–20 and 6 (September 1983): 23–26. The fullest Soviet work on official song is A. Sokhor, *Russkaya sovetskaya pesnya* (Leningrad, 1959).

10. Wolfgang Kazack, "Lebedev-Kumač," in *Lexikon der russischen Literatur ab 1917* (Stuttgart, 1976), pp. 204–205.

11. *Modern Russian Poetry,* ed. Vladimir Markov and Merrill Sparks (London, 1966), pp. 738–41, contains the full original text of the song, with an English translation. The second quatrain of the verse refers to and quotes the "Stalin" Constitution of 1936.

12. On this subject, see Vera Dunham, *In Stalin's Time: Middle-Class Values in Soviet Fiction* (Cambridge, 1976).

13. Pavel Leonidov writes of ". . . the musical mafia that stands guard over the sinecure trough *(kormushka-koryto)* of royalties on songs, the most calorific trough in the country, apart, perhaps, from the aircraft- and rocket-

builders' trough, but they work in secret, while songwriters have fame" (*Vladimir Vysotsky i drugie,* New York, 1983, p. 53). The relations between text writers and musicians are described from an official standpoint in Mikhail Isakovsky, "Istoriya dvukh pesen," collected in his book *O poetakh, o stikhakh, o pesnyakh* (2d ed., Moscow, 1972), pp. 116–24.

14. Felix J. Oinas, "The Political Uses and Themes of Folklore in the Soviet Union," in *Folklore, Nationalism, and Politics,* ed. Felix J. Oinas (Columbus, 1978), pp. 77–95.

15. A good deal of information about the "repertoire sheets" of various variety artists, including the comedian Arkadii Raikin and the very popular singers Muslim Magomaev and Mark Bernes, is contained in Pavel Leonidov, *Vladimir Vysotsky i drugie.* Leonidov asserts that the cabaret singer Aleksandr Vertinsky (1889–1957) had a "repertoire sheet" personally authorized by Molotov, who had been instructed by Stalin to see to his welfare (pp. 128–29).

2. The Middle Ground and the Amateurs

1. Pasternak's lyric "Hamlet" was first published under his own name in the USSR in the annual *Poetry Day* of 1980 (*Den' poezii 1980,* Moscow, 1980, p. 181). In an accompanying note, Andrei Voznesensky asserts that he had earlier published the poem in an article on poetic translation in the journal *Foreign Literature (Inostrannaya literatura).*

2. Alexander Shtein, "Povest' o tom, kak voznikayut syuzhety," *Znamya* 5 (1964): 130, 147. Vertinsky's memoirs, somewhat unctuous and composed throughout with cautious hindsight, make interesting reading: "Chetvert' veka bez rodiny. Vospominaniya," in *V krayakh chuzhikh* (Moscow, 1962), pp. 197–309. His songs have been published most fully abroad: *Pesni i stikhi, 1916–1937gg.* (New York, 1975).

3. Mihajlo Mihajlov, *Moscow Summer* (London, 1966), pp. 51, 61, 205.

4. Vera Sandomirsky [Vera Dunham], "The Sad Armchair: Notes on Soviet War and Postwar Lyrical Poetry," *Harvard Slavic Studies* 3 (1957): 289–327. The theme is further developed in Professor Dunham's *In Stalin's Time: Middle-Class Values in Soviet Fiction* (Cambridge, 1976).

5. B. M. Dobrovol'sky, "Sovremennye bytovye pesni gorodskoi molodezhi," in *Fol'klor i khudozhestvennaya samodeyatel'nost'* (Leningrad, 1968), pp. 176–200.

6. *RSP,* p. 405. The text is dated 1947, but Dobrovol'sky ("Sovremennye bytovye pesni," 187–88) asserts that the song was in fact written in the second half of the 1930s by Mikhail L'vovsky, using the tune of another popular song of the time, Mikhail Svetlov's "Behind the Green Fence" ("Za zelenym zaborikom").

7. *Sovetskie poety, pavshie na Velikoi otechestvennoi voine* (Moscow-Leningrad, 1965), pp. 281–82.

8. Lev Kopelev, "Pamyati Aleksandra Galicha," *Kontinent* 16 (1978): 340. The cultural significance of the virgin lands campaign has not been seriously studied, but it is of considerable interest. The number of young poets who went on geological expeditions in the late 1950s was remarkable; indeed, there has recently been talk of a "geological school" of poets: Konstantin Kuz'minsky, "Geologicheskaya shkola," in *The Blue Lagoon Anthology of Modern Russian Poetry,* vol. 1 (Newtonville, 1980), pp. 387–93.

9. The atmosphere of *samodeyatelnost'* is evoked in E. Ryazanov's delightful film *Beware of Cars (Beregis' avtomobilya),* in which an "honest thief"

and a policeman unwittingly investigating his case are rehearsing a *samode-yatelnost'* production of *Hamlet*. The amateur actors are piquantly played by two of the greatest living Soviet professionals, Innokenty Smoktunovsky and Oleg Efremov.

10. There is an abundant literature in English on this subject; contemporary accounts include *The Soviet Cultural Scene, 1956–1957*, ed. Walter Z. Laqueur and George Lichtheim (New York-London, 1958); George Gibian, *Interval of Freedom: Soviet Literature during the Thaw, 1954–1957* (Minneapolis, 1960); Hugh McClean and Walter Vickery, "Introduction," in their *The Year of Protest, 1956: An Anthology of Soviet Literary Materials* (New York, 1961); Thomas P. Whitney, "Russian Literature and Soviet Politics," in his anthology *The New Writing in Russia* (Ann Arbor, 1964); and the introductory articles in two anthologies edited by Max Hayward and Patricia Blake, *Dissonant Voices in Soviet Literature* (London, 1964) and *Half-Way to the Moon: New Writing from Russia* (London, 1964). The later Khrushchev period is surveyed in Patricia Blake, *Khrushchev and the Arts: The Politics of Soviet Culture, 1962–1964* (Cambridge, Mass., 1965). More recent discussion of the period includes the appropriate sections of the books by Deming Brown and Edward J. Brown (see above, Introduction, Note 3.)

11. R. F. Tumanovsky, "Den' poezii," in *Kratkaya literaturnaya entsikopediya*, vol. 2, col. 593 (Moscow, 1964).

12. Yevgeny Yevtushenko, *A Precocious Autobiography*, trans. Andrew R. MacAndrew (London, 1963), p. 107. See also Anatoly Gladilin, *The Making and Unmaking of a Soviet Writer*, trans. David Lapeza (Ann Arbor, 1979), pp. 78–85.

13. Olga Carlisle, *Poets on Street Corners* (New York, 1968), 15.

14. Yury Andreev, "Chto poyut?" *Oktyabr'* I (1965): 182–92; reprinted in *Literatura i sovremennost', 6: Stat'i o literature 1964–1965 godov* (Moscow, 1965), pp. 257–79.

15. Andreev, *Literatura i sovremennost'*, p. 258.

16. Ibid., p. 276.

17. Dobrovol'sky.

18. Ibid., p. 193. Vladimir Vysotsky used the term *avtorskaya pesnya* to refer to the genre of his songs, contrasting them with the "stage" or "vaudeville" song *(estradnaya pesnya):* "Vladimir Vysotsky o sebe i o svoikh pesnyakh," in Vladimir Vysotsky, *Pesni i stikhi*, vol. 2 (New York, 1983), p. 193.

19. Dobrovol'sky, p. 193.

20. A. A. Bragina, *Neologizmy v russkom yazyke: Posobie dlya studentov i uchitelei* (Moscow, 1973). The lexical group centered on the word *shanson'e* is discussed on pp. 128–35.

21. Bragina, p. 134, quoting an unidentified article from *Sovetskaya kul'tura*, 10 October 1967.

22. The discussions in *Literaturnaya gazeta* are surveyed in Pavel Mikhalevsky, "Russkaya pesnya," *Russkaya mysl'*, 25 September 1975, p. 2.

23. Dmitry Kabalevsky, article in *Komsomol'skaya pravda*, 26 February 1967, reported in Mikhalevsky, p. 2.

24. Mikhail Isakovsky, "Vernut' pesne muzyku i poeticheskoe slovo!" (March 1967), reprinted in his *O poetakh, o stikhakh, o pesnyakh* (2d ed., Moscow, 1972), pp. 125–30.

25. L. Oshanin, untitled speech, in *Chetvertyi s"ezd pisatelei SSSR. 22–27 maya 1967 goda. Stenograficheskii otchet* (Moscow, 1968), p. 194.

26. V. Kukharsky, "V interesakh millionov," *Sovetskaya muzyka* 10 (1968),

reported in anon., " 'Samodeyatel'nye' pesni v Sov. soyuze," *Russkaya mysl'*, 22 May 1969, p. 3.

27. V. Frumkin, "Pesnya i stikh," *Sovetskaya muzyka* 10 (1969): 21–27. In an interview given outside the USSR many years later, Okudzhava implicitly agreed with Frumkin's point; his views on Blanter's settings appear in Larissa Gershtein, "Razgovor s Bulatom Okudzhavoi," *Dvadtsat' dva* 5, no. 25 (1982): 193–94.

28. Frumkin's account of this affair is contained in his émigré edition of Okudzhava's songs: Bulat Okudzhava, *65 pesen/65 Songs* (Ann Arbor, 1980), pp. 11–12. While he was still in Russia, Frumkin also wrote a general essay on the nature of sung poetry, using several examples from the guitar poets. It was accepted for publication but was stopped when the author emigrated. It eventually appeared in the United States: Vladimir Frumkin, "O nekotorykh funktsiyakh muzyki v sinteticheskikh iskusstvakh," in *Papers in Slavic Philology, I: In Honor of James Ferrell* (Ann Arbor, 1977), pp. 77–99.

29. I. Ignat'ev, "Ofitsial'naya sovetskaya pesnya protiv pesennogo samizdata," *Radio Liberty Information Bulletin*, 21(2602), 2 June 1971, passim.

30. Matveeva's poetry is represented in most English-language anthologies of modern Russian verse. See, for example, *Post-War Russian Poetry*, ed. Daniel Weissbort (Harmondsworth, 1974), pp. 183–89; *Russian Poetry: The Modern Period*, ed. John Glad and Daniel Weissbort (Iowa City, 1978), pp. 265–69.

31. *Shkola Okudzhavy* (London, 1971), reprinted from *Kak nadezhna zemlya: Pesennik*, comp. D. Sokolov (Moscow, 1969). *Shkola Okudzhavy* will be referred to in the text as *ShOk*, with page reference.

32. Dobrovol'sky, p. 197, relates that this song was sung from memory by an entire concert audience in Leningrad only days after Gorodnitsky first performed it in public. The song was awarded second prize (the first prize not being awarded) at the All-Union Song Contest in Moscow in 1966.

33. Several singers who perform to their own guitar accompaniment have appeared in Russia since the 1960s; the most talented of them is Zhanna Bichevskaya. In the work of these singers, who are not themselves poets, the influence of guitar poetry is joined by a strong element coming from Western singers using a sophisticated folk-based style, such as Joan Baez and Joni Mitchell. Because of the latter element in Bichevskaya's style, Okudzhava insisted that she give up performing his songs: his account of the confrontation appears in Larissa Gershtein's interview, published outside the USSR (see above, Note 27).

3. Underground Song

1. B. Vol'man, *Gitara v Rossii: Ocherk istorii gitarnogo iskusstva* (Leningrad, 1961), p. 41. See also A. Larin, "Gitara v Rossii (Obzor literatury)," in *Al'manakh bibliofila*, vol. 11 (Moscow, 1981), pp. 142–53. According to Graham Wade, "Only in Russia did the seven-string guitar take root": *Traditions of the Classical Guitar* (London, 1980, p. 98).

2. Vol'man, p. 48.

3. Robert Rothstein, "The Quiet Rehabilitation of the Brick Factory," *Slavic and East European Journal* 39, no. 3 (1980): 374–85.

4. *Pesni i romansy russkikh poetov* (Moscow-Leningrad, 1963), p. 941.

5. Ibid.

6. Vol'man, p. 49.

7. *The New Oxford Book of Light Verse,* ed. Kingsley Amis (Oxford-London-New York, 1978), pp. 163–65. A more decorous version can be found in *W. H. Auden's Oxford Book of Light Verse* (Oxford-New York-Toronto-Melbourne, 1979), pp. 476–77. For a more demotic version of the song, see *Bawdy Barrack-Room Ballads* (London, 1970), pp. 124–26.

8. The most useful accounts are: E. V. Pomerantseva, "Ballada i zhestokii romans," *Russkii fol'klor* 14 (1974): 202–209; Ya. I. Gudoshnikov, *Ocherki istorii russkoi literaturnoi pesni XVIII–XIX vv.* (Voronezh, 1972), pp. 142–49. Both these accounts are condescending, treating the genre as a subliterary phenomenon.

9. D. E. Maksimov, *Poeziya V. Bryusova* (Leningrad, 1940), pp. 127–29.

10. Marina Tsvetaeva, "V moe okoshko dozhd' stuchitsya," in *Stikhotvoreniya i poemy* (Leningrad, 1979), p. 127. See also Simon Karlinsky, *Marina Cvetaeva: Her Life and Art* (Berkeley and Los Angeles, 1966), pp. 188–89.

11. Quoted in I. Timofeev, "Na beregu Nevy," *Novyi zhurnal* 68 (1962): 84–85.

12. Rothstein, p. 376, footnote 13.

13. "Ya byl batal'onnyi razvedchik," in anon. "Narodnye sovetskie pesni," *Student* 2/3 (1964): 81; see also Mikhailo Mikhailov, *Leto moskovskoe 1964* (Frankfurt/M, 1967), pp. 63–64.

14. This text has obviously been distorted by censorship. According to Vladimir Frumkin (private communication), more perfect variants of the song include the following two verses. After the present fifth verse:

> Back home I went, my lads,
> And wasted no time caressing my Shura.
> My false leg really got in the way,
> So I put it under the bed.

And a final verse:

> People say fate is no turkey,
> And that's why I'm singing this song,
> How a vicious little Fascist bullet
> Tore off my ability.

15. Vladimir Markov, *The Longer Poems of Velemir Khlebnikov* (Berkeley and Los Angeles, 1962), p. 44.

16. Ibid., pp. 44–45.

17. "Zhila na Moskve geroinya romana," in anon., "Pesni-stikhi iz SSSR," *Novyi zhurnal* 84 (1966): 146–47.

18. Quoted in Alla Ktorova, "Yurin pereulok," *Grani* 53 (1963): 38. Vladimir Frumkin advises that this song should have a penultimate verse, as follows:

> Once upon a time my own dear mommy
> Went to the hayloft,
> And an awful drama took place:
> The count, my mommy he forced.

The suppression of this verse in the text quoted is a normal example of the prudishness found in émigré Russian journals. The great artist Ernst Neizvestny has asserted that this song, along with several others, was composed by the underground student group of which he was a member in Moscow in the late 1940s: "Katakombnaya kul'tura i ofitsial'noe iskusstvo," *Posev* 11 (1979):

37. The group was called "Love and hunger rule the world (there's hunger enough, but love has to be organized)."

19. Valery Chalidze, *Ugolovnaya Rossiya* (New York, 1977), passim, especially, pp. 51–122.

20. N. Khandzinsky, "Blatnaya poeziya," *Sibirskaya zhivaya starina* 1 (1926): 41–83. I am obliged to Andrew Jameson for a copy of this rare article.

21. Rothstein, p. 379, citing the Russian scholar Viktor Petrov. Rothstein's article contains an interesting discussion of the criminal song, as well as other unofficial songs in the 1920s and 1930s.

22. "Zhuliki i vory, zlye atamany," in anon., untitled song texts, *Student* 5/8 (1967): 146. Punctuation has been inserted in this translation.

23. References to the camps in Soviet literature are surveyed in Mikhail Geller, *Kontsentratsionnyi mir i sovetskaya literatura* (London, 1974). On the particular period of "Ivan Denisovich" there is V. Zhabinsky, " 'Zarubka na veka.' Literatura o lageryakh," *Mosty* 14 (1968): 314–32. In Soviet poetry, "only Tvardovsky" was permitted to discuss the camps, according to Grigory Svirsky: *Na lobnom meste: Literatura nravstvennogo soprotivleniya (1946–1976 gg.)* (London, 1979), pp. 141–42.

24. Boris Thomson, *The Premature Revolution: Russian Literature and Society, 1917–1946* (London, 1972), p. 197.

25. The stage direction at the end of Act IV simply says "Music and dances" *(Muzyka i tantsy);* Nikolai Pogodin, *Sobranie dramaticheskikh proizvedenii,* vol. 3 (Moscow, 1960), pp. 157–60.

26. Aleksandr Vardi, *Podkonvoinyi mir* (Frankfurt/M, 1972), pp. 24–28.

27. "Tovarishch Stalin, vy bol'shoi uchenyi," in anon., "Narodnye sovetskie pesni," *Student* 2/3 (1964): 81–84.

28. Ibid.; Mikhailov, *Leto moskovskoe 1964,* p. 58; the song is attributed to Vladimir Vysotsky in *Pesni russkikh bardov* (Paris, 1977), vol. 3, p. 31. The first authorized publication of the song was Yuzef Aleshkovsky, "Pesni," *Kontinent* 21 (1979): 146–47.

29. Quoted in Mikhailov, *Leto moskovskoe 1964,* pp. 59–60; also in *Na lobnom meste,* pp. 464–65, where it is ascribed to "a convict poet who perished in the camps."

30. B. Zhabinsky, "Fal'sifikatsiya ili fol'klor?" *Mosty* 3 (1958): 266–70.

31. After this section had been written and revised, Yakov Weisskopf's anthology of prison and camp songs came to hand: *Blatnaya lira: Sbornik tyuremnykh i lagernykh pesen* (Jerusalem, 1981). It includes, among other things, a very full text of "Murka" (pp. 22–26).

32. Nadezhda Mandel'shtam, *Vospominaniya* (New York, 1970), p. 205. This passage is omitted from the relevant chapter of Max Hayward's translation, *Hope Against Hope* (New York, 1971).

33. Mikhailov, *Leto moskovskoe 1964,* pp. 56–65. The English edition of his book, *Moscow Summer* (London, 1966), gives these songs only in truncated versions.

34. Yuly Daniel [Nikolai Arzhak], "Atonement," in *This Is Moscow Speaking* (London, 1968), pp. 77–78.

35. S. Frederick Starr has gone even further about the importance of camp songs. He asserts that "incessant propaganda had debased the spoken and written word and turned many young people away from language as such. Significantly, when their interest in verbal communication revived in the late fifties, they turned first to poetry and works by their contemporaries, Andrei Voznesensky and Yevgeni Yevtushenko. A decade of mass songs had also

debased singing. Not until an entirely new genre of songs filtered back from the Siberian labor camps did the sung word return to Russia." *Red and Hot: The Fate of Jazz in Russia* (New York and Oxford, 1983), p. 242. As we have seen, there was always an alternative, underground culture of song in the towns; and the prison-camp element is only one, and not even the most important, of the elements making up the actual "entirely new genre of songs" that returned the sung word to Russia, that genre being the guitar poetry of Okudzhava and his followers.

36. Yevgeny Yevtushenko, " 'Intelligentsiya' poet blatnye pesni," *Druzhba narodov* 7 (1975): 84–85. Krasnaya Presnya is an old working-class district of Moscow, the scene of heroic Communist deeds during the 1905 revolution. The "writers in Pakhra" probably included the famous poet and editor Aleksandr Tvardovsky (1910–71), who had a dacha in Pakhra and was a very able singer of folk songs (Viktor Nekrasov, "Tvardovsky," *Novoe russkoe slovo*, 6 December 1981, p. 5).

37. Vladimir Roslyakov, "Dva rasskaza," *Yunost'* 3 (1969): 34.

38. *The Blue Lagoon Anthology of Modern Russian Poetry*, vol. 1, ed. Konstantin K. Kuz'minsky and Grigory L. Kovalev (Newtonville, Mass., 1980), is a substantial step toward assembling the materials for a history of underground poetry mainly during the 1950s. For the preceding period there is only Boris Filippov's pioneering anthology *Sovetskaya potaennaya muza* (Munich, 1961).

39. Ruf' Zernova, "Elizabet Arden," *Vremya i my* 58 (1980): 64–65.

40. Ibid., p. 67.

41. For example, anon., "Narodnye sovetskie pesni," *Student* 4 (1964): 48. The song is attributed to Vladimir Vysotsky in *Pesni russkikh bardov* (Paris, 1977), vol. 3, pp. 21–22. Many variants of it exist; the first line is usually "Once I was on the lookout" ("Sizhu ya raz na streme").

42. *Blue Lagoon Anthology*, vol. 1, p. 431.

43. See Suzanne Massie, *The Living Mirror: Five Young Poets from Leningrad* (Garden City, 1972), especially pp. 111–65, and *Blue Lagoon Anthology*, passim.

44. Reported by Konstantin Kuz'minsky, in *Blue Lagoon Anthology*, p. 429.

45. For a general survey, see Karl Riha, *Moritat, Bänkelsang, Protestballade: Zur Geschichte des engagierten Liedes in Deutschland* (Frankfurt/M, 1975).

46. On Biermann, see Thomas Rothschild, ed., *Wolf Biermann, Liedermacher und Sozialist* (Hamburg, 1976); Michael Morley, "Hard Times for Poetry: On the Songs and Poems of Wolf Biermann," *Index on Censorship* 2, no. 2 (1973): 23–36.

47. Bulat Okudzhava, "Pamyati Brassensa," *Novoe russkoe slovo*, 22 November 1981, p. 5. The article was acknowledged as a reprint from *Literaturnaya gazeta*, but no details were given.

4. Magnitizdat

1. The following passage is included in my "Modern Russian Dissident Culture," *Strathclyde Modern Language Studies* 3 (1983): 37–50.

2. Abram Terz (Andrei Sinyavsky), "The Literary Process in Russia," in *Kontinent I: The Alternative Voice of Russia and Eastern Europe* (London, 1976), p. 91.

3. For an account of the broadcasts of guitar songs alone from Radio Liberty—over a thousand programs in the ten years from 1971—see R. Pol-

chaninov, "Vysotsky v peredachakh 'Svobody,'" *Novoe russkoe slovo,* 7 February 1982, p. 6.

4. O. Zhadan, "Idem po pelengu," *Komsomol'skaya pravda,* 19 September 1974, p. 4.

5. Anon., "Radioizdat," *Russkaya mysl',* 6 February 1975, p. 5.

6. Gene Sosin, "Magnitizdat: Uncensored Songs of Dissent," in *Dissent in the USSR: Politics, Ideology and People* (Baltimore and London, 1975), p. 277.

7. Aleksandr Zinov'ev, *Ziyayushchie vysoty* (Lausanne, 1976), p. 303 (my translation). The passage is on p. 444 of Gordon Clough's translation: Alexander Zinoviev, *The Yawning Heights* (New York, 1978).

8. A man named V. Kotsishevsky was prosecuted in 1982 for privately producing and marketing cassette recordings; the three tapes he made before being arrested featured: "folklore of the 1920s"; a plagiarized Vysotsky concert recorded by an unknown singer; and a collection of "criminal lyrics." Kotsishevsky made these recordings using Odessa musicians and facilities, and then sold them to street dealers. Yu. Gavrilov, "'Fol'klor' iz podvorotni," *Sotsialisticheskaya industriya,* 16 April 1982, p. 3.

9. All the verse from the three volumes of *Syntax* is translated in *Russia's Underground Poets,* selected and translated by Keith Bosley (New York-Washington, 1969).

10. *Radio Liberty Register of Samizdat, February 1971,* no. R487 (Frankfurt/M, 1971), p. 62.

11. *Pesni russkikh bardov,* 4 vols. (Paris, 1977–78). This collection will be referred to in the text as *PRB,* with volume and page number.

12. One certain fact in this respect is that the songs by Vysotsky that appeared in *Metropol* (see below, Chapter 6) had been submitted for publication and rejected in the USSR. They all appear in *Pesni russkikh bardov.* Remarkably, one of them, "Dialog u televizora," was subsequently published in Vysotsky's posthumous collection *Nerv* (Moscow, 1981), pp. 131–33.

13. In *Pesni russkikh bardov* the song is attributed to Yury Kukin. I owe the correct attribution to Vladimir Frumkin (private communication).

14. In *Pesni russkikh bardov* the song is attributed to Valentin Glazanov; again, I owe my information to Vladimir Frumkin.

5. Bulat Okudzhava

1. See Karl-Dieter van Ackern, *Bulat Okudžava und die kritische Literatur über den Krieg* (Munich, 1976), pp. 25–36; anon., "Okudzhava, Bulat Shalvovich," in John Wakeman, ed., *World Authors, 1970–1975* (New York, 1980), pp. 600–602. The latter article contains a substantial autobiographical statement.

2. An account of how Okudzhava got this job is contained in Martin Dewhirst and Robert Farrell, eds., *The Soviet Censorship* (Metuchen, N.J., 1973), p. 39. According to some sources, he was fired from the job for publishing Yevtushenko's controversial poem about Soviet anti-Semitism, "Babii Yar."

3. Ruvim Rublev, "Mest' Bulata Okudzhavy," *Novoe russkoe slovo,* 10 May 1980, p. 2.

4. For an account of this publication, see Grigory Svirsky, *Na lobnom meste: Literatura nravstvennogo soprotivleniya (1946–1976gg.)* (London, 1979), pp. 217–34. It was translated en bloc into English: *Pages from Tarusa: New Voices in Russian Writing,* ed. Andrew Field (London, 1964); Okud-

zhava's story, the title translated as "Lots of Luck, Kid!" is on pp. 146–213. The story also appears, as "Good Luck, Schoolboy!" in *Half-Way to the Moon: New Writing From Russia,* ed. Patricia Blake and Max Hayward (London, 1964), pp. 149–81.

5. A. G. Dement'ev and M. M. Kuznetsov, eds., *Istoriya russkoi sovetskoi literatury v 4-kh tomakh, 1917–1945,* 2d ed., vol. 4, *1954–1965* (Moscow, 1971), pp. 116–17.

6. van Ackern, passim.

7. Bulat Okudzhava, "'Vse bylo ochen' ser'ezno...,'" *Teatr* 5 (1980): 21–23.

8. Bulat Okudzhava, *65 Songs/65 pesen.* Musical arrangements, selection, and editing by Vladimir Frumkin (Ann Arbor, 1980), p. 155. The translation is my own. The source of the quotation is not identified.

9. For an interesting attempt to relate Okudzhava's prose to his songs as part of an evolving concept that assigns positive values, particularly nobleness *(blagorodstvo),* to the period of Russian history preceding the Great Reforms of the 1860s, see Marran, "Bulat Okudzhava i ego vremya," *Kontinent* 36 (1983): 329–54. Okudzhava has recently made things even more explicit: "The *narodniki* don't interest me as an object of literary inquiry. I think they were filled to the brim with malice, simply boiling with hatred, and that's always bad. Toward the Decembrists, on the other hand, I feel profound affection: they weren't specialists in murder, they were dilettantes, people governed by noble aspirations, not by the thirst for revenge. They were unselfish, decent, and what they did arouses sympathy in me." Bulat Okudzhava, "'My vse rezhe zadumyvaemsya o chesti, chestnosti, chelovechskoi poryadochnosti ...' Interv'yu pol'skogo ezhenedel'nika s Bulatom Okudzhavoi," *Russkaya mysl',* 24 November 1983, p. 8. The implications of this statement with regard to subsequent periods of Russian history are, of course, unmistakable. In the same interview, Okudzhava made equally transparent remarks about his sympathy for Poland's plight.

10. For a list of the main translations to 1975, see the bibliography in van Ackern.

11. *Index on Censorship* 1, no. 3/4 (1972): 120–21.

12. Mikhailo Mikhailov, *Leto moskovskoe 1964* (Frankfurt/M, 1967), pp. 82–92.

13. *Sel'skaya molodezh'* 1 (1966): 33; on the consequences, see *The Soviet Censorship,* ed. Martin Dewhirst and Robert Farrell (Metuchen, N.J., 1973), p. 91.

14. Bulat Okudzhava, *65 Songs/65 pesen* (Ann Arbor, 1980).

15. The accusation of ephemerality is leveled in Gerald Abrahams's review of *65 Songs:* "Unpatriotic Ironies," *The Times Literary Supplement,* 20 February 1981.

16. The best analysis of Okudzhava's melodic gift is contained in V. Frumkin, "Pesnya i stikh," *Sovetskaya muzyka* 10 (1969): 21–27.

17. On the "Khrushchev thaw" see Chapter 2, Note 10 above.

18. This categorization was made in the earliest serious study of Okudzhava's poetry to be published outside the USSR: I. I. Mezhakov-Koryakin, "Osobennosti romantizma v poezii Bulata Okudzhavy," *Melbourne Slavonic Studies* 7 (1972): 58–83; the article concludes with a detailed bibliography of Okudzhava criticism to 1971.

19. References will be given in the text to Bulat Okudzhava, *65 pesen/65*

songs (Ann Arbor, 1980), abbreviated as *65,* with page reference. Translations are my own.

20. The song is also included in *Russkie sovetskie pesni, 1917–1977* (Moscow, 1977), p. 568.

21. Also in *Russkie sovetskie pesni,* p. 567, and *Shkola Okudzhavy,* pp. 19–21.

22. Particular attention is paid to this song in Frumkin, "Pesnya i stikh" (see Note 16 above), and there is a very thorough analysis of the text in A. K. Zholkovsky, "Rai, zamaskirovannyi pod dvor: Zametki o poeticheskom mire Bulata Okudzhavy," in *NRL. Almanach 1978,* edited by V. Len, G. Mayer, and R. Ziegler, pp. 101–120 (Salzburg, 1979).

23. Violetta Iverni, " 'Kogda dvigaetes', staraites' nikogo ne tolknut',' " *Kontinent* 24 (1980): 362.

24. Quoted in anon., "Poeziya, rozhdennaya muzykoi," *Sputnik* 3 (1978): 160. Neither the date of this statement nor the circumstances under which it was made are mentioned in this source.

25. *Literaturnaya Rossiya* 1 (1977): 5.

26. Bulat Okudzhava, *Pesni,* Melodiya S 60-13331-2.

27. "Novye pesni Bulata Okudzhavy," *Literaturnyi Kur'er,* 6 (1983); 3.

6. Vladimir Vysotsky

1. The most substantial source of information on Vysotsky's private life is Pavel Leonidov, *Vladimir Vysotsky i drugie* (New York, 1983), even though only about 40 of its over 250 generously illustrated pages are specifically about him. A considerable number of articles and memoirs, including the orations at Vysotsky's funeral, are collected in vol. 2 of Vladimir Vysotsky, *Pesni i stikhi* (vol. I, New York, 1981; vol. 2, 1983; a third volume is projected). The biographical information in the posthumous Soviet collection, *Nerv* (Moscow, 1981), is restricted to two small paragraphs (p. 233) simply listing the main events in Vysotsky's career.

2. Vladimir Vysotsky, "Pesnya—eto ochen' ser'ezno," *Literaturnaya Rossiya,* 27 December 1974, p. 14; reprinted in *Pesni i stikhi,* vol. 2, pp. 221–25.

3. Grigory Svirsky, *Na lobnom meste: Literatura nravstvennogo soprotivleniya (1946–1976gg.)* (London, 1979), p. 189.

4. Pavel Leonidov, "Do svidaniya, Volodya!" *Novoe russkoe slovo,* 14 August 1980, p. 3.

5. Svirsky, *Na lobnom meste,* p. 189.

6. Alexandr Gershkovich, "Poslednyaya rol' Vladimira Vysotskogo," *Obozrenie* 2 (1982): 38.

7. See Part I, Chapter 2 above.

8. K. Shcherbakov, " 'Gamlet.' Tragediya Shekspira na stsene teatra na Taganke," *Komsomol'skaya pravda,* 26 December 1971, p. 3; A. Bartoshevich, "Zhivaya plot' tragedii: 'Gamlet' v teatre na Taganke," *Sovetskaya kul'tura,* 14 December 1971, p. 2. Vysotsky was scheduled to play Hamlet on the day he died; a recording of the performance was substituted, and a full house at the Taganka heard it through.

9. Andrei Voznesensky, "Sud'ba poeta," *Druzhba narodov* 1 (1982): 136.

10. Yury Lyubimov, quoted in Leonidov, "Do svidaniya, Volodya!" p. 3.

11. On Vysotsky's work in radio, see A. Efros, "Osoboe chuvstvo," in *Pesni i stikhi,* vol. 2, pp. 277–80.

12. For details of Vysotsky's early films, see *Sovetskie khudozhestvennye fil'my: Annotirovannyi katalog,* vol. 4, *1958–1963* (Moscow, 1965), per index. Vysotsky once stated that his favorite film star was Charles Bronson (Leonidov, *Vladimir Vysotsky i drugie,* p. 222).

13. Anon., " 'Chetvertyi,' " *Literaturnaya gazeta,* 1 September 1972, p. 3.

14. Leonidov, "Do svidaniya, Volodya!" p. 3.

15. Voznesensky, "Sud'ba poeta," p. 136.

16. Andrei Voznesensky, "Rekviem optimisticheskii po Vladimiru Semenovu [sic], shoferu i gitaristu," in *Vzglyad* (Moscow, 1972), pp. 147–49. The poem includes the lines: "There he went, more popular than Pele,/Guitar on shoulder," and the epithet "Chansonnier of All the Russias" *(Shanson'e Vseya Rusi).*

17. Leonidov, "Do svidaniya, Volodya!" p. 3. Leonidov has also said that Vysotsky was a morphine addict *(Vladimir Vysotsky i drugie,* pp. 226–27).

18. Efim Etkind, "Sovetskie tabu," *Sintaksis* 9 (1981): 3–20.

19. Agathe Godard, "Marina Vlady: 'Je suis folle de Vladimir parce que je le vois un jour sur deux,' " *Paris Match,* 16 May 1980, pp. 20–21.

20. The Taganka did eventually succeed in performing in Paris, at the Palais de Chaillot in 1978.

21. Leonidov, "Do svidaniya, Volodya!" p. 3. Elsewhere, Leonidov describes a concert given by Vysotsky for the Foreign Faculty of Moscow University in 1959 or 1960, with the implication that it was his first concert appearance as a guitar poet *(Vladimir Vysotsky i drugie,* pp. 111–16).

22. Ruvim Rublev, "Vysotsky nachinalsya tak," *Novoe russkoe slovo,* 6 May 1980, p. 4. Vysotsky's poems, songs, and parodies written for student occasions are described by Roman Vil'dan, his contemporary at the Moscow Arts Theater studio, and by Vysotsky himself *(Pesni i stikhi,* vol. 2, pp. 281–86, 207–208 respectively).

23. "Vladimir Vysotsky o sebe i o svoikh pesnyakh," in *Pesni i stikhi,* vol. 2, p. 193.

24. Voznesensky, "Sud'ba poeta," p. 136.

25. G. Mushta and A. Bondaryuk, "O chem poet Vysotsky," *Sovetskaya Rossiya,* 9 June 1968, p. 3.

26. The song is Vizbor's "Conversation between Engineer Petukhov and an African Prince," which has the famous refrain: "And that's why we make those rockets,/And why we've dammed the Enisei,/And even in the sphere of ballet/ We're ahead of the entire planet." The words of the song have never, apparently, been published; they are not in *Pesni russkikh bardov.*

27. Anon., "Chastnym poryadkom," *Sovetskaya kul'tura,* 30 March 1973, p. 4. See also Hedrick Smith, "Underground in Moscow," *International Herald Tribune,* 6 April 1973, p. 5.

28. A total of seven records was released in the USSR during Vysotsky's lifetime, according to the information in *Nerv* (Moscow, 1981), p. 233. They include: *Pesni Vladimira Vysotskogo,* Melodiya (Leningrad), GOST 5289-73, M62-375/6 ("Skalolazka," "Moskva-Odessa," "Ona byla v Parizhe," and "Koni preveredlivye"); and another record with the same title, Melodiya GOST 5289-68, 33D-00032907 ("On ne vernulsya iz boya," "Pesnya o novom vremeni," "Bratskie mogily," and "Pesnya o zemle"). A set of songs from the film *Begstvo mistera MakKinli (Mr. McKinley's Escape)* was released as no. 11 in the journal *Krugozor* 4 (1976). Vysotsky appeared on several other Soviet records as a performer, notably O. G. Gerasimov's *Alice in Wonderland,* for which Vysotsky also wrote the songs.

29. Daniel Vernet, "Des écrivains soviétiques non-dissidents refusent la censure et éditent une revue dactylographiée," *Le Monde,* 25 January 1979, p. 3, the first substantial report of the affair in the West. Russian émigré comment was rather muted: Vladimir Maksimov, "Metropol' ili metropol," *Russkaya mysl',* 17 May 1979, p. 4.

30. *Metropol': Literaturnyi al'manakh* (Ann Arbor, 1979), p. 191. References will be given in the text to this edition, abbreviated as *M,* with page number, or to *Pesni russkikh bardov,* vols 1–4 (Paris, 1977), with volume and page number. *Metropol'* has been translated *en bloc* into English: *Metropol: Literary Almanac,* foreword by Kevin Klose (New York-London, 1982); Vysotsky's songs, translated by H. W. Tjalsma, appear on pp. 154–75.

31. The north-central Moscow street that from time immemorial had been called Karetnyi ryad (Carriage Row) was renamed in the Soviet period and became part of the Petrovka.

32. The most famous of them is, of course, Isakovsky's "Katyusha" (*Russkie sovetskie pesni, 1917–77,* Moscow, 1977, p. 89).

33. Some information concerning Vysotsky's highly placed patrons and protectors can be found in Leonidov, *Vladimir Vysotsky i drugie* (New York, 1983): they included at different times the KGB general Svetlichnyi, together with Ishkov, the Minister of Fisheries (pp. 85–86); and the Politburo member D. S. Polyansky (pp. 206–207). On Polyansky, see also Chapter 7, Note 12 below.

34. On Vysotsky's death and funeral, see anon., "Des Sängers Fluch," *Der Spiegel* 32 (1980): 121, 124; anon., "Kak khoronili Vysotskogo," *Novyi amerikanets,* 27 August/2 September 1980, p. 18; anon., "Mr. Vladimir Vysotsky" (obituary), *The Times,* 1 August 1980, p. 14; Aleksandr Gershkovich, "Poslednyaya rol' Vladimira Vysotskogo," *Obozrenie* 2 (1982): 37–39.

35. "Ballada o zemle," "Gornoe ekho," in *Den' poezii 1981* (Moscow, 1981), p. 118.

36. Vladimir Vysotsky, "'. . . kak korabli iz pesni,'" *Druzhba narodov* 1 (1982): 137–41.

37. Vladimir Vysotsky, *Nerv* (Moscow, 1981), produced in an edition of 55,000 copies, which is modest in the extreme by Soviet standards, and sold mainly in foreign currency stores and abroad. The book was compiled and supplied with an introduction by Robert Rozhdestvensky. It includes 132 texts. Of them, no less than 44 were commissioned for Soviet plays, films, or records. There are none of Vysotsky's early "underground" songs and very few of the personal lyrics; of the songs discussed in this chapter, "Dialogue" is the only one included in the book (see also Part II, Chapter 4, Note 12 above.) On the way the book distorts Vysotsky's texts, see Leonidov, *Vladimir Vysotsky i drugie,* pp. 232–42, and the very detailed review by Heinrich Pfandl, which also discusses the New York *Pesni i Stikhi: Wiener slawistischer Almanach* 9 (1982): 323–35. The publication of *Nerv* led to a flurry of discussion of Vysotsky's work in the Soviet press; the main articles are summarized in anon., "Vysotsky's Art: How Good? How Bad?" *The Current Digest of the Soviet Press* 34, no. 31 (1982): 10–12 (see Bibliography for further details).

38. A record of Vysotsky songs was published in the United States in 1973 on Voice Records; and a "cover" was published by Nuzgar Sharia the same year: see Petr Kursky, "Pesni Vysotskogo uzhe v Amerike," *Russkaya mysl',* 22 November 1973, pp. 6–7. By far the most extensive collection of Vysotsky songs published in his lifetime is contained in the four volumes of *Pesni russkikh bardov;* it was followed by several smaller publications, for example,

"Dve novye pesni," *Ekho* 3 (1978): 4–7. A record on French Polydor PR 350, with Vysotsky singing mainly in French, was released in 1978. A prose work of 1968, "Zhizn' bez sna," appeared in *Ekho* 2/10 (1980): 7–24; it is reprinted in *Pesni i stikhi,* vol. 2, pp. 123–50, and after it (pp. 150–92) appears another, previously unknown, piece of prose, "Roman o devochkakh"; it is unfinished and undated.

39. For example, Clifford D. May and Alfred Friendly, Jr., "Singing Out," *Newsweek,* 22 March 1976, p. 14; anon., "Protestlieder. Witze von Karl," *Der Spiegel* 13 (1971): 126, 129; V. Maslov, "Tri znakomstva s Vysotskim," *Posev* 1 (1971): 56–60. By far the best critical article on Vysotsky published in his lifetime was Petr Vail' and Aleksandr Genis, "Shampanskoe i politura," *Vremya i my* 36 (1978): 134–42; see also Ruvim Rublev, "Voennye pesni Vysotskogo," *Novoe russkoe slovo,* 8 May 1980, p. 4.

40. This double album, entitled *N'yu-iorkskii kontsert Vladimira Vysotskogo, 1979,* carries no label name, serial number, or liner notes; it contains twenty-seven songs.

41. Bulat Okudzhava, "Pamyati V. Vysotskogo," *Russkaya mysl',* 10 December 1981, p. 8. The text has not been published, apparently, in the USSR. It is reprinted, with the dedication "To Marina Polyakova" [i.e., Marina Vlady], in *Pesni i stikhi,* vol. 2, p. 275.

42. Public tributes in the USSR have been conspicuous by their absence. Tributes in the émigré press include Ruvim Rublev, "O Vladimire Vysotskom," *Novoe russkoe slovo,* 24 January 1981, p. 4; idem, "Spi, shanson'e Vseya Rusi," *Novoe russkoe slovo,* 29 July 1980, p. 3; Nataliya Rubenshtein, "Narodnyi artist," *22* 14 (1980): 193–202; Mikhail Morgulis, "Dusha Rossii," *Novoe russkoe slovo,* 24 July 1980, p. 4; statements by Aleksandr Glezer, Vasilii Aksenov, Vladimir Maksimov, and Misha Shemyakin, with some songs, were published in *Tret'ya volna* 10 (1980): 3–11, and the issue's cover bears a striking picture of Vysotsky; Vladimir Alloi, "Zhivoi," *Russkaya mysl',* 5 August 1982, p. 11.

43. "Trevoga. Razgovor s Vladimirom Maksimovym," *Kontinent* 25 (1980): 412.

44. Bulat Okudzhava, "'My vse rezhe zadumyvaemsya o chesti, chestnosti, chelovecheskoi poryadochnosti . . .' Interv'yu pol'skogo ezhenedel'nika s Bulatom Okudzhavoi," *Russkaya mysl',* 24 November 1983, p. 8.

45. Voznesensky, "Sud'ba poeta," p. 136.

46. "Pamyati Vladimira Vysotskogo," in Andrei Voznesensky, *Bezotchetnoe* (Moscow, 1981), p. 31.

47. Ibid., p. 32.

48. Anonymous editorial, *Ekho* 2/10 (1980): 6.

7. Aleksandr Galich

1. For a detailed account of Galich's life, see my introductory article, "Silence Is Connivance," in Alexander Galich, *Songs and Poems* (Ann Arbor, 1983) pp. 13–54. This book contains verse translations of almost all the songs discussed in this chapter.

2. *Teatral'naya entsiklopediya,* vol. 1, col. 1087 (Moscow, 1961).

3. *Kratkaya literaturnaya entsiklopediya,* vol. 2, col. 45 (Moscow, 1964).

4. Yury Krotkov, "A. Galich," *Novyi zhurnal* 130 (1978): 242.

5. Aleksandr Galich, *General'naya repetitsiya* (Frankfurt/M., 1974), p. 13.

6. Ibid., p. 141. Galich was introduced on this occasion by Vladimir Frum-

kin, who reports that the entire audience was on its feet, "except for the first few rows, where the highest-ranking bosses of Novosibirsk were sitting. They sat there, deafened by the ovation, apprehensively glancing round at the people who were on their feet, sinking their heads down into their shoulders. All this time the movie news team from Chelyabinsk had their camera rolling, making a film (that was never shown, it goes without saying)." Vladimir Frumkin, "Ne tol'ko slovo: vslushivayas' v Galicha," *Obozrenie* 8 (1984).

7. All references to the texts of Galich's songs will be to the most complete collection of them, *Kogda ya vernus': Polnoe sobranie stikhov i pesen* (Frank-furt/M., 1981), abbreviated as *KV*, with page number. This book should not be confused with the smaller *Kogda ya vernus': Stikhi i pesni, 1972–1977* (Frank-furt/M, 1977).

8. Efim Etkind, "'Chelovecheskaya komediya' Aleksandra Galicha," *Kontinent* 5 (1975): 405–26; Andrei Sinyavsky, "Teatr Galicha," *Vremya i my* 14 (1977): 142–50.

9. *Russkie sovetskie pesni, 1917–1977* (Moscow, 1977), pp. 556–57.

10. Raisa Orlova, "'My ne khuzhe Goratsiya,'" *Vremya i my* 51 (1980): 14.

11. Testimony to the significance of Galich's work may be found, for example, in Leonid Plyushch, *History's Carnival: A Dissident's Autobiography* (New York and London, 1977), and Natal'ya Gorbanevskaya, "Golosa Aleksandra Galicha," *Russkaya mysl'*, 16 December 1982, p. 9. Galich is the prototype of "the Singer" *(Pevets)* in Aleksandr Zinoviev's *The Yawning Heights* (*Ziyayushchie vysoty,* 1976).

12. Galich told Hedrick Smith he believed that the actual decision to move against him was taken because at the wedding party for Olga Polyanskaya (the daughter of Dimitry Polyansky, a member of the Politburo) Vysotsky sang some of his own songs—which Polyansky thought amusing—and then some of Galich's, which Polyansky thought less than amusing. He immediately telephoned Demichev, the Politburo's chief of cultural affairs, and ordered him to have Galich silenced. Hedrick Smith, *The Russians* (New York, 1976), pp. 415–16.

13. Gene Sosin, "Then Came Galich's Turn," *New York Times,* 12 February 1972.

14. Sonet Stereo SLP 1427.

15. "Beseda s Aleksandrom Galichem," Radio Liberty Research Department, *RS* 217/74, 17 July 1974, no. 2 of 4 unnumbered pages.

16. A. Galich, "Kul'tura i bor'ba za prava cheloveka," *Russkaya mysl'*, 24 November 1977, p. 7.

17. Ibid.

18. See anon., "Vysotsky's Art: How Good, How Bad?" *The Current Digest of the Soviet Press* 34, no. 31 (1982): 10–12, containing summaries of articles by five Soviet authors; see also the speeches and statements collected in Vladimir Vysotsky, *Pesni i stikhi,* vol. 2 (New York, 1983). It is a token of Okudzhava's political circumspection that after Vysotsky's death he has published a lament for the dead poet and publicly condemned the failure to publish Vysotsky's work during his lifetime; but Okudzhava has never, apparently, uttered a single word in public about Galich.

8. Guitar Poetry as Literary Genre

1. A succinct account of these features is given in Mark W. Booth, *The Experience of Songs* (New Haven and London, 1981), pp. 5–14.

2. Booth, p. 23.

3. G. S. Smith, "The Metrical Repertoire of Russian Guitar Poetry," *International Journal of Slavic Linguistics and Poetics* (in press).

4. A useful introduction to the "unprintable" area is Felix Dreisin and Tom Priestley, "A Systematic Approach to Russian Obscene Language," *Russian Linguistics* 6 (1982): 233–49. Apart from some work on Solzhenitsyn, though, the stylistics of modern Russian dissident literature remain unexplored.

5. Nataliya Rubenshtein, "Vyklyuchite magnitofon—pogovorim o poete," *Vremya i my* 2 (1975): 171. The quatrain means something like: "He's an s.o.b., one of those roving-eyed drivers,/He's a speculator, a profiteer, and a tightwad,/It's a state-owned car he does business with, and he really goes for it,/Sometimes takes money, sometimes does it for a quick lay." This translation does not do justice to the richness of the original. For example, the word *kalymshchik* derives from *kalym,* the Tartar word for "bride-money"; the word translated as "state-owned" is *torgovaya [mashina],* "a car belonging to a state organization whose official name ends with the syllable *-torg,*" e.g., *Voentorg* "Army and Navy Stores." No two native informants have ever given the author the same explanation of all the major elements in this quatrain.

6. Aleksandr Galich, "Pesnya, zhizn', bor'ba," *Posev* 8 (1974): 13.

7. W. H. Auden, "Introduction," in *W. H. Auden's Oxford Book of Light Verse* (Oxford-New York-Toronto-Melbourne, 1979), p. ix.

8. Kingsley Amis, "Introduction," in *The New Oxford Book of Light Verse* (Oxford-London-New York, 1978), p. viii.

9. Auden, p. x.

10. Amis, p. vii.

11. Of course, there are many exceptions to this generalization and those that have preceded it. Russia had an absurdist movement in the 1920s and early 1930s, notably the now rather overrated OBERIU group in Leningrad; and there has been a small but persistent trickle of successors in this tradition down to the present day. And on the other hand, the postmodernist movement in anglophone poetry, in which Auden was the most significant pioneer, tended to favor stricter verse forms, more accessible semantics, and a more colloquial diction (which did indeed lead to accusations that Auden's later poetry is "light"). The work of Amis, Davie, Fuller, Larkin, and in the next generation Harrison continues this tendency.

12. Auden, p. xx.

Conclusions

1. On the rise of rock in the USSR, see S. Frederick Starr, "The Rock Inundation, 1968–1980," in his *Red and Hot: The Fate of Jazz in the Soviet Union, 1917–1980* (New York and Oxford, 1983), pp. 289–315.

Bibliography

Abraham, Gerald. "Unpatriotic Ironies." *The Times Literary Supplement,* 20 February 1981. (Review of Bulat Okudzhava, *65 Songs/65 pesen.*)

Ackern, Karl-Dieter van. *Bulat Okudžava und die kritische Literatur über den Krieg.* Arbeiten und Texte zur Slavistik, no. 11. Munich: Sagner, 1976.

Aczel, T., and Tikos, L. "Introduction: Notes from Underground." In *Poetry from the Russian Underground,* pp. 1–19. New York-Evanston-San Francisco-London: Harper and Row, 1973.

Agursky, Mikhail. "Eshche raz ob Aleksandre Galiche" [Once more about Aleksandr Galich]. *Nasha strana,* 28 May 1978, p. 6.

Aksenov, Vasily. *Zhal', chto vas ne bylo s nami* [A pity you weren't with us]. Moscow: Sovetskii pisatel', 1969.

Aleshin, Yu. "Vopreki interesam razryadki: Radio-diversanty imperializma" [Counter to the interests of detente: imperialism's radio-saboteurs; an attack on the Radio Liberty broadcasting station]. *Pravda,* 13 January 1976, p. 4.

Aleshkovsky, Yuzef. "Pesni" [Songs]. *Kontinent* 21 (1979), pp. 146–53.

Allen, Misha. "Ballads from the Underground." *Problems of Communism* (November-December 1970), pp. 27–30.

———. "Russia's Dissident Balladeers." *East Europe* 20, no. 11 (1971); 26–31.

Alloi, V. "Zhivoi: Pamyati Vladimira Vysotskogo" [The man who is alive: in memory of Vladimir Vysotsky]. *Russkaya mysl',* 5 August 1982, p. 11.

Andreev, Yury. "Chto poyut?" [What's that they're singing?]. *Oktyabr'* 1 (1965): 182–92. Reprinted in *Literatura i sovremennost', 6: Stat'i o literature 1964–1965 godov.* Moscow, 1965, pp. 257–79.

Andreeva, D. "Rossii serdtse ne zabudet . . . O tvorchestve Aleksandra Galicha" [The heart of Russia will not forget . . . on the creative work of Aleksandr Galich]. *Grani* 33, no. 109 (1978); 215–28.

Anon. "Narodnye sovetskie pesni" [Folk Soviet songs]. *Student* 2/3 (1964): 81–84.

———. "Narodnye sovetskie pesni" [Folk Soviet songs]. *Student* 4 (1964): 46–48.

———. "Pesni-stikhi iz SSSR" [Song-poems from the USSR]. *Novyi zhurnal* 84 (1966): 143–47.

———. "Sovetskii fol'klor" [Soviet folklore]. *Student* 5/8 (1967): 127–31.

———. [22 song texts]. *Student* 5/8 (1967): 134–53.

———. "'Samodeyatel'nye pesni v Sov.soyuze" ["Self-made" songs in the Soviet Union]. *Russkaya mysl',* 22 May 1969, p. 3.

———. "Protestlieder: Witze von Karl" *Der Spiegel,* vol. 13, 22 March 1971, pp. 126, 129.

252 / Bibliography

――――. " 'Chetvertyi' " ["The fourth man"; the film featuring Vysotsky]. *Literaturnaya gazeta*, 1 September 1972, p. 3.

――――. "Po povodu publikatsii proizvedenii A. Galicha" [Concerning the publication of A. Galich's works; a warning that Galich owns copyright outside the USSR]. *Vozrozhdenie* 239 (1972): 159.

――――. "Chastnym poryadkom" [On a private basis; on Vysotsky's concerts]. *Sovetskaya kul'tura*, 30 March 1973, p. 4.

――――. "Galich Unsilenced." *Soviet Analyst* 3, no. 4 (1974): 6–8.

――――. "Radioizdat" [Radio publishing; an account of illegal broadcasts in the USSR]. *Russkaya mysl'*, 6 February 1975, p. 5.

――――. "Sovetskaya pesnya" [The Soviet song]. *Pravda* 255(20859), 12 September 1975, p. 1.

――――. "Poeziya, rozhdennaya muzykoi" [Poetry born of music]. *Sputnik* 3 (1978): 157–73.

――――. "Des Sängers Fluch." *Der Spiegel* 32 (1980): 121, 124. (On Vysotsky's funeral.)

――――. "Kak khoronili Vyostskogo" [How they buried Vysotsky]. *Novyi amerikanets*, 27 August/2 September 1980, p. 18.

――――. "Mr Vladimir Vysotsky." *The Times*, 1 August 1980, p. 14.

――――. "Okudzhava, Bulat Shalvovich." In *World Authors, 1970–1975*, edited by John Wakeman, pp. 600–602. New York: Wilson.

――――. "Vysotsky's Art: How Good? How Bad?" *The Current Digest of the Soviet Press* 34, no. 31 (1982): 10–12. (Summaries of Soviet articles and letters by Kireeva, Kunyaev, Tolstykh, Garnik, Lyushy; for details, see under these authors.)

B. A. "Aleksandr Galich v Zheneve" [Aleksandr Galich in Geneva]. *Russkaya mysl'*, 19 September 1974, p. 9.

Bartoshevich, A. "Zhivaya plot' tragedii: 'Gamlet' v teatre na Taganke" [The living flesh of tragedy: *Hamlet* at the Taganka Theater]. *Sovetskaya kul'tura*, 14 December 1971, p. 2.

Bawdy Barrack-Room Ballads, edited by Hugh de Witt. London: Tandem Books, 1970.

Bernst, M. "Opal'nyi poet" [Poet in disfavor; on Galich]. *Nasha strana*, 23 September 1975, 4.

Betaki, Vasily. "Gitara sudit" [Trial by guitar; on Galich]. *Russkaya mysl'*, 15 August 1974, pp. 4–5.

――――. "Repetitsiya, dlinoi v polzhizni" [A rehearsal that lasted half a lifetime; on Galich's *General'naya repetitsiya*]. *Posev* 1 (1975): 58–61.

――――. Biermann, Wolf. *Poems and Ballads.* Translated by Steve Gooch. London: Pluto Press, 1978.

Blatnaya lira: Sbornik tyuremnykh i lagernykh pesen [The bent lyre: a collection of prison and camp songs]. Edited by Yakov Vaiskopf. Jerusalem: privately printed, 1981.

The Blue Lagoon Anthology of Modern Russian Poetry. Vol. 1, edited by Konstantin K. Kuz'minsky and Grigory L. Kovalev. Newtonville, Mass.: Oriental Research Partners, 1980.

Booth, Mark W. *The Experience of Songs.* New Haven and London: Yale University Press, 1981.

Bragina, A. A. *Neologizmy v russkom yazyke: Posobie dlya studentov i uchitelei* [Neologisms in Russian: a handbook for students and teachers]. Moscow: Prosveshchenie, 1973.

Breitbart, Ekaterina. " 'Ne zovi menya . . . Ne zovi—ya i tak pridu!' " [" 'Don't call me . . . Don't call me, I'll come anyway!' "; on Galich]. *Posev* 2 (1978): 4–6.

Brown, Deming. *Soviet Russian Literature since Stalin*. Cambridge: Cambridge University Press, 1978. ("Balladeers," pp. 365–67; "Okudzhava," pp. 98–105.)

Brown, Edward J. *Russian Literature since the Revolution*. Revised and enlarged edition. Cambridge, Mass.: Harvard University Press, 1982.

Bukovsky, Vladimir. *To Build a Castle*. Translated by Michael Scammell. New York: Viking, 1977.

Canzoni/Poesie del dissenso. Tre testimonianze: Wolf Biermann, Aleksandr Galič, Karel Kryl. Venice: Marsilio, 1977.

Canzoni russe di protesta. Edited by Pietro Zveteremich. Milan: Garzanti, 1972.

Carlisle, Olga. *Poets on Street Corners*. New York: Random House, 1968.

Chalidze, Valery. *Ugolovnaya Rossiya* [Criminal Russia]. New York: Khronika, 1977.

Clark, Katerina. *The Soviet Novel: History as Ritual*. Chicago and London: University of Chicago Press, 1981.

Daniel, Yuly [Nikolai Arzhak]. *This Is Moscow Speaking*. London: Collins-Harvill, 1968.

Daniel'son, R. " 'I kazhdyi priyut, kak khram. . .' " ["And every sanctuary is like a temple. . ."; on Galich in Israel]. *Golem* (Studencheskoe ob"edinenie Ierusalim), n.d. [1976?], pp. 17–22.

Delone, Vadim. "Odinnatsat' let tomu nazad" [Eleven years ago; on the "Concert of Bards" in Akademgorodok]. *Ekho* 2–3 (1979): 180–82.

Dement'ev, A. G., and Kuznetsov, M. M. "Predislovie." In *Istoriya russkoi sovetskoi literatury v 4-kh tomakh, 1917–1945*, 2d ed., vol. 4, *1954–65* [sic]. Moscow: Nauka, 1971.

Dewhirst, Martin. "Soviet Russian Literature and Literary Policy." In *The Soviet Union since the Fall of Khrushchev*, edited by Archie Brown and Michael Kaser, 2d ed., pp. 181–95. London: Macmillan, 1978.

Dissonant Voices in Soviet Literature. Edited by Patricia Blake and Max Hayward. New York: Pantheon Books, 1964.

Dobrovol'sky, B. M. "Sovremennye bytovye pesni gorodskoi molodezhi" [The contemporary everyday-life songs of urban youth]. In *Fol'klor i khudozhestvennaya samodeyatel'nost'*, edited by N. V. Novikov, pp. 176–200. Leningrad: Nauka, 1968.

Donatov, L. "Poet Galich, poet Galich" [It's Galich singing, Galich singing]. *Posev* 11 (1969): 52–54.

Dreisin, Felix, and Priestley, Tom. "A Systematic Approach to Russian Obscene Language." *Russian Linguistics* 6 (1982): 233–49.

Dunham, Vera. *In Stalin's Time: Middle-Class Values in Soviet Fiction*. Cambridge-London-New York-Melbourne: Cambridge University Press, 1976.

———. See also Sandomirsky, Vera.

Etkind, Efim. " 'Chelovecheskaya komediya' Aleksandra Galicha" [Aleksandr Galich's *Comédie humaine*] *Kontinent* 5 (1975): 405–26.

———. "Une 'Comédie humaine' en chansons." *Le Monde*, 17 December 1977, p. 42. (On Galich.)

———. "Leonid Brezhnek kak pisatel' " [Leonid Brezhnev as a writer]. *Vremya i my* 30 (1978): 126–41.

———. "Sovetskie tabu" [Soviet taboos]. *Sintaksis* 9 (1981): 3–20.

Frank, Peter. "Poem-Songs: A Soviet Reaction to Pop." *London Magazine* 7, no. 7 (1967): 64–69.

Frolov, V. *Zhanry sovetskoi dramaturgii* [*The genres of Soviet drama*; mentions Galich's early plays]. Moscow: Sovetskii pisatel', 1957.

Frumkin, Vladimir. "Pesnya i stikh" [Song and verse]. *Sovetskaya muzyka* 10 (1969): 21–27.

———. "O nekotorykh funktsiyakh muzyki v sinteticheskikh iskusstvakh" [Some functions of music in the synthetic arts]. In *Papers in Slavic Philology*, vol. 1. *In Honor of James Ferrell*, edited by Benjamin A. Stolz, pp. 77–99. Ann Arbor: University of Michigan Press, 1977.

———. "Tekhnologiya ubezhdeniya: zametki o politicheskoi pesne" [The technology of persuasion: notes on the political song]. *Obozrenie* 5 (1983): 17–20 and 6 (1983): 23–26.

———. "Ne tol'ko slovo: vslushivayas' v Galicha" [Not just the word: listening carefully to Galich]. *Obozrenie* 8 (1984).

Galich, Aleksandr. "Parakhod zovut 'Orlenok'." In *Sovremennaya dramaturgiya* 6 (1958): 131–98.

———. [Four songs from *Sfinksy*]. *Grani* 59 (1965): 24–28.

———. *Pesni* [Songs]. Frankfurt/M: Posev, 1969.

———. *Poema Rosii: Pesni o dukhovnoi svobode. Ironicheskie pesni* [Poem of Russia: songs of spiritual freedom. Ironic songs; not attributed to Galich on the title page]. Paris: Ikhthnos, 1971.

———. *Pokolenie obrechennykh.* [Generation of the doomed; the first authorized collection of Galich's songs]. Frankfurt/M: Posev, 1972.

———. [Poems]. *Grani* 83 (1972): 4–13.

———. "In Memory of Pasternak." Translated by Patrick Dixon. *Russian Literature Triquarterly* 6 (1973): 99–100. Reprinted in *The Ardis Anthology of Recent Russian Literature,* edited by Carl and Ellendea Proffer, pp. 99–100. Ann Arbor: Ardis, 1975.

———. *General'naya repetitsiya* [The dress rehearsal]. Frankfurt/M: Posev, 1974.

———. "Beseda s Aleksandrom Galichem" [A conversation with Aleksandr Galich; with O. A. Krasovsky]. Radio Liberty Research Department, *RS* 217/74, 17 July 1974, 4 unnumbered pages.

———. "Pesnya, zhizn', bor'ba: Interv'yu Aleksandra Galicha spetsial'nym korrespondentam *Poseva* G. Raru, A. Yugovu" [Song, life, struggle: Alexander Galich interviewed by G. Rahr and A. Yugov, special correspondents for *Posev*]. *Posev* 8 (1974): 12–17.

———. "Aleksandr Galich v 'Russkoi mysli' " [Aleksandr Galich at *Russkaya mysl'*]. *Russkaya mysl'*, 7 November 1974, p. 3.

———. "Kul'tura i bor'ba za prava cheloveka: Beseda s A. Galichem" [Culture and the struggle for human rights: a conversation with A. Galich; with K. Pomerantsev]. *Russkaya mysl'*, 24 November 1977, p. 7.

———. *Kogda ya vernus': Stikhi i pesni 1972–1977* [When I return: poems and songs 1972–1977]. Frankfurt/M: Posev, 1977.

———. "Bloshinyi rynok" [The flea market; an unfinished novel]. *Vremya i my* 24 (1977): 5–54 and 25 (1978): 5–54 [sic].

———. *Kogda ya vernus': Polnoe sobranie stikhov i pesen* [When I return: complete collection of poetry and songs]. Frankfurt/M: Posev, 1981.

————. *Songs and Poems.* Translated and with an introduction by G. S. Smith. Ann Arbor: Ardis, 1983.

Gavrilov, Yu. " 'Fol'klor' iz podvorotni" ["Folklore" from under the gate; an account of illegal dealing in cassette recordings]. *Sotsialisticheskaya industriya,* 16 April 1982, p. 3.

Garnik, A. "Pevets na vse vkusy" [A singer for all tastes; on Vysotsky]. *Literaturnaya gazeta,* 7 July 1982, p. 3.

Geller, Mikhail. *Kontsentratsionnyi mir i sovetskaya literatura* [The concentration camp world and Soviet literature]. London: Overseas Publications Interchange Ltd., 1974.

Genina, L. "Otvet pered budushchim" [A response with the future in mind; a reply to Vladimir Frumkin's 1969 article]. *Sovetskaya muzyka* 10 (1969): 28–34.

Gendlin, Leonard. "Poetu sapogami sdavili gorlo: K godovshchine so dnya smerti Vladimira Vysotskogo" [They crushed the poet's gullet with their jackboots: the first anniversary of Vladimir Vysotsky's death]. *Novyi amerikanets,* 10/16 August 1982, pp. 22–25.

Gershkovich, Aleksandr. "Poslednyaya rol' Vladimira Vysotskogo" [Vladimir Vysotsky's last part; by an eyewitness to his funeral who subsequently emigrated]. *Obozrenie* 2 (1982): 37–39.

Gershtein, Larisa. "Razgovor s Bulatom Okudzhavoi" [A conversation with Bulat Okudzhava; conducted in Paris by the Israeli singer]. *Dvadtsat' dva* 5, no. 25 (1982): 191–97.

Gibian, George. *Interval of Freedom: Soviet Literature during the Thaw, 1954–1957.* Minneapolis: University of Minnesota Press, 1960.

Gladilin, Anatoly. *The Making and Unmaking of a Soviet Writer.* Translated by David Lapeza. Ann Arbor: Ardis, 1979.

Glenny, Michael. "The Soviet Theatre." In *An Introduction to Russian Language and Literature,* edited by Robert Auty and Dimitri Obolensky, pp. 271–83. *Companion to Russian Studies,* no. 2. Cambridge: Cambridge University Press, 1977.

Godard, Agathe. "Marina Vlady: 'Je suis folle de Vladimir parce que je le vois un jour sur deux'." *Paris Match,* 16 May 1980, pp. 20–21.

Gorbanevskaya, Natal'ya. "Golosa Aleksandra Galicha" [The voices of Aleksandr Galich]. *Russkaya mysl',* 16 December 1982, p. 9.

Gorbovsky, Gleb. "Pesni Gleba Gorbovskogo" [The songs of Gleb Gorbovsky]. *Ekho* 3 (1978): 50–55.

Grigor'ev, S., and Shubin, F. "Eto sluchilos' na 'Svobode' " [It happened at [Radio] Liberty; a denunciation of the activities of former Soviet citizens]. *Nedelya,* 18(944), 17–23 April 1978, pp. 6–7.

Gudoshnikov, Ya. I. *Ocherki istorii russkoi literaturnoi pesni XVIII–XIX vv.* [Essays on the history of the Russian literary song]. Voronezh, 1972.

Half-Way to the Moon: New Writing from Russia. Edited by Patricia Blake and Max Hayward. London: Weidenfeld and Nicholson, 1964.

Heymann, Daniele. "V. Vissotsky: Le troubadour venu de l'Est." *L'Exprès* 1344 (11/17 April 1978): 21.

Hingley, Ronald. *Russian Writers and Soviet Society, 1917–1978.* London: Weidenfeld and Nicholson, 1978.

Holthusen, Johannes. *Russische Gegenwartsliteratur,* vol. 2. Berne-Munich, 1968. ("Okudzhava," pp. 128–32).

Hosking, Geoffrey. *Beyond Socialist Realism: Soviet Fiction since Ivan Denisovich.* London-Toronto-Sydney-New York: Paul Elek/Granada, 1980.

Ignat'ev, I. "Ofitsial'naya sovetskaya pesnya protiv pesennogo samizdata" [The official Soviet song versus *samizdat* songs]. *Radio Liberty Information Bulletin,* 21(2602), 2 June 1971, 5 unnumbered pages.

Isakovsky, M. *O poetakh, o stikhakh, o pesnyakh* [Poets, poems, and songs; by the venerable Soviet songwriter] 2d ed. Moscow: Sovremennik, 1972.

Iverni, Violetta. "Chas miloserdiya (Razmyshleniya o proze Bulata Okudzhavy)" [The hour of mercy (thoughts on Bulat Okudzhava's prose)]. *Kontinent* 12 (1977): 353–64.

———. " 'Kogda dvigaetes', staraites' nikogo ne tolknut' ' " ["When you move, try not to bump into anyone"; on Okudzhava's prose and poetry]. *Kontinent* 24 (1980): 358–63.

———. "Opera nishchikh Aleksandra Galicha" [Aleksandr Galich's beggars' opera]. *Russkaya mysl',* 16 December 1982, p. 8.

James, C. Vaughan. *Soviet Socialist Realism: Origins and Theory.* London: Macmillan, 1973.

Johnson, Priscilla. *Khrushchev and the Arts: The Politics of Soviet Culture, 1962–1964.* Cambridge, Mass.: M.I.T. Press, 1965.

Karabchievsky, Yu. "I vokhrovtsy i zeki: Zametki o pesnyakh Aleksandra Galicha" [Both guards and convicts: notes on the songs of Aleksandr Galich]. *Vremya i my* 65 (1982): 144–59.

Karlinsky, Simon. *Marina Cvetaeva: Her Life and Art.* Berkeley and Los Angeles: California University Press, 1966.

Kassis, V. B.; Kolosov, L. S.; Mikhailov, M. A.; and Pilyatskin, B. A. *Poimany s polichnym* [Caught red-handed; allegations of anti-Soviet activities by ex-Soviet citizens, including Galich]. Moscow: Izvestiya, 1976.

———. *Sovershenno sekretno* [Top Secret; further allegations by the same team]. Moscow: Izvestiya, 1977.

Kazack, Wolfgang. *Lexikon der russischen Literatur ab 1917.* Stuttgart: Alfred Kroner, 1976.

Khandzinsky, N. "Blatnaya poeziya" [Underworld poetry]. *Sibirskaya zhivaya starina* 1 (1926): 41–83.

Kireeva, A. "Ostanovit'sya, oglyanut'sya" [Stop and look around; on Vysotsky]. *Yunost'* 3 (1982): 97–100.

K. K. "Blatnye lagernye pesni" [Underworld camp songs]. *Novyi zhurnal* 116 (1974): 190–96.

Kopelev, Lev. "Pamyati Aleksandra Galicha" [In memory of Aleksandr Galich]. *Kontinent* 16 (1978): 334–43.

Kratkaya literaturnaya entsiklopediya. Edited by A. A. Surkov. 9 vols. Moscow: Sovetskaya entsiklopediya, 1962–78.

Krotkov, Yury. "A. Galich." *Novyi zhurnal* 130 (1978): 242–45.

Ktorova, Alla. "Yurin pereulok" [Yura's lane; a short story]. *Grani* 53 (1963): 33–43.

Kunyaev, Stanislas. "Ot velikogo do smeshnogo" [From the sublime to the ridiculous; discusses Vysotsky]. *Literaturnaya gazeta,* 9 June 1982, p. 3.

Kursky, Petr. "Pesni Vysotskogo uzhe v Amerike" [Vysotsky's songs are already in America]. *Russkaya mysl',* 22 November 1973, pp. 6–7.

Lamont, Rosette C. "Horace's Heirs: Beyond Censorship in the Secret Songs of *Magnitizdat.*" *World Literature Today,* Spring 1979, pp. 220–26.

Leonidov, Pavel. "Do svidaniya, Volodya!" [Au revoir, Volodya!—on the death of Vysotsky]. *Novoe russkoe slovo,* 14 August 1980, p. 3.

———. *Vladimir Vysotsky i drugie.* New York: Russica, 1983.

Larin, A. "Gitara v Rossii (Obzor literatury)" [The guitar in Russia (a survey of the literature)]. In *Al'manakh bibliofila* 11 (1981): 142–53.

Lert, Raisa. "Podstupy k 'Ziyayushchim vysotam': Opyt nenauchnogo analiza" [The foothills of *The Yawning Heights:* an attempt at an unscholarly analysis]. *Grani* 108 (1978): 279–91.

Lyusy, A. "Pevets dlya vsekh!" [A singer for everyone!—on Vysotsky]. *Literaturnaya gazeta,* 7 July 1982, p. 3.

Maksimov, D. E. *Poeziya V. Bryusova* [The poetry of V. Bryusov]. Leningrad, 1940.

Maksimov, Vladimir. "Do svidaniya, Sasha" [Au revoir, Sasha; on the death of Galich]. *Russkaya mysl',* 29 December 1977, p. 2.

———. *Farewell from Nowhere.* Translated by Michael Glenny. Garden City, N.Y.: Doubleday, 1978.

———. "Metropol' ili metropol'" [Metropolis or *Metropol';* mentions Vysotsky's songs]. *Russkaya mysl',* 17 May 1979, p. 4.

———. "Trevoga: razgovor s Vladimirom Maksimovym" [Alarm: a conversation with Vladimir Maksimov; mentions Vysotsky]. *Kontinent* 25 (1980): 389–419.

Mal'tsev, Yury. *Vol'naya russkaya literatura, 1955–1975* [Independent Russian literature, 1955–1975; includes a chapter on guitar poetry]. Frankfurt/M: Posev, 1976.

Malyshev, Aleksandr. [Untitled remarks on *magnitizdat*], *Studies on the Soviet Union,* n.s. 8, no. 3 (1969): 73–77.

Mandel'shtam, Nadezhda. *Vospominaniya.* New York: Chekhov Press, 1970. Translation: *Hope against Hope: A Memoir.* New York: Atheneum, 1970.

Markov, Vladimir. *The Longer Poems of Velemir Khlebnikov.* Berkeley and Los Angeles: California University Press, 1962.

Marran. "Bulat Okudzhava i ego vremya" [Bulat Okudzhava and his time]. *Kontinent* 36 (1983): 329–54.

Maslov, V. "Tri znakomstva s Vysotskim" [Three acquaintanceships with Vysotsky]. *Posev* 1 (1971): 56–60.

Massie, Suzanne. *The Living Mirror: Five Young Poets from Leningrad.* Garden City, N.Y.: Doubleday, 1972.

May, Clifford D., and Friendly, Alfred Jr. "Singing Out." *Newsweek,* 22 March 1976, p. 14. (On Vysotsky.)

McLean, Hugh, and Vickery, Walter. "Introduction." In *The Year of Protest, 1956: An Anthology of Soviet Literary Materials,* pp. 3–34. New York: Vintage Books, 1961.

Metropol': Literaturnyi al'manakh. Ann Arbor: Ardis, 1979. Translation: *Metropol: Literary Almanac.* Foreword by Kevin Klose. New York-London: W. W. Norton, 1982.

Mezhakov-Koryakin, I. I. "Osobennosti romantizma v poezii Bulata Okudzhavy" [Specifics of romanticism in the poetry of Bulat Okudzhava]. *Melbourne Slavonic Studies* 7 (1972): 58–83.

Mikhailov, Mikhailo. *Leto moskovskoe 1964.* Frankfurt/M: Posev, 1967. Translation: *Moscow Summer.* London: Sidgwick and Jackson, 1966 [sic].

Mikhalevsky, Pavel. "Russkaya pesnya" [The Russian song]. *Russkaya mysl',* 25 September 1975, p. 2.

Modern Russian Poetry: An Anthology with Verse Translations. Edited and with an introduction by Vladimir Markov and Merrill Sparks. London: MacGibbon and Kee, 1966.

Morgulis, Mikhail. "Dusha Rossii" [The soul of Russia; on Vysotsky] *Novoe russkoe slovo,* 24 July 1980, p. 4.

Morley, Michael. "Hard Times for Poetry. On the Songs and Poems of Wolf Biermann." *Index on Censorship* 2, no. 2 (1973): 23–36.

Mushta, G., and Bondaryuk, A. "O chem poet Vysotsky" [What Vysotsky is singing about]. *Sovetskaya Rossiya,* 9 June 1968, p. 3.

Naumov, Vladimir. "Tot samyi Galich, kotoryi poet pesenki" [That Galich who sings the songs]. *Russkaya mysl',* 16 November 1972, p. 5.

Neizvestny, Ernst. "Katakombnaya kul'tura i ofitsial'noe iskusstvo" [Catacomb culture and official art]. *Posev* 11 (1979): 37–38.

Nekrasov, Viktor. "Sasha Galich." *Ekho* 1 (1978): 81–82.

———. "Tvardovsky." *Novoe russkoe slovo,* 6 December 1981, p. 5.

The New Oxford Book of Light Verse. Chosen and edited by Kingsley Amis. Oxford-London-New York: Oxford University Press, 1978.

The New Russian Poets, 1953–1966: An Anthology. Selected, edited, and translated by George Reavey. London: Calder and Boyars, 1966. (Ten poems by Okudzhava, including one song, pp. 145–65.)

Ocherki istorii russkoi sovetskoi dramaturgii. Edited by S. V. Vladimirov and G. A. Lapkina. 3 vols. Leningrad-Moscow: Nauka, 1966–68.

Oinas, Felix J. "The Political Uses and Themes of Folklore in the Soviet Union." In *Folklore, Nationalism, and Politics,* edited by Felix J. Oinas, pp. 77–95. Indiana University Folklore Institute Monograph Series, vol. 30. Columbus, Ohio: Slavica, 1978.

Okudzhava, Bulat. *Veselyi barabanshchik: Kniga stikhov* [The merry drummer: a book of poems]. Moscow: Sovetskii pisatel', 1964.

———. "Bud' zdorov, shkolyar!" In *Tarusskie stranitsy: Literaturnoillyustrirovannyi sbornik,* edited by K. Paustovsky, pp. 50–75. Kaluga: Kaluzhskoe knizhnoe izdatel'stvo, 1961. Translations: "Lots of Luck, Kid!" In *Pages from Tarusa: New Voices in Russian Writing,* edited by Andrew Field, pp. 146–213. London: Chapman and Hall, 1964; "Good Luck, Schoolboy!" In *Half-Way to the Moon: New Writing from Russia,* edited by Patricia Blake and Max Hayward, pp. 149–81. London: Weidenfeld and Nicholson, 1964; "Good-bye, Schoolboy!" Translated by Helen Colaclides. In *Fifty Years of Russian Prose: From Pasternak to Solzhenitsyn,* edited by Krystyna Pomorska, vol. 2, pp. 171–244. Cambridge, Mass. and London: M.I.T. Press, 1971.

———. [Eight songs]. *Sel'skaya molodezh'* 1 (1966): 32–33.

———. *Mart velikodushnyi: Stikhi i poemy* [Magnanimous month of March: short and long poems]. Moscow: Sovetskii pisatel', 1967.

———. "Vremya idet" [Time goes on; an autobiographical statement]. *Voprosy literatury* 8 (1967): 64–66.

———. *Proza i poeziya* [Prose and poetry; the fundamental edition of Okudzhava's songs until Vladimir Frumkin's of 1980]. 2 vols. Frankfurt/M: Posev, 1968 and subsequent editions.

———. *Arbat, moi Arbat* [Arbat, my Arbat; a collection of poems]. Moscow: Sovetskii pisatel', 1976.

———. "Pishu istoricheskii roman" [I'm writing a historical novel; a song]. *Literaturnaya Rossiya* 1 (1977): 5.

————. *65 pesen/65 Songs*. Musical arrangements, selection, and editing by Vladimir Frumkin. English translations by Eve Shapiro. Ann Arbor: Ardis, 1980. 2d edition, revised, 1982.

————. " 'Vse bylo ochen' ser'ezno . . .' " ["Everything was very serious . . ."; a discussion of the war theme in Okudzhava's life and writing]. *Teatr* 5 (1980): 21–23.

————. [Seven poems]. *Russkaya mysl'*, 10 December 1981, pp. 8–9. (Includes "Pamyati V. Vysotskogo" [In memory of V. Vysotsky]; the remainder are from the 1960s, none, apparently, published in the USSR.)

————. "Pamyati Brassensa" [In memory of Brassens; reprinted from *Literaturnaya gazeta*, no details given]. *Novoe russkoe slovo*, 22 November 1981, p. 5.

————. "Novye pesni Bulata Okudzhavy" [New songs by Bulat Okudzhava; three texts]. *Literaturnyi kur'er* 6 (1983): 3.

————. " 'My vse rezhe zadumyvaemsya o chesti, chestnosti, chelovecheskoi poryadochnosti . . .' Interv'yu pol'skogo ezhenedel'nika s Bulatom Okudzhavoi" [" 'Ever more seldom do we give thought to honor, integrity, human decency . . .' An interview with Bulat Okudzhava by a Polish weekly." A conversation between Okudzhava and the Polish journalist Anna Zebrowska, first published in *Polityka*, October 1983]. *Russkaya mysl'*, 24 November 1983, pp. 8–9, 14.

Orlova, Raisa. " 'My ne khuzhe Goratsiya' " [We're no worse than Horace; on Galich]. *Vremya i my* 51 (1980): 5–26.

O. S. "Bryussel': Vystuplenie A. A. Galicha" [Brussels: an appearance by A. A. Galich]. *Russkaya mysl'*, 26 September 1974, p. 9.

Oshanin, L. [Untitled speech]. In *Chetvertyi s"ezd pisatelei SSSR. 22–27 maya 1967 goda: Stenograficheskii otchet*, pp. 193–95. Moscow: Sovetskii pisatel', 1968.

Pages from Tarusa: New Voices in Russian Writing. Edited and with introduction by Andrew Field. London: Chapman and Hall, 1964.

Paperny, Z. "Za stolom semi morei (Bulat Okudzhava)" [At the table of the seven seas (Bulat Okudzhava)]. *Voprosy literatury* 6 (1983): 31–52.

Pesni i romansy russkikh poetov [Songs and romances of the Russian poets]. Edited by V. E. Gusev. Biblioteka poeta, bol'shaya seriya. Moscow-Leningrad: Sovetskii pisatel', 1963.

Pesni russkikh bardov [Songs of the Russian bards; the only substantial collection of guitar poetry]. 4 vols. Paris: YMCA, 1977 (vols 1–3), 1978 (vol. 4). With 34 cassette recordings.

Pfandl, Heinrich. Review of Vladimir Vysotsky, *Pesni i stikhi* (New York, 1981) and *Nerv* (Moscow, 1981). *Wiener Slawistischer Almanach* 9 (1982): 323–35.

Plyushch, Leonid. "Ukhodyat druz'ya" [My friends are going away; on Galich]. *Russkaya mysl'*, 29 December 1977, p. 2.

————. *History's Carnival: A Dissident's Autobiography*. Edited and translated by Marco Carynnyk. New York and London: Harcourt Brace Jovanovich, 1977.

Poetry from the Russian Underground: A Bilingual Anthology. Translated and edited by Joseph Langland. New York, Evanston, San Francisco, London: Harper and Row, 1973. (Four songs by Galich, pp. 96–111; six songs by Okudzhava, pp. 158–73.)

Pogodin, Nikolai. *Aristokraty* [The aristocrats; a play]. In *Sobranie dra-*

maticheskikh proizvedenii v pyati tomakh, vol. 3, pp. 85–171. Moscow: Iskusstvo, 1960.

Polchaninov, R. "Vysotsky v peredachakh Svobody' " [Vysotsky in broadcasts by [Radio] Liberty]. *Novoe russkoe slovo,* 7 February 1982, p. 6.

Pomerantsev, Kirill. " 'Kogda ya vernus' ' " [When I return; on Galich's death] *Russkaya mysl',* 26 January 1978, pp. 10–11.

Pomerantseva, E. V. "Ballada i zhestokii romans" [The ballad and the cruel romance]. *Russkii fol'klor* 14 (1974): 202–209.

Post-War Russian Poetry. Edited and with an introduction by Daniel Weissbort. Harmondsworth: Penguin Books, 1974. (Six poems by Okudzhava, including three songs, pp. 93–97.)

Primak, Anatoly. "Pesni Galicha" [The songs of Galich]. *Novoe russkoe slovo,* 23 October 1982, p. 6.

Proffer, Carl R. "A Disabled Literature." *The New Republic,* 14 February 1981, pp. 27–34.

Radio Liberty Register of Samizdat, February 1971. #R487. Compiled by Albert Boiter and Peter Dornan. Frankfurt/M.: Radio Liberty, 1971.

Reddaway, Peter. "The Development of Dissent and Opposition." In *The Soviet Union since the Fall of Khrushchev,* edited by Archie Brown and Michael Kaser, pp. 121–56. 2d ed. London: Macmillan, 1978.

Riha, Karl. *Moritat, Bänkelsang, Protestballade: Zur Geschichte des engagierten Liedes in Deutschland.* Frankfurt/M.: Fischer, 1975.

R[omanov, E.], " 'Erika' beret chetyre kopii" [The "Erica" [machine] makes four copies; on Galich]. *Posev* 1 (1968): 59–61.

———. "Vozvrashchenie: Pamyati Aleksandra Arkad'evicha Galicha" [Return: Aleksandr Arkad'evich Galich in memoriam]. *Posev* 2 (1978): 2–3.

Roslyakov, Vladimir. "Dva rasskaza" [Two stories; one includes a party scene where songs are sung]. *Yunost'* 3 (1969): 30–36.

Rothstein, Robert. "The Quiet Rehabilitation of the Brick Factory: Early Soviet Popular Music and Its Critics." *Slavic and East European Journal* 39, no. 3 (1980): 374–85.

Rubenshtein, Nataliya. "Vyklyuchite magnitofon—pogovorim o poete" [Switch off the tape recorder—let's talk about the poet; on Galich]. *Vremya i my* 2 (1975): 164–77.

———. "Narodnyi artist" [People's actor; on Vysotsky]. *Dvadtsat' dva* 14 (1980): 193–202.

Rublev, Ruvim. "Vysotsky nachinalsya tak" [This is how Vysotsky began]. *Novoe russkoe slovo,* 6 May 1980, p. 4.

———. "Voennye pesni Vysotskogo" [Vysotsky's war songs]. *Novoe russkoe slovo,* 8 May 1980, p. 4.

———. "Mest' Bulata Okudzhavy" [Bulat Okudzhava's revenge]. *Novoe russkoe slovo,* 10 May 1980, p. 2.

———. "Evgeny Klyachkin—piterskii bard" [Evgeny Klyachkin, bard of Petersburg]. *Novoe russkoe slovo,* 28 May 1980, p. 4.

———. "Galich proshchaetsya s Leningradom" [Galich takes his leave of Leningrad]. *Novoe russkoe slovo,* 18 June 1980, p. 2.

———. "Yury Vizbor—poet i reporter" [Yury Vizbor, poet and reporter]. *Novoe russkoe slovo,* 16 August 1980, p. 8.

———. "Podpol'nye ansambli" [Underground bands]. *Novoe russkoe slovo,* 28 October 1980, pp. 1–2.

————. "Spi, shanson'e vseya Rusi" [Sleep, chansonnier of all the Russias; on the death of Vysotsky]. *Novoe russkoe slovo,* 29 July 1980, p. 3.
————. "O Vladimire Vysotskom" [About Vladimir Vysotsky]. *Novoe russkoe slovo,* 24 January 1981, p. 4.
————. "Vladimir Vysotsky i parodisty" [Vladimir Vysotsky and the parodists]. *Literaturnoe zarubezh'e* 11/12 (1981): 11.
Russian Poetry: The Modern Period. Edited by John Glad and Daniel Weissbort. Iowa City: University of Iowa Press, 1978. (Four poems by Okudzhava, including two songs, pp. 216–19; two songs by Galich, pp. 339–42.)
Russian Writing Today. Edited by Robin Milner-Gulland and Martin Dewhirst. Harmondsworth: Penguin Books, 1977. (One poem by Okudzhava, pp. 371–72.).
Russia's Underground Poets. Selected and translated by Keith Bosley, with Dimitry Pospielovsky and Janis Sapiets. Introduction by Janis Sapiets. New York and Washington: Praeger, 1969. (Seven songs by Okudzhava, pp. 55–59; three songs by Galich, 32–34.)
Russkie sovetskie pesni, 1917–1977 [Russian Soviet songs, 1917–1977]. Compiled by N. Kryukov and Ya. Shvedov. Moscow: Khudozhestvennaya literatura, 1977.
Sandomirsky, Vera [Vera Dunham]. "The Sad Armchair. Notes on Soviet War and Postwar Lyrical Poetry." *Harvard Slavic Studies* 3 (1957): 289–327.
Sapiets, Janis. "Introduction." In *Russia's Underground Poets,* selected and translated by Keith Bosley, with Dimitry Pospielovsky and Janis Sapiets, pp. xv–xxvi. New York and Washington: Praeger, 1969.
Seeger, Murray. "Russian Satirist Takes Art and Bitterness Underground." *International Herald Tribune,* 2 April 1974, p. 5. (On Galich.)
Shcherbakov, K. " 'Gamlet'. Tragediya Shekspira na stsene teatra na Taganke" [*Hamlet.* Shakespeare's tragedy on the stage of the Taganka Theater]. *Komsomol'skaya pravda,* 26 December 1971, p. 3.
Shkola Okudzhavy [The school of Okudzhava]. London: Flegon, 1971. Reprinted from *Kak nadezhna zemlya: Pesennik* [How reliable the earth is: a songbook], compiled by D. Sokolov. Moscow: Muzyka, 1969.
Shomina, V. G. "Poeticheskie osobennosti pesen tyur'my, katorgi i ssylki" [The poetic specifics of prison, hard-labor, and exile songs]. *Izvestiya akademii nauk SSSR,* seriya literatury i yazyka 25, no. 4 (1966): 341–46.
Shtein, Aleksandr. "Povest' o tom, kak voznikayut syuzhety." *Znamya* 5 (1964): 130–47.
Shtromas, Aleksandr. "Mir Aleksandra Galicha" [The world of Aleksandr Galich]. *Vremya i my* 45 (1979): 106–20.
S. I. "Iz perepiski s Rossiei" [From correspondence with Russia; mentions Galich's songs]. *Grani* 70 (1969): 213.
Sidel'nikova, A. V. "N. G. Tsyganov i ego pesennoe tvorchestvo" [N. G. Tsyganov and his creative work in song]. *Uchenye zapiski moskovskogo pedagogicheskogo instituta* 455 (1971): 143–59.
Sinyavsky, Andrei. See Terz, Abram.
Smith, G. S. "Whispered Cry: The Songs of Alexander Galich." *Index on Censorship* 3, no. 3 (1974): 11–28.
————. "Modern Russian Underground Song: An Introductory Survey." *Journal of Russian Studies* 28 (1974): 3–12.
————. "Underground Songs." *Index on Censorship* 7, no. 2 (1978): 67–72. (Review of *Pesni russkikh bardov.*)

———. "Literature and the Arts." In *The Soviet Union,* edited by R. W. Davies, pp. 148–59. London: George Allen and Unwin, 1978.

———. "Modern Russian Dissident Culture." *Strathclyde Modern Language Studies* 3 (1983): 37–50.

———. "Silence is Connivance: Aleksandr Galich." In Aleksandr Galich, *Songs and Poems,* pp. 13–54. Ann Arbor: Ardis, 1983.

———. "Galich in Emigration." In *Russian Literature in Emigration: The Third Wave,* edited by Olga Matich and Michael Heim. Ann Arbor: Ardis, in press.

———. "The Metrical Repertoire of Russian Guitar Poetry," *International Journal of Slavic Linguistics and Poetics* (in press).

Smith, Hedrick. "Underground in Moscow." *International Herald Tribune,* 6 April 1973, p. 5. (On Vysotsky.)

———. *The Russians.* New York: Quadrangle/The New York Times, 1976.

Sokhor, A. *Russkaya sovetskaya pesnya* [The Russian Soviet song]. Leningrad: Muzyka, 1959.

Solzhenitsyn, Alexander. *The Oak and the Calf: Sketches of Literary Life in the Soviet Union.* Translated by Harry Willets. New York: Harper and Row, 1980.

Sosin, Gene. "Then Came Galich's Turn." *New York Times,* 12 February 1972.

———. "Lament for a Poet." *New York Times Magazine,* 11 November 1973. (On Galich.)

———. "Alexander Galich: Russian Poet of Dissent." *Midstream* 4 (1974): 29–37.

———. "Magnitizdat: Uncensored Songs of Dissent." In *Dissent in the USSR: Politics, Ideology, and People,* edited by Rudolf L. Tökés, pp. 276–309. Baltimore and London: Johns Hopkins University Press, 1975.

Sovetskaya potaennaya muza [The Soviet secret muse]. Edited by Boris Filippov. Munich: Posev, 1961.

Sovetskie khudozhestvennye fil'my: Annotirovannyi katalog [Soviet art films: an annotated catalog; lists work by Galich, Okudzhava and Vysotsky]. Vol. 4, *1958–1963.* Moscow: Iskusstvo, 1965.

Sovetskie poety, pavshie na Velikoi otechestvennoi voine [Soviet poets who fell in the Great Patriotic War]. Compiled by V. Kardin and I. Usok. Biblioteka poeta, bol'shaya seriya. Moscow-Leningrad: Sovetskii pisatel', 1965.

The Soviet Censorship. Edited by Martin Dewhirst and Robert Farrell. Metuchen, New Jersey: Scarecrow Press, 1973.

The Soviet Cultural Scene, 1956–1957. Edited by Walter Z. Laqueur and George Lichtheim. New York-London: Atlantic Books, 1958.

Sparre, Viktor. "Aleksandr Galich ne umer" [Aleksandr Galich has not died]. *Russkaya mysl',* 29 December 1977, p. 2.

Starr, S. Frederick. *Red and Hot: The Fate of Jazz in the Soviet Union, 1917–1980.* New York and Oxford: Oxford University Press, 1983.

Svirsky, Grigory. *Na lobnom meste: Literatura nravstvennogo soprotivleniya (1946–1976 gg.).* London: Novaya literaturnaya biblioteka, 1979. Translation: *A History of Post-War Soviet Writing: The Literature of Moral Opposition,* translated and edited by Robert Dessaix and Michael Ulman. Ann Arbor: Ardis, 1981.

Swayze, Harold. *The Political Control of Soviet Literature, 1946–1959.* Cambridge, Mass.: Harvard University Press, 1962.

Tarusskie stranitsy: Literaturno-illyustrirovannyi sbornik. Edited by K. Paustovskii. Kaluga: Kaluzhskoe knizhnoe izdatel'stvo, 1961. (Translation: see *Pages from Tarusa.*)

Telesin, Yu. "Predislovie" [Foreword]. In Petr Yakir, *Detstvo v tyur'me* [A prison childhood; by the dissident Petr Yakir; includes information about underground culture], pp. 5–13. London: Macmillan, 1971.

Tendryakov, V. "Troika, semerka, tuz." In *Nakhodka,* pp. 71–117. Moscow: Sovetskaya Rossiya, 1966. Translation: "Three, Seven, Ace." In *Dissonant Voices in Soviet Literature,* edited by Patricia Blake and Max Hayward, pp. 205–35. New York: Pantheon, 1964.

Terz, Abram [Andrei Sinyavsky]. *On Socialist Realism.* Introduction by Czeslaw Milosz. New York: Pantheon Books, 1960. Translation of: "Chto takoe sotsialisticheskii realizm," collected in *Fantasticheskii mir Abrama Tertsa,* pp. 399–446. London: Inter-Language Literary Association, 1967.

————. "The Literary Process in Russia." Translated by Michael Glenny. In *Kontinent I: The Alternative Voice of Russia and Eastern Europe,* pp. 73–110. London: Andre Deutsch, 1976.

————. "Teatr Galicha" [Galich's theater] *Vremya i my* 14 (1977): 142–50.

————. "Anekdot v anekdote" [The anecdote in the anecdote; on contemporary underground culture]. *Sintaksis* 1 (1978): 77–95.

————. "Samizdat and the Rebirth of Literature." *Index on Censorship* 9, no. 4 (1980): 8–13.

Thomson, Boris. *The Premature Revolution: Russian Literature and Society, 1917–1946.* London: Weidenfeld and Nicolson, 1972.

Timofeev, L. "Na beregu Nevy" [On the bank of the Neva]. *Novyi zhurnal* 68 (1962): 84–85.

Tolstykh, V. "Paradoksy populyarnosti" [The paradoxes of popularity; mentions Vysotsky]. *Literaturnaya gazeta,* 16 June 1982, p. 3.

Tsvetaeva, Marina. *Stikhotvoreniya i poemy.* Leningrad: Sovetskii pisatel', 1979.

Tumanovsky. R. F. "Den' poezii." In *Kratkaya literaturnaya entsiklopediya,* vol. 2, col. 593. Moscow: Sovetskaya entsiklopediya, 1964.

Uncensored Russia. Edited by Peter Reddaway. London: Cape, 1972.

Vail', Petr, and Genis, Aleksandr. "Shampanskoe i politura" [Champagne and varnish; on Vysotsky. Varnish *(politura)* is used to make home-distilled spirit by Russians, especially in the armed forces]. *Vremya i my* 36 (1978): 134–42.

Vanshenkin, K. "Iz pesni slova ne vykinesh' " [You can't throw the words out of a song; a Russian proverb]. *Pravda,* 4 March 1967, p. 2.

Vardi, Aleksandr. *Podkonvoinyi mir* [A world under guard; memoirs of the GULag, with much information about underground song]. Frankfurt/M.: Posev, 1971.

Ventsov, Lev. "Poeziya A. Galicha" [The poetry of A. Galich]. *Vestnik russkogo studencheskogo khristianskogo dvizheniya* 104–105 (1972): 211–28.

Vernet, Daniel. "Des écrivains soviétiques non-dissidents refusent la censure et éditent une revue dactylographiée." *Le Monde,* 25 January 1979, p. 3. (On the *Metropol* affair.)

Vertinsky, A. "Chetvert' veka bez rodiny. Vospominaniya" [A quarter of a century without my motherland; the memoirs of his émigré years by the great cabaret singer]. In *V krayakh chuzhikh,* pp. 197–309. Moscow, 1962.

———. *Pesni i stikhi, 1916–1937gg.* [Songs and poems, 1916–1937]. New York: Globus, 1975.

Vladimirov, Leonid. *Rossiya bez prikras i umolchanii.* Frankfurt/M.: Posev, 1969. Translation: *The Russians.* New York: Praeger, 1968.

Vol'man, B. *Gitara v Rossii: Ocherk istorii gitarnogo iskusstva* [The guitar in Russia: an essay in the history of the art of the guitar]. Leningrad: Gosudarstvennoe izdatel'stvo khudozhestvennoi literatury, 1961.

Voznesensky, Andrei. *Vzglyad* [Glance; a collection of lyric poems]. Moscow: Sovetskii pisatel', 1972.

———. *Bezotchetnoe* [Something unaccountable; a collection of lyric poems]. Moscow: Sovetskii pisatel', 1981.

———. "Sud'ba poeta" [The fate of a poet; echoing Pushkin's poem on Lermontov; on Vysotsky]. *Druzhba narodov* 1 (1982): 136–37.

Vysotsky, Vladimir. "Pesnya—eto ochen' ser'ezno" [Song—that's something very serious]. *Literaturnaya Rossiya,* 27 December 1974, p. 14. Reprinted in *Pesni i stikhi,* vol. 2, pp. 221–25.

———. "Tri pesni." *Tret'ya volna* 2 (1977): 44–50.

———. "Dve novye pesni." *Ekho* 3 (1978): 4–7.

———. "Zhizn' bez sna" [Life without sleep; a prose work of 1968]. *Ekho* 2/10 (1980): 7–24. Reprinted in *Pesni i stikhi,* vol. 2, pp. 123–50.

———. [Two poems]. in *Den' poezii 1981,* p. 118. Moscow: Sovetskii pisatel', 1981.

———. " '. . . kak korabli iz pesni' " ["Like the boats in the song"; two poems]. *Druzhba narodov* 1 (1982): 137–41.

———. *Nerv* [Nerve: a collection of songs and poems]. Moscow: Sovremennik, 1981.

———. *Pesni i stikhi* [Songs and poems; the second volume contains autobiographical and memoir material, including the speeches at Vysotsky's funeral]. New York: Literary Frontiers Publishers. Vol. 1, 1981; vol. 2, 1983.

Wade, Graham. *Traditions of the Classical Guitar.* London: Calder, 1980.

W. H. Auden's Oxford Book of Light Verse. Oxford-New York-Toronto-Melbourne, 1979. (Originally published as *The Oxford Book of Light Verse.* Oxford: Oxford University Press, 1938.)

Whitney, Thomas P. "Russian Literature and Soviet Politics." *In The New Writing in Russia,* pp. 3–51. Ann Arbor: University of Michigan Press, 1964.

Wolf Biermann, Liedermacher und Sozialist. Edited by Thomas Rothschild. Hamburg: Rowohlt, 1976.

Woll, Josephine, and Treml, Vladimir. *Soviet Unofficial Literature: Samizdat. An Annotated Bibliography of Works Published in the West.* Durham, N.C.: Duke University Press, 1978.

———, ———. *Soviet Dissident Literature: A Critical Guide.* Boston: G. K. Hall, 1983.

Yershov, Peter. *Comedy in the Soviet Theater.* New York: Columbia University Press, 1956.

Yevtushenko, Yevgenii. *A Precocious Autobiography.* Translated by Andrew R. MacAndrew. London: Collins and Harvill, 1963.

———. " 'Intelligentsiya' poet blatnye pesni" [The "intelligentsia" is singing underworld songs; a poem]. *Druzhba narodov* 7 (1975): 84–85.

Zernova, Ruf'. "Elizabet Arden." *Vremya i my* 58 (1980): 51–94. Reprinted in Ruf' Zernova, *Zhenskie rasskazy,* pp. 9–52. Ann Arbor: Ermitazh, 1981.

Zhabinsky, V. "Fal'sifikatsiya ili fol'klor?" [Falsification or folklore?—shows that a Soviet-published song, alleged to be of Nazi origin, is in fact an underground Russian song]. *Mosty* 3 (1958): 266–70.

———. " 'Zarubka na veka'. Literatura o lageryakh" ["Felling for the Ages." Literature on the camps]. *Mosty* 14 (1968): 314–32.

Zhadan, O. "Idem po pelengu" [We follow the bearing; on radio hams in the USSR]. *Komsomol'skaya pravda,* 19 September 1974, p. 4.

Zholkovsky, A. K. "Rai, zamaskirovannyi pod dvor: Zametki o poeticheskom mire Bulata Okudzhavy" [Paradise disguised as a back yard: notes on Bulat Okudzhava's poetic world]. In *NRL. Almanach 1978.* Edited by V. Len, G. Mayer, and R. Ziegler, pp. 101–120. Salzburg, 1979.

Zinov'ev, Aleksandr. *Ziyayushchie vysoty.* Lausanne: L'Age d'Homme, 1976. Translation by Gordon Clough: *The Yawning Heights.* New York: Random House, 1978.

Index